The E-Aligned Enterprise

THE
E-Aligned Enterprise

How to Map and Measure

Your Company's Course

in the New Economy

Jac Fitz-enz

AMACOM

American Management Association

New York • Atlanta • Boston • Chicago • Kansas City • San Francisco • Washington, D. C.

Brussels • Mexico City • Tokyo • Toronto

This publication is designed to provide accurate and authoritative information in regard to the subject matter covered. It is sold with the understanding that the publisher is not engaged in rendering legal, accounting, or other professional service. If legal advice or other expert assistance is required, the services of a competent professional person should be sought.

Library of Congress Cataloging-in-Publication Data

Fitz-ens, Jac.
    The e-aligned enterprise: how to map and measure your company's course in the new economy / Jac Fitz-enz.
        p.   cm.
    Includes bibliographical references and index.
    ISBN 0-8144-0625-4
    1. Electronic commerce.   I. Title.

HF5548.32.F57   2001
658.8'4—dc21

                                                                                    2001016041

Printing number

10 9 8 7 6 5 4 3 2 1

To
The Saratoga Institute staff.
Their insights continually add value.
Thank you all.

Contents

SAME PEOPLE—DIFFERENT WORLD

Despite all the hype about e-world—our new fast-paced, electronic-driven, information-rich milieu—human nature has not changed at its core. We are in a very true sense carbon copies of our grandparents, the inhabitants of i-world. In both e-world (the electronic world) and i-world (the industrial world), the inhabitants have similar needs. At the core of our being, we still have needs for survival, safety, social contact, and achievement, just like our grandparents. We have belief systems, motivations, aspirations, and a sense of ethics along with passive or aggressive personalities. We are, in short, still human beings.

What is different today from the opening of the 20th century is that we have been beamed up to this new planet called e-world. In this place, technology, transportation, community, businesses, family, and all the other institutions, which are hallmarks as well as creations of humanity, are a world apart from that of our grandparents. In e-world, technology has evolved from an electromechanical to an electronic base. The velocity of transportation has increased from horses and locomotives to automobiles and supersonic aircraft. Communities once marked by their permanence are now more transitory. Businesses that focused on domestic markets now trade worldwide. Families that huddled close together are now spread across great distances. The good news is that the connectivity of the World Wide Web links everyone at light speed. The other news is that it has imposed a pace of life that is almost intolerable.

While some e-world differences are slight, others are off the scale. It is the differentiations these new systems bring that drive changes in processes, inhibit or liberate, empower or restrain, and make us say, correctly, "life is different." People are the same at their center, but their world is morphing into a new form. Adjusting to this causes confusion and distress to some but releases and exhilarates others.

Young people welcome change and usually drive it. They want and need to play with the world as though it were a lump of clay. They want to reform it in ways that will serve their value systems, the evolving technological requirements, and the changes in social and economic circumstances. Older people tend toward maintaining the familiar. They've set up their world to suit their needs and prefer not to change unless it is obviously necessary or clearly better. Both young and old have to coexist. As the young mature, they take on the characteristics of their forebears and become more resistant to changing the world they formed not that long ago. In turn, the next generation grabs the clay and starts to reshape it.

Within living memory we can see how society opened up after World War I. Then, like an enthusiastic child with little experience, it overshot in its enthusiasm for the new possibilities. This led to the market crash of 1929 and a dozen years of economic depression. World War II broke the Great Depression and spawned social change again. The affluence of the 1950s gave life to the flower children of the 1960s, who distrusted everyone over 30 and became intent on creating a brave new world of peace and sharing. Twenty years later, they had traded their tie-dyes for suits, were running competitive businesses, and were wondering at what to them seemed to be the lethargy and detachment of Generation X. And so life evolves, changing its processes and yet remaining consistent at its human core: everyone still seeking safety, comfort, a little fun, and love.

Today there is great discomfort in the land. This anxiety stems from a new source, but it is no less intense than it was during the waning days of the industrial world. Discomfort arises when strongly held beliefs or new information or experience contradicts assumptions. It's called cognitive dissonance, or, in the vernacular, "Things don't add up like they used to!" We try to relieve the discomfort by convincing ourselves that it does not exist, that we will soon go back to the comfortable past, or by rationalizing or reconciling the differences. When it becomes too much, we drop out mentally and emotionally or try a new way of life in a new place.

People do this at all levels up to and including the executive suite. Cases of CEOs who believed the industrial world had not changed are rampant. Consider the executives at IBM and DEC who missed the PC revolution; executives at Ford, GM, and Chrysler who scoffed at the VW Beatle and Honda Civic; leaders at railroads who ignored interstate trucking; Swiss watchmakers who dismissed electronics as toys; Wall Street stuffed shirts who ignored discount brokerages; and those at Big Steel who laughed at the minimills. It's a long list, and it reflects an all too predictable behavior.

Management must acknowledge its discomfort with e-world and respond with new approaches to leadership, strategy, employees, technology investment, infrastructure, customers, competition, and vendors—in short, all stakeholders. Most of all, management must deal with e-world inside their organizations in terms of policies, processes, people, and power. Policies must be open in nature, fostering communication and innovation. Processes must be simplified and updated, applying technology to move information quickly to the fingertips of employees. People need to be developed and managed as the most precious and elusive assets of the company. As for power, the associates are truly the principal drivers of innovation and productivity. Power has to be put into their hands so they can leverage technology and information.

E-World Map

The map of the e-world organization is markedly different from its i-world predecessor. Its main features are clear. Key distinctions are several. It is flexible. The days of rigid, permanent roads are gone, probably forever. It's collaborative. We cannot operate in isolation in e-world. It's open. This supports collaboration and speeds processes. It's outwardly oriented. Market vigilance is essential. It's knowledge driven. The speed and complexity of a high-technology service-obsessed organization demands instant access to masses of data that can be converted to intelligence.

How to design and build strategic and tactical components of an organizational vehicle that can travel efficiently and effectively through this territory is the point of this book. And to know how well we are doing on this new and never-ending journey, micro- and macro-measures of costs, time, distance, quality, and satisfaction are scoreboarded.

THE TASK AT HAND

The most difficult part of writing this book has been the mountain of data available. In addition to my personal experience in companies, at conferences, and in meetings with thought leaders, I found myself drawn into the flood of research and speculation that threatens to inundate all of us. There is hardly time to scan all of the sources available, from the traditional (such as *Fortune, Forbes, The Economist,* and *Business Week*) to the spin-offs (like *Forbes ASAP* and the new generation of *Wired, Fast Company, Red Herring,* and *Upside*) to the focused journals (*Information Week, CIO, CFO*) to the many trade association publications, plus the constant flow of books. Even more difficult is having time to absorb and compare what I've read, seen, and heard. I am continually faced with the question of what makes sense and what is wild-eyed pap designed only to shock or sell copies. Furthermore, with change coming at such a frenetic pace, how can anyone write a book today that will be useful by the time it hits the market next year?

Whenever I find myself in the midst of overload or caught on the horns of an apparent dilemma, I have learned the best way to cope is to drop back to basic questions. Fundamentals always apply whether you're talking about hitting a golf shot, baking a cake, or leading a commercial enterprise. To me, the fundamentals of a successful business are leadership, strategy, employees (or associates as we now call them), customers and other external relationships, and of course, execution—the ability to bring it all together better than the competitor. Accordingly, I have organized the book this way and coalesced the information flood into a meaningful and comprehensible map for navigating your company through e-world and evaluating the stops along the way.

FINDING SOLID GROUND

The solution to e-world's new challenges will not come from Wall Street or from Silicon Valley. Money and machinery have roles to play. However, cash and technology are by their nature inert. Despite the fact that some computers now talk to others without ongoing human intervention, only people can meet the challenges of e-world. This implies that top management must turn inward toward the employees, associates, cast members, staff, or whatever euphemism it uses to describe labor. The executive team has to find more efficient and effective ways to put people in touch with leveragable resources—mainly information and other people.

People who are in contact with each other normally find ways to work out mutually satisfactory solutions. People out of contact with each other normally look for ways to maximize their reward at the expense of the strangers or competitors. In the first case, they work continually to find balance—the so-called win-win solution. In the second, they strive for imbalance, me versus them, which is by definition destabilizing and in the long run destructive for all parties.

No matter how high or fast a company flies, every company eventually declines. Some disappear while others find ways to renew themselves. But no one's success line rises uninterrupted. Industrial giants like IBM and General Motors and even whole industries such as textiles, railroads, utilities, and banking have experienced significant disruption and the need to restructure to survive. Your company and mine are no exception to this natural, undeniable rule of cycles. While competition is at the heart of business, it must also support and nurture a kernel of respect for others, at least enough to maintain stability in the market.

THE STRUCTURE

This book is divided into six Parts, labeled Parts I through V, and an Epilogue. The Parts contain two to four short chapters designed for easy, quick reading.

Part I is an introduction starting with two brief chapters that look at how the marketplace is changing from the old, industrial world that I title i-world to the new, electronic world, titled e-world. It offers a quick overview of the effects of "e" on people and organizations. Chapter 3, on intellectual capital, provides the foundation for my exposition of how to build and evaluate an e-driven business. Intellectual capital becomes more than an esoteric concept when we see how it can be applied to practical business situations. I use it as a criterion tool to help me find, apply, and evaluate opportunities.

Parts II through IV consist of chapters covering leadership, strategy, and human capital. In each the focus is on what is the same, what is different, what new problems and opportunities e-world brings. Within each chapter there is a discussion of what is happening along with recommendations on how to respond to the emerging dynamics of e-world. Each of these Parts ends with a summary and a scorecard providing sample metrics and suggesting ways to measure performance for the topic covered.

Part V is the how-to-do-it arena with specific statements on the central issues. The objective is achieved by bringing all the previous commentary together into a model for e-aligning the enterprise. It concludes with a scorecard of macro measures for e-world business, which are in turn composed of several micro- or tactical-level measures.

The Epilogue is a look into the future with some fanciful as well as practical examples of what will come in the next century. It is capped off with my view about how to cope with the basic changes in life and commerce that are certain to come.

The book concludes with two Appendixes. One is on Performance Measurement and the other is a Bibliography. Performance measurement is essential if we are to be efficient in our transformation to the e-market. We need new metrics as well as different ways of looking at traditional measures.

Acknowledgments

THIS PROJECT WAS THE MOST grueling writing assignment I have ever taken on. The e-world topic is so new, complex, and rapidly evolving that it was difficult to find solid, unshifting ground from which to start. There is an overwhelming amount of information flooding the market. Every day, new inventions and processes are popping up, promising to change the way we work and live. Sorting through the hype for the kernels of future truth has not been easy. I would have drifted off into cyberspace long ago if it had not been for the support given by a number of people.

The foundation of my work was always my partner, Ellen Kieffer, who provided encouragement in the dark days and brought me back to reality when I went off the deep end. My acquisitions editor, Adrienne (The Noodge) Hickey, keeps after me with practical advice and good humor. One of her most annoying characteristics is that she is almost always right. The staff at Saratoga Institute, particularly Barbara Davison, Michelle Deneau, Marcela Echeverria, and Melodye Serino, provided research and comments to help me sort through the mountain of data available on this topic. I thank each of them profusely. Outside of my personal and business family, so many people have been so generous with their time and knowledge that I can't begin to mention or thank all of them individually. Nevertheless, key contributors in Europe include Markus Raebsamen at Zurich Financial Services, Peter Heinold at Seimens, and Anne Jubert at the European Commission. In the United States, the list is way too long, but a special thank you must go to John Macy at General Management Technologies for sharing its research with me. So many other discussions with so many people helped me test my ideas and focus my exposition. You all know who you are and to you I say thank you for your selfless generosity.

Part I

ENFOLDING THE NEW WORLD

Chapter 1

What a Trip!

UNQUESTIONABLY, E-BUSINESS IS THE MAJOR management issue today. Yet predicting the evolution of "e-biz" is like being present at the creation of the world on Monday and not having any idea what else God is planning for the rest of the week. We see only "the Heavens and the Earth," cyberspace and organizations. What else could God have in mind? Flowers, trees, animals, people . . . what next?

The big noise transcends business. It's not just e-biz but e-world that we are facing. At this point we are sticking our collective toes into a murky, swirling stream, filled with unseen currents and eddies, which at the same time looks rather inviting. We know we have to get wet sooner or later, but some of us are a bit apprehensive as to the temperature and the unknowns that lurk below the surface.

E-world is going to be a trip, a hell of a trip—an unimaginable trip, on which we have already begun and from which we can never turn back. But before we scare ourselves into a catatonic state, let's put it in perspective.

CHAOS AND COMPLEXITY

Margaret Wheatley tells us that chaos and complexity are now part of our daily awareness.[1] But chaos is not a new idea. The Greeks believed that the first power in the universe was a vast dark area known as Chaos. It seems they viewed it as a diffuse mass of disorganized bits and pieces, energy and matter without form. Today, from what's happening globally to what's happening in our personal lives, this disorganization is now the norm. The challenge—indeed, our imperative—is to discover new ways of coming together in order to create lives and organizations worthy of "human habitation."

THE NEW CHAPTER IN THE HUMAN HISTORY BOOK

E-world is the latest stage in the evolution of human life, business organizations, and economies. If we look back through the 20th century, we can see other situations that at the time were as profoundly confusing, upsetting, and stimulating as e-world promises to be. Think about the huge change that took place November 11, 1918, the day World War I ended. The 1920s exploded into a cultural and technological upheaval that stunned the nation. Flappers and jazz music were as scary to many people then as techno-geeks are today. Along came Prohibition, speakeasies, widespread ownership of that great liberator the automobile, and then whammo—the big crash of 1929. The Great Depression lasted until the involvement of the United States in World War II in 1942. Millions rode the economic and emotional roller coaster up and down through the 1920s and 1930s.

> *E-world is the latest stage in the evolution of human life, business organizations, and economies.*

In the 1950s the GI Bill and the Federal Housing Administration made it possible for people to obtain college educations and own homes. Those too were earthshaking changes in America. Before World War II, widespread college education and home ownership were not privileges of the masses, which may seem strange to someone born to the affluence that this social-economic shift drove. We settled into the appliance-rich, television-based, new suburbia of the 1950s and listened to Dion and the Belmonts, Harry Belafonte, and the Kingston Trio. All of a sudden, *bebopaloobopalopbamboom*: And there was Little Richard, James Brown, Jerry Lee Lewis, Chuck Berry, and finally that hip-shaking demon, Elvis Presley. I remember reputable people claiming that the heavy beat of rock music would cause long-lasting physical damage to our young people. But then, my grandparents said that about the jungle rhythms of jazz.

The Civil Rights Act, the Vietnam War, Flower Power, LSD, and a man on the moon delivered the most resounding sociological shock wave the United States had yet endured. The late 1960s and the 1970s were as tumultuous as any period. Soon after, the economy drifted downward, hitting bottom in stagflation by 1980. Then, Wall Street kickstarted us with junk bonds and the savings and loan debacle. By the end of the decade, we were dealing with over 7 million of our neighbors losing their jobs and the dissolution of the industrial age psychological contract at work.

Enter 1995 and Mosaic, then Netscape, and away we go on WWW, the World Wide Web. We hit the millennium break with a roaring economy, the Y2K threat, and dot-com mania. This made Huxley's *Brave New World* look like kindergarten. So, my friends, as FDR said in 1933, "the only thing we have to fear is fear itself."

KEEPING IT IN PERSPECTIVE

History is nothing more than a series of jolts. It is a succession of changes that send us off on new journeys into the unknown and unknowable. To enjoy this latest trip happily and gainfully, we need to change our view of life. Just as the industrial revolution tore the old order apart, so too is the electronic revolution reordering existence.

The invasion of technology is changing the way we work, and demographic forces are dictating who will be available for work. *The Futurist* magazine recently offered a list of twenty-four trends reshaping the workplace.[2] Several of the more interesting predictions are:

- Resumes will be put on microchips and implanted in people's bodies.
- Retirees and teenagers will be the new entrepreneurs.
- Advanced technologies will offset some of the labor shortages.
- Degreed, experienced women will shatter the glass ceiling.
- Telecommuting will drive up productivity.

- Many people will work flexible schedules and be available 24/7.
- Generation Xers will produce a new Baby Boom from 2000 to 2012.

Chris Meyer and Stan Davis suggest that as the new world brings with it higher risks, so too does it offer new opportunities to individuals.[3] They believe people will come to view themselves as capital to be invested rather than workers looking for a job. In this scenario, people will auction their services just like they auction hard goods. They will offer their knowledge and skills to the highest bidder on either short- or long-term contracts. Organizations will build and—although the authors don't suggest this—perhaps even trade portfolios of human capital just as they do financial instruments. The difference is that the individual will have the final say in the decision to invest.

Always controversial economist Jeremy Rifkin claims that we are headed for a fundamental change in the way we relate to things.[4] His premise is that soon we will no longer own but rather will lease, rent, or otherwise pay for an experience or product. According to him, the world will become a vast service network residing in cyberspace. Companies are already on this track, selling off hard assets like real estate and inventories and outsourcing noncore activities. A precursor to the new service company might be Exult. Less than two years after its founding as an outsourcer of human resources and other administrative services, it has booked over $1 billion in long-term outsourcing contracts from the likes of BP Amoco/Arco, Bank of America, Tenneco, and Unisys.

If this is to be the new world, we need to stop right now and rethink everything. We must shift our focus from isolated tasks to holistic process strategies. Assuming that something like the service world is coming, the implication is that soon, more than ever in history, life will be about fostering relationships. This means we need to be better at listening, conversing, and respecting one another's uniqueness. We are now all truly connected, like it or not. It is a sobering thought that we probably have to change our view of the world of human relations at the most basic level. But think about the possibilities when we master the connections.

Paul Saffo, director of the Institute for the Future, tells us to brace ourselves because we are entering a new era that will continue for a couple of decades.[5] In my opinion, it could be that the human race has shifted from unhurried evolution to impulsive transformation as the new steady state of the world. We may no longer be going from there to here. Possibly, we have just entered our final infinite state: a high-speed journey of never-ending transformation.

Either way, this journey is going to be a fantastic trip, so get a grip and hang on tight!

REFERENCES

1. Margaret J. Wheatley, *Discovering Order in a Chaotic World* (San Francisco: Berrett-Koehler, 2nd ed., 1999).
2. John Challenger, "24 Trends Reshaping the Workplace," *The Futurist,* September–October 2000, pp. 35–41.
3. Stan Davis and Chris Meyer, *Future Wealth* (Cambridge, Mass.: Harvard Business School Press, 2000).
4. Jeremy Rifkin, *The Age of Access* (New York: Tarcher/Putnam, 2000).
5. Paul Saffo, "State of the New Economy," *Fast Company,* September 2000.

Chapter 2

I-World Meets E-World

BOB ROGERS, FOUNDER AND CHAIRMAN of BRC Imagination Arts, described the core issue that the new millennium has pushed to the forefront of business and society: "The 20th century was a century of machines—the airplane and the telephone and the computer and the satellite. Those things got us going faster than ever before. So, in the 21st century we're faster and we're bigger and we're smaller and we're taller. The question is, Why? The 21st century will be a search for meaning."

The media have allied with the techno-geeks in the construction of a maniacal argument that e-world is totally different from i-world. This is not true, and saying it is a disservice to managers, associates, suppliers, and customers who are trying to understand what is happening. There are several dimensions that are different in e-world than in i-world. In some cases, the difference is exclusive. In others, it is only a matter of degree. In e-world:

- *Scope* is global versus local or regional.
- *Time cycles* are faster.
- *Structures* are more complex.
- *Prime resources* are talent and information versus machinery.
- *Innovation* is more important.

- *Risks* are higher.
- *Systems* are connected and open versus discrete and closed.

As a result, *people desperately need to find more meaning in their work and in their lives. This is the central issue of organizational life in the 21st century.*

Cisco Systems states that the new world model is similar to an ecosystem. The rules of the Internet ecosystem support broad and unlimited market participation while conversely encouraging market anarchy—making up the rules as we go along. Value networks are supplanting value chains. Instead of a linear hierarchy, the ecosystem is a web. By their nature, webs are inclusive rather than exclusive. Each node or connection point is accessible to and from all other points with no formal protocols required. The system has almost no barriers to entry and is self-organizing and self-reorganizing with the addition of each new player. Finally, the power is on the periphery, not at the center. Cisco claims there is already over $1 trillion worth of technical infrastructure in place and available for anyone to access, at any time, free of charge. These open and free characteristics invite everyone to play and in playing to add to the utility and value of the system. While this new system is growing at warp speed, the old system is simultaneously still in place in many places. The result is at the same time stimulating and confusing.

Although technology is exploding at a record pace, all the bricks and mortar companies of the past 200 years have not suddenly disappeared into a black hole. In fact, after the April 2000 collapse of dot-com hysteria, some of the old companies caught their breath and have started to respond. Figure 2-1 illustrates the fantasy and reality of the "i" versus "e" phenomena.

I-world and e-world are not two separate, distinct entities. In actuality, the two worlds are merging into an integrated new world. When the dot-com fever took over the stock market in the last years of the 1990s, the absurd valuations of start-ups sent the i-world masters reeling. It was a frightening, often paralyzing, event to spend a career building a business and find it now valued at less than a figment of a twenty-something's imagination. However, the mavens of i-world are not totally stupid. They did what they have always done: They analyzed the threat. What they saw was that although the bar-

Figure 2-1. I-world versus e-world.

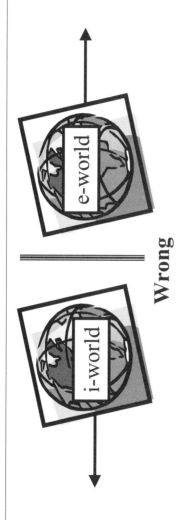

i-world

e-world

Wrong

New World

Right

riers to entry in e-world are virtually nil, the barriers to economic success are higher than ever. While the Internet lets any merchant reach and serve customers worldwide overnight, it is still only a new channel for conducting business. Through all the technobabble, our revenues must still exceed our expenses if we are going to stay in business over a long period.

NEW LIGHT

Seeing the light at the end of the tunnel, the i-world executives began to notice the underlying weakness of many dot-coms and to discern ways in which they could compete. As of the end of 2000, they were hitching up their collective trousers and marching back into the fray. But as they enter the new arena, they are finding that the power has shifted from a producer-driven market to a consumer-driven one. This is the single greatest difference between the old and the new order, spawned by the open, accessible, and free aspects of the Web. To be successful in e-world, the bricks-and-mortar folk have to accept and work with the principle that they are now naked before the demanding consumer.

> **To be successful in e-world, the bricks-and-mortar folk have to accept and work with the principle that they are now naked before the demanding consumer.**

STRATEGY FOR THE NEW MARKETPLACE

Already there is a flood of books telling us how to build a strategy for this new marketplace. Some are cogent dissertations. Others are anthologies of war stories: "How I Did It." Nearly every one of them has a list of rules or principles. Most of them overlap to some degree. But as is typical in a rush to publish, the story told is incomplete and unbalanced. Strategists write about strategy and ignore execution. Sales and marketing types focus on customer relations to the neglect of employee relations: the people who deal with the customers. Finance advocates overemphasize return on capital invested while forgetting leadership. This should not surprise us. It is natural for each of us to think and communicate from our professional discipline. But we need to step outside of that and look at all sides of the story: leadership, strategy, customers, human capital, and, most importantly, how to put it all together with an integrating alignment plan. The result will be a map for navigating around the shoals and through the safe passages of e-world. Included are scorecard—we may liken them to time and distance—headings. These will alert us to approaching dangers as well as tell us how far we have come along our voyage. So let's start by examining the central issues that make the transformation from i-world to e-world so fascinating.

Along about 1998, as the dot-com epidemic began to build, people were claiming that business success was a simple process: Go online with your business and the world will make you rich. They sang the "better mousetrap" theme and waited for the world to beat a track to their Web site. This was going to be the new better business model, all paid for by a bottomless purse of advertising funds. However, it was soon clear that there is much more to e-biz than putting up a Web site. That technology, although evolving at light speed, is relatively simple and available to anyone. But Web-based marketing brings with it new requirements. Outside in the marketplace, the principal demands are for speed and convenience. As B2B and B2C customers become more familiar with Web purchasing, they are expecting levels of performance that were laughable a decade ago. They want buying to be more than easy and they want response time to be zero. In addition, they expect that if the product is not what they anticipated, there will be rapid service response, no matter what it takes.

Inside the company, given growing demands for exceptional service, the organization must be able to turn on the proverbial dime as well as dance on the head of a pin to keep up with and satisfy the customer. Business executives are already recognizing that to be truly competitive, they have to be ahead of the customer. This calls for a massive amount of information that is very focused, not only on customers' current needs but also on their future requirements. The challenge is that the future requirements are not even evident to the customers today. All this points to a prerequisite for the rapid acquisition, cataloging and distribution, of information for constant knowledge growth.

A passive database is only the starting point. Companies are working on learning what the relevance of a data point is or could be and pushing that out to everyone in the organization who might need it. This includes information on all aspects of what is now called intellectual capital: organizational, relational, and human. It assumes that people will be willing to share information and add to the knowledge exchange. However, this is the major failing point of many knowledge initiatives. Only very slowly are companies coming to realize that e-biz is as much, if not more, an intellectual capital/knowledge management issue as a marketing and distribution contest. The unseen requirement is a culture change driven by information and demanding constant learning to support the technology investment.

Today, employees in all functions, including administration, need to work at lightning speed if the company is to be a highly competitive e-business. Finding an answer and responding to a customer's query must be nearly instantaneous. If it takes as much as an hour to locate the person who has the knowledge to answer the query, there is a good chance that today's impatient customer may have already found it through another supplier, and the sale is jeopardized. Designing a system to respond to this is the challenge.

As yet, only a very few have attempted to tie knowledge management directly to e-biz goals. For the most part, first attempts often look like knowledge for knowledge's sake. This should not be a surprise. As I said before, we all look at the world from the base of our professional discipline and experience. The intellectual capital movement is a telling example. Lawyers are looking at patents, engineers are redesigning structure, marketing people are concentrating on customer relations, and human resources is thinking about employees. Attempts at interlacing all aspects of intellectual capital have been feeble to nonexistent. To optimize intellectual capital, all the facets have to be connected in a synergistic manner. Intellectual capital data is the key because it is the grist for the knowledge management mill.

Rather than simply calling attention to the magnitude and subtleties of the problem, this book provides direction for solving it. Knowledge management is grounded in intellectual capital data and connected with learning. It is operationalized through a description of how data from all corners of the business need to be collected, organized, and distributed to give the company an e-biz competitive advantage—in other words, how to steer your company's course in this exciting—and often frightening—new economy.

TIMELINESS AND CHANGE

There are two technical challenges before us. One is that information must be available *now*. The other is that the information is constantly changing. To solve the timeliness problem, the information system must enable every employee to access whatever he needs quickly from a 24/7/365 platform from any point in the globe in which he finds himself. The operative term is speed. As for the change problem, realize that the half-life of useful information is very short. How short is an irrelevant question: It is short with a capital S. Yesterday's information may be obsolete already. For example, consider the constant flow of titillating articles about technological advancements. By the time such prognostications are published, a significant portion of them are already out-of-date. Therefore, state-of-the-art information must be constantly discovered, reconfigured, and literally put at the fingertips of the employee. How to set it up so that we can measure our return on investment is the challenge.

THE BREAKTHROUGH

For the first time in history, businesses are able to overcome the richness versus reach dilemma. Until the development of the World Wide Web, organizations had to make a choice between penetrating deeply into a market segment or working thinly and broadly across it. Only the very largest corporations could afford to cover an entire market. Examples of these are Standard Oil, which at one time was totally integrated from exploration through retailing, and the General Motors Corporation, which built the full range of automobiles from inexpensive Chevrolets to luxury Cadillacs and also made components like batteries and filters. Henry Ford set the model by having everything from rubber plantations to supply raw materials and a fleet of ships to deliver raw material and components to assembly plants and retail distributorships.

However, with the information and communications technology underlying the World Wide Web, many companies can now serve both broad and diverse customer bases deeply using a combination of sales and distribution channels including the Web. Rather than being forced to build a large field sales force, a company can sell products over the Web while simultaneously selling through distributors, retailers, or field salespeople. This is the good news. The other news is that they have to figure out how to do it.

CHANGING THE RULES OF ENGAGEMENT

With so much change occurring at such a rapid rate, writers are having a field day. Every issue of every newspaper, newsletter, journal, magazine, and electronic publication is filled with hyperventilating stories of the latest technological wonder. Many of these will never reach the market. Some will be shams and some will be scams. A small number will actually fulfill their promise and significantly affect a business or personal process. The central question in all this is not what is coming or how it will improve an operation, but what it will contribute to changing the way we live.

Fax machines are handy but they didn't affect our lives like the personal computer did. Personal digital assistants are useful but until voice recognition becomes more reliable and wireless connectivity more pervasive, they will not fulfill their Dick Tracy wrist-radio potential. The likelihood that 90 percent of the new gadgets will change our lives is slim. If we want to get the jump on this fascinating new world, we have to become more insightful. We want to slip behind the hype and try to imagine what it implies for different aspects of our lives and our business practices.

WORDS AND MEANING: A QUESTION OF IMPLICATION

My wife's favorite episode of *Star Trek* is "Spock's Brain." In one scene, the alien woman replies to Captain Kirk's question about

Spock's brain by saying, "Brain and brain. What is brain?" In our case, we need to ask, "What are the following":

- E-economy
- Connectivity
- Clicks and bricks
- Net everything
- Digital capital
- Intellectual capital
- Deflection points
- Virtual anything
- Disaggregation
- Disintermediation
- All the other terms of the e-lexicon

It is not a question of definition. It is a question of implication. How will the factors that these terms describe change our organizations, our customer relations, our associates, and our personal lives? We know that the Web allows a person to exist in a seemingly infinite space and communicate with anyone on the net, anywhere, at any time, for free. Don't let anyone tell you that's not going to change our lives. In the following chapters, we look at the essential elements of business—leadership, strategy, associates, customers, and knowledge/learning—to see what is required so far as we currently understand the rules of the new global, electronic economy.

One thing is certain amid this new jargon. All business, whether i-world– or e-world–initiated, must become one integrated system. Labels often obscure operations. To label something *knowledge management* and create a Chief Knowledge Officer makes the management of knowledge someone else's job. The same reaction applies to all functions, whether they be mainline activities such as production, sales, and service, or support functions like information systems, finance, or human resources. Business is an integrated system in e-world. Everyone must think of all of it as his or her job, not the sole responsibility of a staff function or a specialized unit. To compete, management must view it this way. It must first learn itself, and second, teach every associate how he or she is part of the internal and external web.

What has long been a business cliché—"We're all part of one team"—must now become a reality. Everyone in every position needs to see, feel, and accept how the consequences of her actions, no matter how humble or mundane, ripple throughout the enterprise and eventually impact its ability to attract, serve, and retain customers. Labeling units as line versus staff or expense centers versus revenue producers violates this imperative. Where isolation and introversion are the case, no one owns the business and critical activities deteriorate from neglect, spite, or the not-invented-here syndrome.

> *What has long been a business cliché—"We're all part of one team"—must now become a reality. Everyone in every position needs to see, feel, and accept how the consequences of her actions, no matter how humble or mundane, ripple throughout the enterprise.*

THE NEW BOTTOM LINE

To be successful in e-world, we have to recognize how it differs from what we knew and counted on in the past. Figure 2-2 shows the hallmarks of e-world. You can reflect on how they differ from i-world. It's not a question of better—only different. E-world is bigger, faster moving, open to everyone, more demanding, continually and rapidly changing, talent-dependent, information-driven, and customer-centric.

Many of the proven techniques of the industrial age will fall back into minor roles in e-world. Although incremental improvements in processes using quality control and reengineering are useful, they will not produce the types of gains that e-world speed demands. We can't keep up if we persist in continual tweaking to gain minute increments of efficiency. Process improvement may wring another percent out of operating cost, which does improve margins slightly. But while we dedicate resources to that exercise, competitors will be changing the market on us. We might wake up one day to find ourselves being the low-cost producer of a bleeding-edge product.

In e-world, the better we get at one thing, the more vulnerable we are to the new thing. Extreme competence blinds us to new possibilities for competitive advantage. There is a natural tendency to focus on things we do well while ignoring the discomfort of our weaknesses. Ted Williams, the last man to bat .400 in the major

Figure 2-2. The hallmarks of e-world.

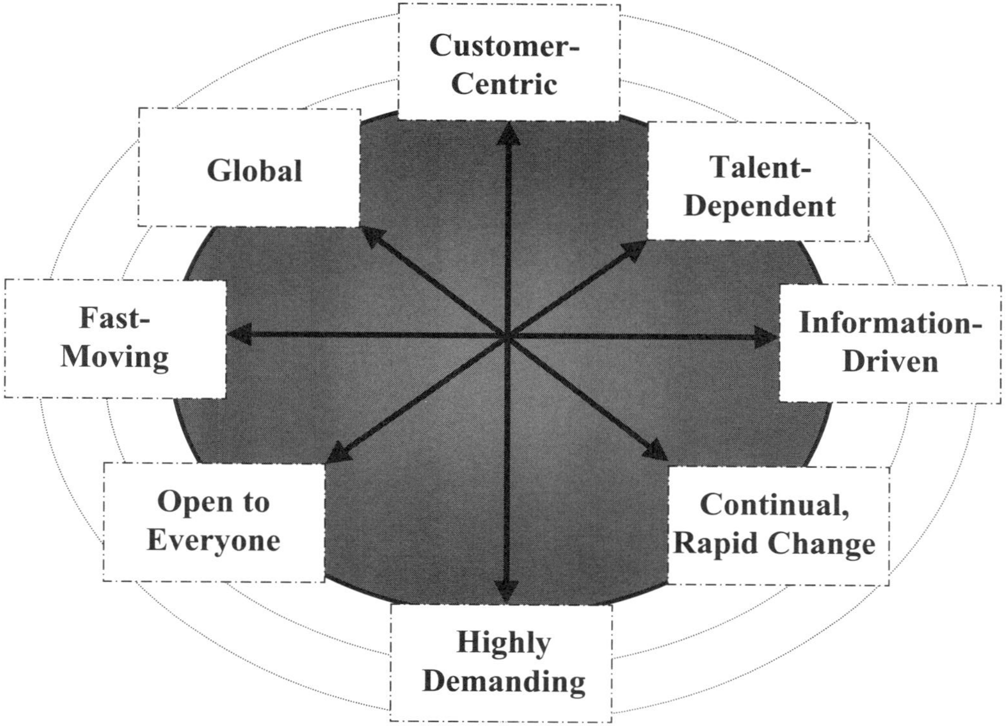

leagues sixty years ago, said that the good hitters continually practice hitting and the good fielders continually hone their fielding skills, and it should be the other way around. When we focus only on doing what we do well better, innovation blindsides us.

Kevin Kelly, executive editor of *Wired* magazine, states that "To achieve sustainable innovation you need to seek persistent disequilibrium. To seek persistent disequilibrium means that one must chase after disruption without succumbing to it, or retreating from it."[1] He goes on to claim that there are three types of change:

1. Change in the game
2. Change in the rules of the game
3. Change in how the rules are changed

In the first case, there are visible changes: new winners and losers. Examples are Wal-Mart and Dell Computer, which displaced Sears and Compaq. In the second case, there are new kinds of business. Examples are Federal Express and Amazon.com, which declared a new set of rules for package delivery and retailing. The third type of change is when change accelerates still more change. It is like the old ramjet engine: The faster it went, the faster it went . . . until it was ready to blow itself apart. In the third-order change, we find creative destruction. We don't do something better; we make it obsolete. The old is blown apart by the new. The key question is, "Are we going to blow apart our old methods, or are we going to let someone else do it to us?"

Despite the differences and in many cases improvements in e-world versus i-world, we need not abandon i-world. A great body of truth and value has been built during a century of experience in the marketplace. I-world simply needs to be updated to serve 21st-century conditions. Just as railroads connected industry with consumers and expanded commercial possibilities in the 19th century, the Internet is making connection ubiquitous today. To operate effectively—to be highly competitive—management must merge the best of the two worlds.

The winners will be the traditional companies that are able to combine the fleeting, intangible, dynamic qualities of the digital world with their hard-won capabilities, experience, and physical assets. Chris Meyer and Randy Love wrote about these qualities of what they termed the dot companies.[2] They claimed the dot companies would bring together the growth prospects of the young Internet companies with the infrastructure of the traditional, profitable corporations. The combining will spawn a new species of organization that is stronger, faster, and better equipped to deal in e-world than either of the parents. The risk-adverse parent will be prodded by the upstart to trade some stability for adaptability. Enron is cited as an example of this new species. It transformed itself from a traditional energy company into an energy trader and risk manager. Since the defining characteristic of the e-world economy is disequilibrium, the concept of stability is an anachronism. The lesson behind the dot-com phenomenon is: *Evolve or die.*

Retiring General Electric CEO Jack Welch brought a note of reality to the e-world hypemeisters when he said: "Old companies thought this was Nobel Prize–type work. This is not rocket science. It's just like breathing. The existing business already has sales and expenses. Digitize it and costs fall. Sales climb. Instantly (the old guy) gets to break even. Then the margins just pour in."[3]

Who was it that said that the more things change, the more they stay the same? The laws of physics have not changed. Gravity still rules. Integrity is still inviolable. Choose carefully the star you follow.

REFERENCES

1. Kevin Kelly, *New Rules for the New Economy* (New York: Viking, 1998), p. 114.

2. Chris Meyer and Randy Love, "Meet the Connected Economies New Species: The Dot Companies," *Perspectives on Business Innovation* (Cambridge, Mass.: Cap Gemini Ernst & Young, Center for Business Innovation, 2000), pp. 13–20.

3. "The E-Gang," *Forbes,* July 24, 2000, p. 148.

Chapter 3

The Practical Side of Intellectual Capital

INTELLECTUAL CAPITAL: FAD, HYPE, OR REALITY?

In 1994, Tom Stewart wrote a cover article for *Fortune* entitled "Your Company's Most Valuable Asset: Intellectual Capital," which popularized this latest addition to the management lexicon.[1] This was followed in the next few years by a flood of books, conferences, and seminars on intellectual capital (IC). IC's contribution to the evolution of the art of management is its focus on information as a capital asset of the organization. At the time it was first proposed, this was a unique angle and one that fit the emerging recognition that intelligence is an increasingly important element in all work from aerospace to zoo management. In addition, it later became evident that the missing element was the role that motivation plays in capturing and disseminating information.

Despite all the commotion, intellectual capital is not new. When Homo sapiens first learned how to control fire, that was intellectual capital at work, and this applied knowledge raised humankind above the beasts. So it has always been. Data plus human comprehension equals knowledge—and knowledge is the driving force behind progress. Within organizations, knowledge embodied in human beings, programs, and processes is their key competitive advantage.

Paradoxically, IC has been identified both as the intangible asset that stays behind when employees leave and as the intellectual asset that goes home with the employees every night. Both definitions are partly true, and therein lies the fundamental issue underlying this phenomenon. Although IC is central to organizational progress as a management model, it has yet to be translated into a form that is useful in daily operations. Essentially, it is an accepted but underutilized concept. This is ironic in that there is great practical potential in IC if organizations learn how to translate it into operational strategies and tactics.

THE FOUNDATION OF KNOWLEDGE MANAGEMENT

Intellectual capital is very important for e-world since the new economy runs more on intelligence than on any other asset. IC is the content within knowledge management. IC is the information that resides within intellectual property, associates, products, processes, and corporate culture, as well as on databases. It is that which knowledge management programs purport to manage. IC is management's most powerful tool. The challenge of knowledge management is to capture this information, structure it, and put it into various transmission media so that associates can use it and add to it. Intellectual capacity—what I refer to as IC^2—is the ability to manage that process and extract value from IC.

To date, many knowledge management programs have not consciously used IC as the content structure of their programs. Nevertheless, IC is important because it gives us the framework for understanding and classifying, discussing, and applying the information that is the grist of knowledge management. With the right information, practically anyone can obtain money to start or build a business enterprise. Without the right information, all the money in the world cannot create or sustain a viable business.

THE BUILDING BLOCKS OF IC

IC data can be placed into three categories: organizational, relational, and human. The following are examples of the types of data residing within those categories:

- **Organizational.** Intellectual property such as patents, copyrights, trademarks, and brands; the infrastructure, including process capability and communications; the corporate culture, which contains critical information for associates on how things work in the company
- **Relational.** Knowledge of and acquaintance with customers, suppliers, partners, competitors, governments, and communities in which the company operates
- **Human.** Attitudes, skills, and knowledge of employees, their motivation and commitment to the company, and the depth of talent

The test for IC is whether the data:

- Have relevance and purpose for human beings who can agree on the data's meaning.
- Can be transmitted and shared with other people.
- Are understood by other people.
- Have utility for other people in relation to their work objectives and personal growth.
- Have the potential to add value to the enterprise.

When these conditions are met, IC truly becomes an asset of the enterprise. IC's potential is exploited when an organization learns how to systematize and institutionalize the movement of IC in a way that achieves competitive advantage. That is the central point, which turns IC from an interesting academic topic to a business tool. Competitive advantage can be assessed in terms of economic value added (EVA). EVA is calculated as net operating profit after tax minus the cost of capital. Intellectual capacity is proven when EVA is achieved.

BARRIERS TO GETTING FULL VALUE FROM IC

To create and extract value from IC, managers have to adopt a broad view of the workplace. We need to overcome our natural tendency to approach a problem from our particular professional viewpoint. Engineers, salespeople, accountants, and human resources managers each concentrate on a different aspect of any given issue.

So it is with IC. When legal, finance, engineering, sales, and human resources see only their part of IC, it suboptimizes any reaction to the data. Therefore, the first tenet of IC management is integration. If we want the best results, we have to work each opportunity from all viewpoints.

The second limitation is time perspective. It is not that we don't have enough time—that is granted. It is that we tend to look at the present when we should be looking at the future. By the time we get to work in the morning, it is already the next day on the other side of the world. We have to build IC for tomorrow because it will be tomorrow before we can collect and use it.

> By the time we get to work in the morning, it is already the next day on the other side of the world. We have to build IC for tomorrow because it will be tomorrow before we can collect and use it.

My experience is that the winners in business do two things better than most people. First, they see beyond the obvious. They are not blinded by their discipline nor by the surface data. They exhibit a passion for asking *why* as well as *what*. The second thing they do well is manage the future from today. They are always a step ahead of the crowd, planning and positioning for the next big opportunity. So it must be with IC. We have to look beneath the surface of the data presented to us, and we have to work on tomorrow, today.

INTELLECTUAL CAPACITY IN ACTION

Intellectual capacity (IC^2) management locates, integrates, and communicates the information—the IC—needed to create competitive advantage. It answers several questions:

- How do we know IC when we see it?
- When we find it, how do we determine where it has potential value?
- Finally, how do we apply it for competitive advantage?

The answers to these questions take us from a list of dormant assets to something of practical economic value. The three actions, performed during different phases, are finding (or discovery), valuing, and building.

Phase One: Discovery

The IC search focuses on the value potential of the massive amounts of data that lie within organizational, relational, and human capital activities. For each data type, we ask ourselves, "What is the value potential of this?" For example, "What is the economic value in the information inherent within a patent, a work process, a relationship, or a person?" Is there something that we can sell outright or combine with other information to create a competitive advantage and realize economic value added?

Using intellectual property as an example, we can ask, "What is the value potential of this patent, copyright, or brand?" To answer that accurately and fully, we consider how it can be applied with organizational, relational, and/or human capital simultaneously. For example, what does our knowledge of the market, of our customers, and of our competitors tell us about the potential value of this patent? Knowing our customers' needs as well as the strategy and work in progress of our competitors tells us something of the potential market value of our patent. Next, understanding the capability of our workforce to turn the patent into a product at a competitive cost suggests that we should either attempt to manufacture it ourselves, outsource the building of the product, or simply license or sell the patent.

This simple example gives you a glimpse of the need for and the value of knowledge. With the wrong information, we might pass up an opportunity, spend resources on a product that our customers don't want, produce a product that is not as good as a competitor's offering, or let a potentially valuable asset lie dormant in the vault. Dow Chemical Company was one of the first concerns to recognize the value of its patent portfolio. Dow has subsequently made millions of dollars by licensing some of its patents to other companies.

There are many basic discovery questions. The following are just a few examples.

INTELLECTUAL PROPERTY

- Is the production and filing of patents linked to corporate strategy and goals?
- Which of our patents or copyrights have market value, and in what form?
- What is the current and future ROI (return on investment) of each existing active patent?
- What are the values of our brands?
- What is the state of the current franchise and license agreements we have?

INFRASTRUCTURE

- Are our production and administrative processes state-of-the-art?
- Are our communications systems effective and reliable?
- Is quality a program or a way of life?
- Does our corporate culture help to attract and retain good people?
- Does the compensation program reward learning as well as performance?

Integration

Each item that seems to have significant value potential should be judged against all other relevant items inside and outside its own sector. Assume for the sake of an example that we have a patent on a new type of stapler. Our stapler patent describes a handheld machine that can sense the thickness to be stapled as soon as it makes contact with the stack. It has a roll of thin staple wire, rather than precut staples, inside the body of the stapler. The machine advances the right amount of staple wire, cuts it, and drives the staple into the stack. The advantages are that the user has just the right length of staple in every case, saving time in trying to staple very thick stacks. In addition, the wire reel is cheaper than cut staples and it also holds more wire than the standard precut stapler. To determine if this patent is an economically valuable intellectual capital asset, we need to view it across all sectors. Figure 3-1 is a graphic example of a patent being considered in relationship to the issues within the three IC sectors (organizational, relational, and human).

The point of this simple example is twofold. First, there is great

Figure 3-1. Cross-sector considerations of a patent.

		IC SECTORS	
ITEM	ORGANIZATIONAL	RELATIONAL	HUMAN
Patent No. XXX	Copyrights	Customers	Manufacturing skills
	Other patents	Suppliers	Productivity level
	Brands	Competitors	Turnover rates
	Reputation	Government regulators	Morale
	Process capability	Community groups	Commitment

value to be found within the intellectual capital of the organization. Second, this is a simple, practical way to organize the investigation. There are many considerations regarding the potential value of this patent. For example, we might ask these questions about it:

- What is the potential size of market for the products using this patent?
- What is our competitor's product offering in those market niches?
- What is our manufacturing process capability (capital investment, process efficiency)?
- What would be the effect of this product on our other products already on the market?
- What would be the effect on our brand identity in the market?
- What would be the effect on our company's reputation?
- What would be the likely response capability of the competition?
- What is the level of customer awareness/desire for this type of product?
- What is the likelihood of resistance from the government or a community group?
- What is the current ability of employees to produce this product?
- What is the trainability of employees to produce it?
- What is the motivation of employees to produce it?
- What is the sustainability of production (employee retention rate)?
- What is the ability of our suppliers to provide a steady source of raw material?

Let's assume that it looks like a business opportunity and the preliminary decision is to go ahead. Are there any environmental or legal concerns with this production process? Suppose, because of our close relationships with our suppliers, we can induce them to commit to warehousing the wire inventory and stapler parts, and to meeting a just-in-time delivery schedule with a response time of no more than eight hours. Great, but do we have the competencies within the workforce to build it? Can we hire, train, and motivate our people to do the job fast enough to make it to the market window for this product? Or should we look into outsourcing the production? If production is initially successful, can we sustain or increase production levels? Assume further a total cycle time from booking the order to receiving material to assembling and shipping the product of four hours for 98 percent of orders. This would mean that we could promise delivery within twenty-four hours and have virtually no inventory cost.

If we have positive answers to all of the above, it appears that we have a good product and the ability to produce it. Among the many values are customer satisfaction and a near-zero inventory expense that reduces product cost. It appears that in meeting this scenario, there is a potential price/performance competitive advantage with this product. Now, we are moving toward valuing the potential of that patent—Phase Two of putting intellectual capacity into action.

Phase Two: Valuing IC

There is no inherent value in any intellectual capital asset such as a patent. Each asset—whether it be intellectual property, process efficiency, a relationship, or a human skill—has only potential value. It is through its use or application that the actual value appears and can be measured. The challenge of valuing intellectual capital can be solved by tracing it through examples of outcomes. Activity is expense. Results are value.

The Value Measurement Path

Companies that have struggled with the idea of quantitatively assessing the value of their intellectual capital assets have foundered on three points:

1. Unclear description of the asset(s) under study
2. Lack of understanding of the connections between an activity and a result
3. Vague or often subjective goals that have no link to competitive advantage

It is necessary to quantitatively assess the value. One way is with a measurement matrix. Figure 3-2 is a specific application of the general measurement matrix described in Appendix A, here used to determine the value of the stapler patent we have been discussing. In this case, we can easily see where the value lies, and, more importantly, we can put dollar signs on each of those values. This is an exercise in intellectual capacity (IC^2), our ability to put a piece of intellectual capital to work to generate economic value. In Figure 3-2 we can see several values. The product is an advance on the competition. There are no environmental hurdles. By developing a strong, positive relationship with a quality supplier, the company is able to ship product on short notice, which makes the customer happy and saves money through minimal inventory cost. Last, we can produce the stapler at a competitive price because we have the people who do the job or can acquire the necessary skills at an acceptable cost. In summary, we have acceptable if not superior margins on the product; the ability to sustain production; reliable, high-quality suppliers; and probably exceptional customer satisfaction. In the case of customer satisfaction, repeat sales, referrals to new customers, and reduced marketing expenses are additional measurable values. When we actually perform on this, we will have a practical example of intellectual capacity.

Figure 3-2. Patent value matrix.

	Service	*Quality*	*Productivity*
Cost			Low Unit Cost
Time	Quick Delivery		
Volume			Lower Inventory
Defect Rate		Acceptable Level	
Reaction	Customer Satisfaction		

Relational and Human Values

Valuing products and processes is easier than valuing relationships and human skills. Still, relationships between our associates and outsiders have clear value. Knowing customers, having a close connection with a supplier, being on friendly terms with local and federal officials, and having strong alliance partners is obviously valuable. Having firsthand information from direct and indirect contact with the competition's attitudes as well as its plans is useful. How much value lies within those relationships depends on the application of the information we extract from the relationship.

When we move to associates as assets, the problem is a bit more complex. Valuation of training programs has long been a deficient area. It is fair to ask how we can put a monetary value on skills training, supervisory development, or executive education. Let's look at each opportunity to evaluate and build human capital.

- **Skills Training.** The first case is relatively easy. If we conduct basic skills training, we can watch the trainees exercise the skill later and see the result. When the trainees can assemble products faster, with less waste, and with fewer errors, the economic value is obviously found in the product's cost, our ability to ship on time, and the customer's satisfaction with its quality.

- **Supervisory Development.** If we move up to supervisory development, we want to know how much the exercise of the supervisor's skills affects employee performance. Saratoga Institute's retention surveys have shown that the behavior of the supervisor is extremely important in terms of both productivity and associate retention. Depending on what we are teaching supervisors, we should be able to identify more efficient scheduling of work, higher employee morale, increased productivity, and, in time, lower turnover. By observing the work environment closely, we can determine if extraneous factors affected the results. In twenty years of measuring and evaluating performance, I have seldom had to resort to statistical methods to show face valid evidence of a measurable return on investment.

- **Executive Education.** When we reach the level of executive education, we have to work quite hard to find the economic value. The problem is that the focus of this type of education concentrates on strategic and long-term issues rather than on daily operations. Nevertheless, we are not lost. If we are teaching leadership, we must define it in terms of actions or behaviors that enlist people to follow the leader's plan. Examples might include ability to formulate a compelling vision for the enterprise, effective communications skills to stimulate employee commitment to the vision, ability to recruit and develop executive-level personnel, and determination and perseverance when difficulties or setbacks are encountered. In short, what visible, measurable value do those behaviors produce in the people being led? It is the response of the followers that reveals the value measure of leadership. In Part II, we look at the ROI of effective leadership.

The valuation questions are simply as follows:

1. What happened to cause service, quality, or productivity to change?
2. How much did it change in cost, time, volume, defects, or human reaction?
3. Was it the training that caused the improvement, was it an extraneous factor, or was it a combination of both?

These questions have been answered in a training valuation process that Saratoga Institute tested with eleven companies in the United States in 1994. In all the cases above, reference to the value matrix is a handy way to find visible change that can be evaluated.

Phase Three: Building Intellectual Capacity

Intellectual capacity is a managerial process skill—not a specific organizational, relational, or human factor. Operationally, IC^2 expands as organizations learn the most efficient and effective ways to:

• Obtain relevant data (data that have potential utility).
• Convert data into knowledge.

- Put data into the hands of the people who need the data.
- Train them to convert the data into value-adding intelligence.
- Reward them for being good IC data managers.

We've seen how IC^2 functions in a product example. The following is an example of IC^2 at work in the area of building human capital for the organization. For the foreseeable future, there will be a shortage of skilled personnel in almost all job groups, from entry-level workers through technicians and professionals to managers. Competitive advantage rests largely on the ability to cost-effectively recruit and retain needed human capital. Yet if we want to know how to manage and measure the economic value of human capital, we have to consider the totality of its effect on the enterprise. This includes everything from workforce planning to measures of associate productivity. The following brief example will be confined to outlining the factors antecedent to productive associate behavior, namely finding and keeping human skills.

Starting Point

The first step is to determine the value adding goals and objectives of three workforce management functions—planning, staffing, and retention—as they relate to the enterprise's goals. Typical generic examples of the three functions are as follows:

- **Planning.** Quantifying the number, type, and availability of human capital needed to meet the enterprise's objectives
- **Staffing.** Acquiring that human capital in the most cost-effective manner, which can be through hiring, renting, or training (buy or make)
- **Retention.** Keeping a target percentage of that human capital

Information Needs

The second step is to identify information needed for each function and task. The base of intellectual capital is information, not cash or equipment. This requires describing data through information specification and mapping:

1. **Data Needs.** List the data needed for each task within these functions:
   - **Planning.** The business plan, which outlines labor needs
   - **Hiring.** Information on current associate skills and external labor availability
   - **Retaining.** Exit interview data on reasons for voluntary associate separations
2. **Data Sources.** Internal sources include business plans and hiring managers; external sources include government, industry, and regional sources.
3. **Data Recipients.** Who needs what information?
4. **Data Schedule.** When does each user need it?
5. **Data Acquisition.** Processes for data gathering include surveys, interviews, and benchmarking.
6. **Data Dissemination.** This can be one-to-one, through teams, broadcast, electronic, and paper and personal reports.
7. **Barriers and Bottlenecks.** These are current and potential impediments to data acquisition and dissemination.
8. **Information Costs.** What is the most cost-effective approach?
9. **Information Values.** What is the value of having accurate data?

Application

With these information specs, each function can begin to develop the organizational, relational, and human capital data it needs to carry out its work and meet its specific ROI objectives. Over time, the data decisions can be empirically tested for their validity within and across the functions. Ultimately, the test is: Did the line managers have the information they needed to hire, effectively apply, and retain key personnel?

Information is the fuel of intellectual capacity. Having the right information in the right place at the right time is the critical starting point. It is the essence of intellectual capital management. Understanding the implications within the information converts it into operating intelligence. The ability to use the information in conjunction with the corporate vision and strategy to manage effectively is the essence of intellectual capacity.

> *Information is the fuel of intellectual capacity. Having the right information in the right place at the right time is the essence of intellectual capital management.*

CONCLUSION

Intellectual capacity is based on an appreciation of the complexity and interdependencies of information assets. Just as organizations have traditionally invested capital in machines and people to achieve competitive advantage, it is now imperative to invest in information tools and processes. With insightful application of information rapidly becoming a key performance differentiator, it is clear that new methods and procedures for information acquisition, dissemination, and application are needed. Bigger and faster computers and larger databases add little incremental value to people who don't understand the interdependencies of data from different sectors.

Although information management might seem like a time-consuming and complicated task, experience has shown that it is not. It simply demands discipline, perseverance, and knowledge gained through experience on how information and activity variables interact. If there is no time to perform a full valuation potential on each task, the following quick questions will at least open the door to new insights:

1. What is the competitive advantage that the company seeks in service–quality–productivity?
2. Will completing this task contribute more to that competitive advantage goal than completing another task?
3. What evidence is there to support that conclusion?

Working harder is not the answer, since activity is expense. Value comes from achieving relevant results.

Intellectual capacity can be achieved by looking beneath the surface of each information-bearing item that resides within an enterprise. The most potent way to uncover, transform, and leverage data is to integrate all three perspectives—organizational, relational, and human—as closely as possible.

REFERENCE

1. Thomas Stewart, "Your Company's Most Valuable Asset: Intellectual Capital," *Fortune,* October 1994, pp. 68–72.

Part II

LEADERSHIP IMPERATIVES

IN E-WORLD

Leading: The Inside Game

BY FAR THE MOST POPULAR topic in organizational literature is leadership. Whether the venue is government, the military, or commerce, more speeches, books, and seminars have been produced on the mysteries of leadership than on any other topic. The issue has been attacked from philosophical, genetic, and skill perspectives. The traits and behaviors of Alexander the Great, Jesus, Genghis Khan, Mohammed, Otto von Bismarck, Benjamin Disraeli, Douglas MacArthur, Golda Meir, John F. Kennedy, Margaret Thatcher, Ronald Reagan, and hundreds of others across recorded history have been debated in search of an answer to the elusive question, "What makes an exceptional leader?" There are as many hypotheses as there are proponents. At the end of the day we are left with a broad consensus but no generally accepted, detailed model. Now the issue is complicated with the question of how leadership differs, if it does, in e-world versus i-world.

There is no question that certain aspects of leadership are unchangeable. People, being what they are, have a set of expectations about their leaders. Some of these expectations are the same today as they were one hundred years ago. The unchanging parts are those characteristics and behaviors that are of the most personal nature. On the other hand, the environment has changed and, in doing so, is driving people toward some new expectations of leaders. The dilemma is: What is the same and what is different?

WHY LEADERSHIP IS IMPORTANT IN E-WORLD

Given the uncertainty of many new businesses—both joint ventures and start-ups—plus the reconfiguration of traditional businesses, the uniqueness of the market revolution intensifies the importance and hence the interest in leadership. Since intangibles are a key part of many current projects, the first question asked about a new venture is who is going to lead it. Who is the CEO? According to leadership researcher Leslie Gaines-Ross, the reputation of the CEO can account for as much as 45 percent of the company's market capitalization. While this might sound outlandish, consider the before-and-after market value of Merck & Co. under Ray Vagelos, Coca-Cola under Robert Goizueta, or Motorola under Robert Galvin.

When we think about corporate strategy, we think of a plan that sits there until the CEO gives it life. Clearly, the person is more important than the plan. It is the chief executive whose reputation and skills attract top people, influence investors, and cultivate partnerships. We see evidence of this in advertising. CEOs are now common spokespersons for their companies in television and print ads. The trend to emphasize the personality of the CEO has gone so far as to cause some to claim strategy is dead; it's all about leadership. This is a typical overreaction so prevalent in the media today. The more useful approach is to look at how leadership and strategy fit into e-world.

E-WORLD LEADERSHIP ESSENTIALS

Dealing with fundamental questions such as the nature of leadership in e-world calls for a look at basic elements. There are a number of seminal thinkers and practitioners who have offered their beliefs for consideration. Charles Handy, Warren Bennis, James

O'Toole, Jack Welch, and John Chambers are a few of the more familiar.

Another person with an interesting theory who I believe has something very important to add to the mix is Peter Koestenbaum, who is essentially a philosopher in executive-coach clothes. He approaches the topic by starting at a point over which others often leap. Given the question of leading in a profoundly new environment, I believe we cannot afford to skip over his lessons. Koestenbaum's starting point is how effectively the leader considers the central issues of life. He writes: "Unless the distant goals of meaning, greatness and destiny are addressed, we cannot make an intelligent decision about what to do tomorrow morning—much less set strategy for a company."[1]

When lists of great current business leaders are compiled, we seldom see the names of any of the high-profile CEOs of technology companies. This is because they do not address this fundamental question of meaning, greatness, and destiny. If you ever have a chance to engage them in conversation, you find them totally preoccupied with technical and marketing issues. They seldom talk about the basics that led Bill Hewlett and Dave Packard to set out "The H-P Way" fifty years ago. When they do talk about the basics, it is most often mouthing of clichés without any thoroughly considered personal belief system underpinning them. In the political arena, since Watergate, the United States has desperately sought to reaffirm its values. But because of the tragedy of that incident and its aftermath, we have lost faith in subsequent administrations to provide that type of leadership.

Koestenbaum notes that the more we understand the human condition, the more effective we are as human beings and as businesspersons. Herein lies the path to understanding how leadership in e-world is and is not different than in i-world. The underlying truth is that the forces of the new global economy alienate the average person. It is easy to see why. On the one hand, we are told how fortunate we are to live in this time of unprecedented freedom, opportunity, and exploding wealth. On the other hand, the stress level brought on by impossible demands for ever better quality, ever higher productivity, and ever faster response is often unbearable. In the end, the probability that 99 percent of the population will participate in a millionaire-making initial public offering is virtually nil. What this comes down to is a demand on the top team to deal with the brutality of the marketplace while simultaneously supporting human values. It ain't an easy task, my friend.

Koestenbaum offers a path through the chaos. He suggests that we think of leadership as the sum of two drivers: (1) competence (skills, knowledge, know-how) and (2) authenticity (identity, character, attitude). When we are stuck on the horns of the latest dilemma, we usually rededicate ourselves to working harder. This often gives us short-term, relative success as defined by only a dampening of the fire, not the acquisition of new knowledge—in short, nothing learned. Koestenbaum prescribes a path of greater lasting value. He states that if we feel trapped in a vortex, we need to do two things. One is to understand better at a basic level what it means to exist as a human being in this world. This is a time-consuming and potentially uncomfortable task that takes some deliberation. But in the long run it can contribute greatly to peace of mind.

The second thing we need to do is to change our habits of thought, what we value, how we work, how we connect with others, how we learn, what we expect from our lives, and how we manage our frustrations. Koestenbaum describes these two acts as the fundamentals of a leadership mind.

TWO PERSPECTIVES OF LEADERSHIP

Leadership can be viewed from two perspectives: (1) what we do and (2) how we do it. We can get people to do what we want if we have the power to coerce or bribe them. In the short term, we get the behavior we want—but at a high price. Recently, I was talking about performance metrics (ROIs) with a group of managers from one of the *Fortune* 50 companies. After I presented my views, one of the executives said, "That's all interesting and valid, but if you want performance you simply provide an incentive, such as a bonus." He went on to illustrate his position with an example from the previous year, where generous performance bonuses were dangled in front of senior managers who responded accordingly and met their goals. After congratulating him, I asked what effects those behaviors were having on the company this year. He said they had not checked. Is this leadership or is it bribery? How big do the bribes have to be next year—and five years from now? How many times can this type of short-term, single-minded, thoughtless behavior be repeated until the organization crumbles from within? Does this style of leadership build lasting shareholder value? I think not. Less than one year after this company's bonus bonanza, cracks are starting to appear in the organization. A recent publication of the top ten companies in its industry did not include this company. Discussions with some managers confirmed the mounting confusion and disarray. I expect that we will see significant management turnover there in the near term.

> *We have well-educated, mobile, values-driven associates throughout our technical and professional ranks, and we are stressing them to the limits of their tolerance.*

In e-world, we must recognize that we are dealing with a paradox. We have well-educated, mobile, values-driven associates throughout our technical and professional ranks, and we are stressing them to the limits of their tolerance. Offering on-site dry cleaning and day care services, bring your pet to work days, and other forms of stress relief are helpful, but they are not the ultimate solution. We must address our associates' human needs for respect, recognition, meaningful accomplishments, growth opportunity, and authentic communication in the course of meeting increasingly difficult performance objectives. If we don't, we will suffer high absenteeism followed by high turnover and a lack of commitment to customers at a time when we need commitment most. The fact that a person stays in the company does not necessarily mean he is committed to its vision. He might just be hiding out and offering minimally acceptable performance.

PEOPLE PUZZLE: DEMOGRAPHICS AND DOWNSIZING

A number of studies have shown that there is a demographic problem within the U.S. population that will severely affect the ability of corporations to find or develop leaders for the new millennium.

McKinsey and Company surveyed 400 corporate officers and 6,000 executives and concluded that "many American companies are already suffering a shortage of executive talent."[2] A study by Development Dimensions International (DDI) claims that a significant number of our larger, old-line companies will lose at least 40 percent of their executives through retirement by 2005, sixty years from the start of the Baby Boom. This predicament will be exacerbated by another population demographic. Between the years 2000 and 2015, the number of 35- to 40-year-olds in the United States will drop by 15 percent—the effects of the Baby Bust.

If that isn't enough, corporations have done much to contribute to the shortfall. From 1989 through the middle of the 1990s, downsizing was the order of the day. In fact, i-world companies that have been slow on the draw are still handing out wholesale pink slips. Outplacement firms report that more than half of their clients are middle managers, the successors to the retiring executives. Since downsizing has been in vogue, succession planning has largely disappeared. This means not only that are there no depth charts being kept, but that little succession-focused development has been attempted. Finally, the alienation felt by many workers has caused some midlevel associates to pass on management opportunities. Their attitude is, what is the point of sticking our necks out and taking on more stress and responsibility when the company shows no signs of loyalty toward us?

Bill Byham, president of DDI, wraps up the situation thus: "Corporations can neither hunt future talent as they once did, nor relegate action to the back burner, as many have done in recent years. They would do well, in fact, to take a cue from GE's Jack Welch, who spends 50 percent of his time on the development of his corporation's future leaders."[3]

A LEADERSHIP KIT

In June 1999, the cover story of *Fast Company* was leadership.[4] They interviewed a wide range of people from bankers to B-school professors to dot-com CEOs. In the end they coalesced their findings into a "Do-It-Yourself Kit." Figure 4-1 is a distillation of the elements of leadership they suggest as appropriate for e-world. Keep these in mind as we work through this chapter.

Figure 4-1. Elements of leadership appropriate for e-world.

1. Leaders are both confident and modest. They leave their ego in the cloakroom.
2. Leaders are authentic. They show integrity in all cases.
3. Leaders are listeners. They are fueled by curiosity.
4. Leaders are good at giving encouragement, and they are never satisfied. They test and build courage and stamina.
5. Leaders make unexpected connections—innovative people connections.
6. Leaders provide direction—in touch and out front, but not in control.
7. Leaders protect their people from danger and expose them to reality. They eliminate fear of change.
8. Leaders make change and stand for precious values that don't change.
9. Leaders lead by example. They exhibit their principles under a microscope.
10. Leaders don't blame. They learn, try, fail, learn, and try again.
11. Leaders look for and network with other leaders. They are not Lone Rangers. They help others to become better.
12. The job of the leader is to make more leaders. The team with the most and best wins.

FINDING AND MAKING LEADERS

The most common method for addressing a shortage of any type or level of talent is to raid the competition. This is a short-term action with long-term consequences. Raiding talent from other companies creates two problems. The first is that now-famous quote from the movie *Forrest Gump*: "Life is like a box of chocolates. You never know what you're going to get."

Many a mistake is made in recruitment. The most outrageous cases occur when inadequate background checking takes place. I've seen several cases of outright fraud on resumés that top management accepted at face value. The ensuing termination was not only costly but embarrassing as well. Even when the new hire is OK, raiding is only a stopgap method. New hires take some time to acclimate themselves to the company. Precious time is lost breaking them into our way of doing things. Saratoga Institute's research shows the learning curve for new managers takes at least six months and most often a year or more to reach standard performance levels. In the meantime, customers are not well served and associates are not well managed.

The second problem with raiding is that while we are raiding to fill a hole somewhere in the company, someone else from another place is abducting our talent. Unless the national economy collapses, talent raiding and the growth of new businesses are going to make headhunters very rich and corporations talent poor. We have to recoup for the decades of hands-on experience we flushed out in our downsizing mania. The only sustainable long-term solution is to grow our own talent as rapidly as possible.

Organizations have to dedicate resources to identifying associates who have the potential and interest in ascending to upper-level positions. This implies more sophisticated selection and testing methods than we've applied in most companies over the past decade. Having selected the high potentials, obviously without bias, we have to focus on their development. This means someone has to be responsible for monitoring and/or mentoring these candidates. Possible career paths need to be identified and discussed. Developmental experiences have to be planned. These can take several forms, such as stretch assignments, job rotation, outside alliance program assignments, formal educational experiences, or other developmental opportunities. If this is conducted as a planned activity with associates being viewed as corporate rather than departmental assets, acceleration can be accomplished. It leaves us with the one original question: *What does it take to be a leader in e-world?*

EXECUTIVE CONFUSION

Not only is there a shortfall of future leaders, there is also extreme confusion within the ranks of present-day leaders. Saratoga Institute's retention service interviewed over 60,000 current and departed employees from 1996 to 2000. Recently, we have seen a steady rise in the number of associates who claim that "upper management" is a major source of irritation and problems. The complaints are clustered around vagueness of vision and values, lack of consistency in word and deed, not listening to employees, showing no respect, and being "lightweight, tactical folk." Our conclusion is that many of today's leaders are bewildered, flustered, and even dazed by what they are facing. In fairness to them, they were not prepared for e-world. No one was or is.

Jim Bracher, one of the preeminent executive counselors in the United States, seconds our conclusions. In a recent conversation, he claimed that after over more than two decades of working with CEOs and their direct reports, he has never seen this level of frustration. Driven by the hyper growth rate of many companies in this superheated economy, people are promoted some levels above their capability. As a result, the boss is picking up the work of others who are functionally or marginally incompetent. Bracher put it this way:

> *Increasingly, executives are finding that the curse of the clock [demand for rapid response] causes them to be overwhelmed by data, much of which is irrelevant to the leadership and decision making for which they are paid. Hounded by voice-mail, e-mail, and unprepared followers, they burn their energies in the endless pursuit of resolving conflicts for others. They are tired, frustrated, and isolated. And it ain't gettin' better, pal.*

PRINCIPLES AND MODELS

Every writer on leadership to date has a list of leadership traits and behaviors, which are touted as essential. If we put every known list side by side and analyze the content, I suspect we would find at least 75 percent overlap.

James O'Toole at Stanford University believes that focusing on a leader's style or personality is doomed to failure because each leader is a different person (*in a different situation,* I would add).[5] His premise is that focusing on traits obscures the fact that leadership isn't a solo act. What matters is the organization's overall *leadership capacity* throughout its ranks. O'Toole claims that the common behavior of effective leaders is that they don't do a lot of unfocused things. They concentrate on a small set of acts necessary to cascade leadership down through the organization. These actions are learnable and replicable. By observing examples of successful acts rather than personal traits, anyone with insight and ambition can grow into leadership at some level.

O'Toole talks about developing leaders who can work through other people to create institutions that are not dependent upon them and who can create legacies of innovation and entrepreneurship that live on. He describes leaders who can look into the future, beyond their company and industry, to the communities of which they are a part. This is where he admits to a character trait essential for effective leadership, which he calls *appropriate ambition*. This is an internal force that motivates one to risk all in the pursuit of a worthy corporate goal—not just a personal goal. All effective leaders have the compelling desire to help their own nation, company, or organization achieve its highest potential. Moreover, they are willing to put themselves on the line to achieve it.

James Citron and Thomas Neff of Spencer Stuart claim that the fundamental characteristics that make for outstanding business leadership in e-world are the same as those in i-world. Then, they add a coda.[6] Briefly, they state that effective leaders live by enduring principles and augment them with new qualities that focus on speed, flexibility, risk taking, customer obsession, and internal communication. They offer six enduring principles that carry over from i-world into e-world. These are also a good summation of the factors listed by most leadership authors:

1. Exhibit personal integrity of word and deed.
2. Offer a *Big Idea* with a winning strategy behind it.
3. Build a great management team to execute it.
4. Excite associates with the *Big Idea*.
5. Create a flexible, responsive organization.
6. Build an infrastructure of management and compensation systems.

I am assuming that within the first principle listed above is the self-examination of values that Koestenbaum demands.

Citron and Neff follow up with six new principles for e-world:

1. Obsessing about the customer
2. Building a flat, cross-functional organization

3. Managing via a fluid business model versus the old annual strategic plan
4. Evangelizing and generating positive buzz
5. Truly encouraging risk taking
6. Rolling up the sleeves and working hard

My view is that of these six new principles, 1, 2, 3, and 5 are spot-on. Number 6 goes without saying. Number 4 can be confusing depending on how we read it. If the focus is external, I believe that actions speak louder than buzz. Look what happens when a company misses quarterly earning expectations. No explanation can restrain the fall of the stock price. It could be that I am too old to understand how important buzz is in e-world. However, I hear from every corner that there is entirely too much hype and overpromise in the market today. "Ship it and fix it in the field" is the war cry. Associates complain that upper management does not walk its talk. I don't believe customers are accepting that any more either. I would be more comfortable with a principle that focuses internally on listening and responding to associates. Given what we know about the stress that everyone is experiencing, it is absolutely critical to sustained success that leaders bond more closely with associates at all levels. To me, this is one of the most important differences in leadership between the two worlds.

GETTING TO THE HEART OF IT

Ram Charan and Geoffrey Colvin stepped into the leadership debate with their *Fortune* report on "Why CEOs Fail."[7] In search of the reasons, they looked at thirty-eight high-profile people who had failed. Six general reasons for failure were developed. The six and the frequency with which each occurred across the group were:

Bad earnings news:	30—Awash in red ink, poor performance

Lifer syndrome:	20—Too long in the job, lost touch with the market
People problems:	17—Put the wrong people in key jobs
Decision gridlock:	15—Analysis paralysis
Off-the-deep-end financials:	6—Overemphasis on financials, missing the rest
Missing in action:	4—Too much time away from the job

The authors determined that while the problems above were known and contributed to the CEOs' downfall, and while bad earnings may have triggered the board's decision to terminate, none of them were the primary cause behind the symptom. What were the key reasons for their failure? To use Charan and Colvin's words: "It's bad execution . . . not getting things done, being indecisive, not delivering on commitments." When asked how most CEOs blew it, the answer was, "By failure to put the right people in the right jobs—and the related failure to fix people problems in time." They went on to make a most interesting point. Successful CEOs never hesitate to fire when they must, but they're deeply interested in people—far more than failed CEOs are. Their implied motto is: "People first, strategy second."

Jim Kouzes and Barry Posner wrote what in my opinion is the most practical book on leadership of all time: *The Leadership Challenge*.[8] It is based on their leadership workshops at Santa Clara University, where they collected data from thousands of working managers and supervisors over many years. They followed that work with another book that concentrated on what they believed to be one of the seminal issues: recognition.[9] When they asked participants if they needed encouragement to perform at their best, only 60 percent said yes. This flew in the face of the expected answer. The majority believed in themselves and their ability to perform without outside stimulation. Given that finding, the authors reframed the question. They asked, "When you get encouragement, does it help you perform at a higher level?" This time 98 percent said yes.

A number of other studies over the past fifty years have shown the same types of results. People want to be acknowledged. Less than half of all workers surveyed in the United States say they get any recognition for a job well done. About 40 percent claim they *never* get any recognition for outstanding performance. Going deeper, long-term research into leadership and leaders

> **Leaders as well as those led crave recognition and—dare we say it?—affection.**

continually shows that leaders as well as those led crave recognition and—dare we say it?—affection. Why is recognition essential for performance? It is a two-step process. Recognition builds self-esteem, and self-esteem drives productivity. In Chapter 11, I will describe our research into the relationship between self-esteem and productivity. For now, take my word for it.

The conclusion now must be that to be an effective leader, a person must be comfortable expressing appreciation and showing outright affection for the people with whom she comes in contact. In order to do this honestly, the leader must know herself, be comfortable with that self, and in the long term be able to communicate that to others. I grant that there are people leading *Fortune*-level companies who are shallow, totally mercenary, and making tons of money in the process. However, in every case where I have personal knowledge, the individual is not fooling anyone. People follow only because they too are making a good living. But for the most part, they neither respect nor are committed to the leader as a human being. It is undeniable: Effective leadership starts inside.

We are left with a new list of keys to effective leadership, which will help you guide your company in the new e-economy.

LEADERSHIP KEYS
1. Leadership is at least as important, if not more so, in e-world as it was in i-world.
2. Leadership today requires all the inherent capabilities as in the past, plus several new skills and sensitivities.
3. The e-world leader must have a thorough knowledge of him- or herself in terms of personal values and behavior style.
4. The personality of the e-world leader is important because of the need for the leader to be more visible internally and externally.

5. Due to the extremely large workload and the criticality of the position, the leader must become very focused and efficient.

A NOTE TO THE BOARD OF DIRECTORS

Given the intense competitiveness and speed of the market, along with the criticality of the leader in an e-world company and his or her personal fiduciary responsibility, I believe the board of directors should be involved in the enterprise beyond quarterly meetings. This implies that directors cannot sit on a large number of boards and fulfill their responsibilities as directors. I realize this is not a welcome idea. Nevertheless:

1. Directors must be knowledgeable of the industry in which the company operates.
2. Directors must have the time and the willingness to take a personal, active role in support of the CEO, when needed. Leaders need all the help they can get, and allegedly the board is populated by people who have proven themselves to be effective managers if not leaders.
3. Directors have a responsibility to the associates as well as to external stockholders. The associates, whose welfare is dependent on the viability of the company, should receive a short report from the board of directors at least semiannually. This should follow immediately after the first- and third-quarter board meetings. The director's report to associates should inform them of the state of the company and of progress against financial, marketing, and structural plans. The chair of the board should report, simultaneously and personally to the associates, the same matters that are reported to the general public. Most important, the report should focus on what these data mean to the associates. It should also recognize and celebrate extraordinary achievements by an associate, a team, or a business unit. In cases where the CEO is the chair, an outside director should deliver the report in the most personal manner practical.

REFERENCES

1. Polly Labarre, "Do You Have the Will to Lead?" *Fast Company*, March 2000, pp. 222–230.

2. Elizabeth Chambers, Mark Foulon, Helen Handfield-Jones, Stephen Hankin, and Edward Michaels III, "The War for Talent," *McKinsey Quarterly 3*, 1998.

3. William C. Byham, "Executive Help Wanted, Inquire Within: The Leadership Dearth Is the Real Dilemma," *Employment Relations Today*, Autumn 1999.

4. *Fast Company*, June 1999, special supplement following p. 128.

5. James O'Toole, *Leadership A to Z: A Guide for the Appropriately Ambitious* (San Francisco: Jossey-Bass, 1999).

6. James Citron and Thomas Neff, "Digital Leadership," *Strategy and Business*, First Quarter 2000.

7. Ram Charan and Geoffrey Colvin, "Why CEOs Fail," *Fortune*, June 21, 1999, pp. 69–78.

8. James Kouzes and Barry Posner, *The Leadership Challenge* (San Francisco: Jossey-Bass, 2nd ed., 1995).

9. James Kouzes and Barry Posner, *Encouraging the Heart* (San Francisco: Jossey-Bass, 1999).

Chapter 5

Leading Others into E-World

TRUE LEADERSHIP IS BASED ON the belief that people are assets—beings who add value. For decades, if not centuries, demagogues as well as many managers have believed that people are a nuisance, a self-absorbed mass to be exploited and an expense meant to be minimized. Leaders who think that way are probably self-absorbed martinets who themselves should be minimized. For most people, leadership is a combination of hoping and settling. We hope for great leaders, yet much of the time we settle for mediocrity. One look at the political scene confirms this. Business does slightly better, some of the time.

The great majority of people want only a few basic things out of life. First is certainly safety and security. We all want a life as free from worry about survival as possible. Second, people want a modicum of worldly goods so that they might have a degree of comfort and self-respect. Third, they want family and friends to share life with them. Last, they would like to find meaningful work so they have a sense of accomplishment. For many people, anything more than that is frosting on their cake. If a leader can contribute to those human needs, the people gladly follow, support, and perhaps even come to defend the leader in his or her time of need.

In a business organization, the leader provides two essentials.

First, the leader articulates a compelling vision and a practical strat-egy—a goal with a path to reach it. Second, the leader creates a culture based on his or her values and behavior that shows the pre-ferred way to live and work together in attaining that goal. The semi-nal skill underlying both essentials is communication, both verbal and nonverbal. All great leaders, no matter their moral character, have been exceptionally adept communicators. That is the focus of this chapter.

LEADERSHIP COMMUNICATION

There have been thousands of books and articles written about how leaders communicate. Nevertheless, this topic deserves another look because of where we are today. We are launching ourselves into the most wide-ranging, rapidly changing, risk-laden era in the history of humankind. Building a strategy and a culture that will not only survive the transformation from i-world to e-world but also thrive during it is surely a task worthy of discussion.

Since e-world is possible only because of the new communica-tions technology, the e-economy is an exercise in communication. Communication has always been the foundation on which a society is laid. It supports not only our interpersonal discourses: It is also the primary channel of commerce. In the earliest times, commerce was conducted on a one-to-one barter basis. As people gathered them-selves into villages, the local market became the focus of trade and social life. There, people came to see, touch, taste, inquire, gossip, and negotiate. Now the World Wide Web has expanded trade for the common person beyond the boundaries of the village market or city bazaar. The net is the new medium of communication and trade for all of us. It is the marketplace. The Internet is the new communi-cations system, and communication is the lifeblood of human ex-change.

It is clear to everyone already that the net is affecting almost every aspect of life, yet it has been in operation for the general population since only 1995. In its first five years, it succeeded in in-stantaneously connecting 300 million people around the globe. That communication is not the prime issue here. The Internet is merely a communications system. We are talking here about leadership communication. Too often, executives fund the development of communications systems and believe that they have filled the communications void. In many cases, all they have done is highlighted the vacuum. It is akin to laying out a plumbing system and forgetting to turn on the water. Nice pipe—no water.

Communication is a personal art first and a system science second. In practically every employee survey ever taken, communication comes up with a poor score. How many times have you heard someone lament, "We have a communication problem"? You may remember the Paul Newman movie *Cool Hand Luke*, where he is a prisoner in a Southern prison. After he is knocked down by a guard for some transgression, the warden looks down at him and says, "What we have here is a failure to communicate." Why is it that the most natural of all human behaviors is sorely lacking in organizations? It could be that this is merely a manifestation of our general inability to communicate effectively in many situations. Marriages fail, children are alienated, workers are demotivated, partnerships collapse, customers are lost—all because of poor communication. In e-world, ineffective communication is both an intolerable condition and a potentially tremendous competitive disadvantage.

THING OR PROCESS?

James Gleick has pointed out that we often think and act as though information is a thing.[1] I believe that this may be a major source of the problem. When leaders think of communication as a thing, they tend to ignore its *humanness*. Communication is a constant process, a weaving of qualitative judgment with the sharing of facts. There is as much emotion and socialization to most communication as there is fact. The personality, needs, and concerns of the discussants come through, even when they are discussing accounting figures or statistical data. Effective communication is to a degree a function of the medium used, as Marshall McLuhan described more than thirty-five years ago. Each medium affects the message it is carrying. The same words (message) delivered by telephone, radio, or television sound(s) and feel(s) different.[2] That notwithstanding, effectiveness is much more a matter of the character of the communicator, the content of the message, the context in which it is happening, and the desired response. Information transmitted does not just lie there. It is absorbed, compared, and responded to by every being who receives it. If you say "sit" to your dog, you may get the behavior you want. If you say "sit" to your child, you probably get a different behavior. If you say "sit" to your spouse, you most likely get a response you certainly don't want. The point is that as a leader, our words, tone, timing, and medium, as well as our relationship with our associates, all affect our communication. People speak of credibility in communication. If communication were a thing, credibility would not be an issue. But information coming from a human being is energy, and that makes it an entirely different matter.

People make their reality by constantly processing incoming information from all the five senses as well as the sixth sense, intuition. Margaret Wheatley points out that all life uses information to organize matter and energy into form or substance.[3] She states that we often confuse a system's physical manifestation with the processes that gave birth to it. Yet the true living system is the processes that continually form and reform it. We need to keep open systems that continually take in new information and reform themselves and their by-products. This is what innovation depends on. Closed systems that do not allow all available information to course through them wind down and decay, victims of the Second Law of Thermodynamics. Information is the life force of organizations. No one person or group is so omniscient that he knows what can and cannot be usefully communicated. Even if he did, he could not totally exclude outside information from insidiously finding cracks in the system and upsetting the internal order. Information from the free world is what finally brought down the Iron Curtain. It was not the number of nuclear warheads in NATO, it was Mikhail Gorbachev seeing what was going on in the free world and realizing that the Soviet Union could no longer keep it out.

> *Information is the life force of organizations. No one person or group is so omniscient that he knows what can and cannot be usefully communicated.*

With the nature of information and human communication being what it is, it is nearly impossible for a leader to fool the associates. As Mr. Lincoln said, "You can fool some of the people all of the time and all of the people some of the time, but you can't fool all of the people all of the time." On the other side is W. C. Fields, who claimed, "You can fool some of the people some of the time and fortunately that is enough to make a good living." Management has always tried, in vain, to control information—to fool some of the people some of the time. (It's called investor relations.)

The latest attempt to control information is called *knowledge management*. In e-world, information is freely moving among millions of people every second of the day 24/7/52/365. So please, let's drop this notion that we can control or even manage it. The best we can do is capture some of the information, codify it, and put it into the hands of the people who need it. That is what I would like to call *knowledge organization*. It is unquestionably useful, but to call it knowledge management might be a bit of an overstatement. However, it looks like we are stuck with this term, at least for a while. So for the sake of clarity, I will reluctantly use it. But keep in mind I am thinking of organization, not control.

To be effective, we must accept that information and communication are personal matters of cooperation and collaboration. No matter what I write in this book, you are going to respond to it idiosyncratically based on everything that makes you what you are today. If you read it tomorrow under different circumstances, you might respond differently. Have you ever read something and said to yourself that it was a bunch of hokum, and then read it again at a future date and seen it as wisdom? Information and communication are live, self-organizing issues. The only way a leader can be an effective communicator is to operate from this premise.

FUNDAMENTALS OF COMMUNICATION

Unequivocally, the most important element in communication, especially a leader's communication, is trust. Where there is trust, the listener is much more likely to believe and support the vision and strategy of the leader. On a day-to-day basis, trust leads associates to accept the leader's statements and directions. Trust can be built only on honesty and authenticity. To the degree that the leader stands aloof, trust is diminished. This is not to say that an aloof person cannot be a leader. Generals Douglas MacArthur and Charles De Gaulle were aloof as could be. Nevertheless, they were great leaders because they were authentic. Soldiers could see and appreciate the military intelligence of those two men, so they could follow them. George Patton and Omar Bradley were quite different and equally effective leaders. Patton was a man of great passion as well as intelligence. Bradley was a soldier's general because of his warmth and personal nature. All these men could lead because soldiers could see what they were as human beings.

Underneath trust is great caring. MacArthur and De Gaulle did care a great deal about their soldiers although you could not see it in their public persona. That didn't mean that they necessarily wanted to have dinner or share private moments with the rank and file. But they cared about the welfare of their people. Ask yourself this: When an employee has a special problem that falls outside of the policies of the company, how do you respond? Do you go by the book, or do you see to it that the person is taken care of? The following is an example from my recent experience.

There is an employee in our company who had a personal physical problem. His problem was not covered under the company's medical plan. I paid for it without question, and it wasn't cheap. I did this for two reasons. First, he was and is a deserving person. He works hard for us and makes a significant contribution. I was pleased to be able to help him. Second, I believe that organizations should think first of the welfare of their people and second of policy. We should "walk our talk" if we want commitment. Policy is set for guidelines, but we don't develop commitment through policy. There is no question that this person now has an extraordinarily high level of trust and commitment to our company. The lesson is that if you truly care about me as a human being as well as an economic unit, I will tend to trust you. If I trust, I follow. Without trust there is only suspicion, fear, and maybe resentment. (About six months after the man's treatment was completed, I talked to our benefits manager and explained the situation. I said I was glad to pay for the treatment but I believed that the corporation should find a way to reimburse me. After some discussion, it was determined that I could be reimbursed through another avenue.)

Trust is a prerequisite of empowerment, and it is the heart of team building. With trust, people feel comfortable taking risks. Trust is built through engagement. Engagement is a function of personal presence and emotional attention. Trust is as much an emotional as an intellectual factor. Emotion demands a high touch style, at least in the beginning of a relationship. If I am to gain your trust, I must get into your space somehow. If I can't physically be there because of distance, I have to use a personal medium such as the telephone or teleconference to touch you. You want to know me. An e-mail message or an internal all-hands letter is cold and impersonal no matter what the words. You can't hear my tone or see my expression. Only people of extraordinary presence can gain trust without personally engaging others.

One of the best examples of engagement in recent history was President Franklin Roosevelt's "fireside chats" during the depression. Roosevelt took office four years into America's worst depression. Over 20 percent of the workforce was without jobs. Fear, anger, and resentment typified the citizenry. Roosevelt used the still relatively new technology of radio to communicate with America. This was the first time that many Americans had heard their president speak. The title of the talks, fireside chats, was a trust-building label. Roosevelt made the people feel like they were sitting around the fire chatting with a strong, wise man who was going to take care of them. Even though he took drastic measures to advance his program, from closing the banks to attempting to reconstitute the Supreme Court, he won the minds and the hearts of many Americans in those critical early days after his inauguration. His predecessor, Herbert Hoover, was a man of extraordinary intelligence and wide-ranging experience, yet his personality was such that he never touched the hearts of the populace. He did not have the ability to engage that Roosevelt possessed.

The other side of engagement is listening. Robert Rosen claims that communication has two goals.[4] One is to clarify things: what needs to be done. The other is to set the right tone: help people feel good about doing it. He states that achieving this listening is as important as talking. Listening is probably people's worst skill. We all love to hear the sound of our voice and the brilliance of our opinion. Many people defend to the end their opinion when it is clear to everyone that they are wrong, yet they are so committed to defending and selling their position that they fail to hear the evidence that destroys them.

The leader has to truly listen to the associate. If the leader asks for thoughts and feelings, he or she must listen to and deal authentically with the responses. This is as applicable with an employee attitude survey as it is in a group or one-to-one discussion. You know how you feel when you believe someone is ignoring you or just isn't listening to you. Leaders who don't listen, who ignore, who don't like to confront, who avoid, and who delegate the uncomfortable sooner or later lose trust. The message is that the person is trying to avoid us or simply doesn't care enough about us to acknowledge our concern. Many leaders suffer from this habit. They appear, speak, and disappear, believing that they have won the hearts and minds of the associates. I was in a meeting recently where the leader came in, spoke strongly for a few minutes about something, and then left without giving the associates a chance to ask questions or even to add value and support. The result was not commitment; it was resentment.

The only action worse than not engaging is to equivocate or not admit that we don't have the answer. Some people feel that they need to hide things. If we are describing a finding and the listener asks how we came upon it, it is OK to say that it was by luck. If we are willing to admit that sometimes we just get lucky, we are affirming that we are human beings. This admission or affirmation builds a bond with the listener. The associate or customer says to herself that here is a *mensch*, a true and authentic human being who is willing to expose his ignorance. I can trust someone like that. But if on the other hand the person brags about how clever he was, and I learn later that he was just lucky, I know I can't trust him. W. C. Fields notwithstanding, remember what Lincoln said about trying to fool people.

THE LEADERSHIP SECRET

Although there are many actions a leader must take in order to be successful, there is none more important or more essential than to recognize the performance of the associates. We all have experienced the letdown when we have done something truly exceptional and received no positive feedback regarding it. Our reaction is, "Why should I try? No one cares."

Leaders must be positive. Everyone is watching them. When the boss arrives in the morning, everyone takes note of her arrival. They look for signs. Is she feeling good, smiling, gregarious, or is she clearly upset, scowling, close-mouthed? I worked for a man many years ago who habitually came in and went directly to his office, often with nothing more than a brusque greeting, and closed the door. When my colleagues did something noteworthy, they never heard a word of praise from him. As a result, we worked for ourselves and to some extent for the company, but certainly not for him.

We all need encouragement, recognition, and a pat on the back to carry us through the tough times. James Kouzes and Barry Posner offer a tool for leaders to assess the degree to which they encourage others.[5] Their Encouragement Index is shown in Figure 5-1. Kouzes and Posner offer a scoring method that generates ranges by which we can rate ourselves. This comes from their research with over 100,000 respondents in nearly twenty years of leadership work. The score ranges and an interpretation are as follows:

186 to 210: You're doing great. You're probably seeing a lot of your people producing at high levels. People like working with you, and their morale is high because you keep the environment positive.

126 to 185: You're doing pretty well. Although most of your people are doing well, you may feel that they could be doing better. There is an undertone of negativism in some places, but overall people are generally happy to be working in your unit. You might have a feeling that you could be doing more to motivate, but you aren't sure exactly what it is.

66 to 125: Your people are not working at their highest level. You might even feel that the only time they are truly putting out is when they think you are watching them.

21 to 65: Your score probably is not this low. If it is, the odds are there is a fair amount of discontent, low productivity, and high turnover.

Figure 5-1. The Encouragement Index.

How frequently do you typically engage in this behavior? Write the number from the scale below that best describes your response to each statement.

1	2	3	4	5	6	7	8	9	10
Almost Never	Rarely	Seldom	Once in a while	Sometimes	Fairly often	Often	Usually	Very Often	Almost always

1. _____ I make certain we set a standard that motivates us to do better in the future than we are doing now.
2. _____ I express high expectations about what people are capable of accomplishing.
3. _____ I pay more attention to the positive things people do than to the negative.
4. _____ I personally acknowledge people for their contributions.
5. _____ I tell stories about the special achievements of the members of the team.
6. _____ I make sure that our group celebrates accomplishments.
7. _____ I get personally involved when we recognize the achievements of others.
8. _____ I clearly communicate my personal values and professional standards to everyone on the team.
9. _____ I let people know I have confidence in their abilities.
10. _____ I spend a good deal of time listening to the needs and interests of other people.
11. _____ I personalize the recognition I give to another person.
12. _____ I find opportunities to let people know the why behind whatever we are doing.
13. _____ I hold special events to celebrate our successes.
14. _____ I show others, by my own example, how people should be recognized and rewarded.
15. _____ I make it a point to give people feedback on how they are performing against our agreed-upon standards.
16. _____ I express a positive and optimistic outlook even when times are tough.
17. _____ I get to know, at a personal level, the people with whom I work.
18. _____ I find creative ways to make my recognition of others unique and special.
19. _____ I recognize people more in public than in private for their exemplary performance.
20. _____ I find ways to make the workplace enjoyable and fun.
21. _____ I personally congratulate people for a job well done.

THE SEVEN REQUISITES FOR MAKING PEOPLE FEEL SPECIAL

Kouzes and Posner offer seven steps drawn from their subjects' observations that make people feel special.[6] Leaders win the support of their people when they practice these. When leaders work on encouragement, they:

1. **Set clear standards.** Constant reinforcement of performance standards without haranguing lets associates know where their focus should be. This reduces ambiguity and uncertainty—the major drags on performance.

2. **Expect the best.** Dedication to the idea that people are innately good and want to do a good job brings out the best in them. Continually reinforcing this expectation in person and to the group lets people know we believe in their ability.

3. **Pay attention.** Leaders are on the lookout for things that matter. Not only do they watch for problems, they watch for examples of extraordinary behavior. When they see it, they celebrate it.

4. **Personalize recognition.** Emphasis on the individual makes praise much more potent. The person gets the feeling that the leader knows him and cares about him in a very personal way. Nothing can take the place of that feeling.

5. **Tell the story.** Stories capture attention. They excite. They teach. Stories evoke emotion. Stories are personal. Everyone can get involved in a story. The lesson learned in a story of exceptional performance is not forgotten.

6. **Celebrate together.** Public celebrations bring people together around the reason for the event. Everyone wants recognition and respect from her peers. By sharing the moment with everyone, each person sees that there is a genuine caring, as well as the possibility that she could be next—if she earns it.

7. **Set the example.** Leaders take the lead in encouragement, from public events to private conversations. They practice what they preach. They are authentic. They show by their consistent behavior what is appreciated, what is expected, and what is rewarded. People are smart. They catch on quickly when the leader's behavior is consistent with his or her talk.

SPONSORING THE DIALOGUE

Leaders don't have to be solitary heroes. No longer are they expected to be Superman or Wonder Woman. The facts of e-world do not force managers into being the all-knowing, macho leader. Given the complexity and pace of change, no one can know everything. Most of the knowledge needed to fulfill the strategic goals of the organization lies within the associates. One of the key tasks of the leader today is to sponsor a dialogue among the associates and between associates and managers. This is why we talk about e-world as a knowledge-based economy and about managing that knowledge. We need open dialogue to move and share that knowledge.

> *Leaders don't have to be solitary heroes. No longer are they expected to be Superman or Wonder Woman.*

Dialogue is different from debate. Debate implies using logic to win and is a win-lose contest. Dialogue is deeper than debate. It is not about winning versus losing. It is about sharing and growing knowledge. Ikujiro Nonoka points out that dialogue comes from the gut.[7] It is built of the simultaneous exchange of ideas, instantaneous feedback, and continuous collective enhancement. It is a sincere expression of one's philosophy. It is based on collective respect and collaboration. Since it is so real, it depends on trust. A leader is on the road to being a successful communicator if he or she can stimulate, support, and participate in honest dialogue.

There are many opportunities to stimulate a dialogue. On every occasion when two or more people are together, dialogue is taking place. If the leader is willing to hear the truth, as seen by the associates, a valuable dialogue can happen. However, there is no dialogue if the leader is simply "managing by walking around" but not truly engaging, caring, listening, and discussing. Consider the many times during a day when we can engage our associates. Every setting from our office to their workplace to the kitchen, the cafeteria, the parking lot—you name it. Bob Galvin, son of the founder of Motorola and former chairman of the company, always ate lunch in the employee cafeteria. I saw people walk up to him, interrupt his lunch, talk to him for a few minutes, and move on. This is a man everyone trusts. If he can put himself on the line like that, so can we. Trust is built on authentic communication.

CULTURE: THE LEADER'S SHADOW

Culture and communication are so tightly interwoven that it is impossible to separate them. Culture is built first by the leader expressing his values and then giving them life through his behavior. Figure 5-2 is a graphic example of how leadership, communication, and culture intertwine.

In forty-plus years in business, I have yet to find a culture that differs from the values of the leader. There have been many cases where a new leader came into a strong culture and failed to perform because his or her values did not fit the engrained culture. There have been other cases where a new leader came in and changed the culture. In these cases, the leader explained his values and what that meant in terms of management and associate interaction. Then he reinforced it with his own consistent behavior. According to anthropologist Edward Hall, communication is the core of culture.[8] The other side of it is anthropologist Edmund Leach's statement that "culture communicates."[9] The two are as inseparable as the ingredients in a cake.

Figure 5-2. Leadership link.

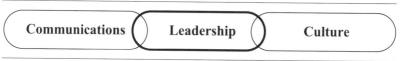

The leader's communication provides examples of values, enhances and encourages behaviors that fit those values, and builds a common base on which social relationships can flourish, nourish, and reinforce each other. As Phillip Evans and Thomas Wurster state, "Culture defines the corporation. And that is uniquely the creation of leadership."[10]

TEN IMPERATIVES OF E-WORLD LEADERSHIP

If we review everything from this chapter and Chapter 4, we find that there are fundamentals that occur time and again. We might rightfully call them leadership imperatives.

1. **Provide a clear vision and strategy for people to follow.**
   The foundation of leadership is the vision and strategy that we
   lay out in the beginning. Everything builds on that, aligns with
   that, supports that, and fulfills that. Anything we do that is not
   directly connected to the vision and strategy is at best confusing
   and at worst a waste of resources.

2. **Communication is our first priority as well as our best
   tool.** The most important point within that is: Cut out the platitudes. With the arrival of the Web, insincerity doesn't work any
   more. Nothing is accepted at face value. Everything is open to
   questioning, and it will be questioned. Inquiring people know as
   much about our company as do many executives. In fact, because many executives don't browse the net, outsiders and associates often know more things about the company and how its
   employees and customers feel than do the executives. So, first
   and foremost, be honest!

3. **Use stories to implant the message.** Stories have an emotional tone that facts and figures miss. People remember emotional experiences more than factual ones. Use stories and
   pictures to pass on the history of the company. What was it like
   the first year with a small number of crazy people dedicated to
   an idea? What were some of the funny things that happened?
   What mistakes did we make and survive? Remember that expensive ad we ran that no one responded to? Telling such stories
   makes an indelible stamp of humanity on the company. It says
   that we are all just fallible human beings, but we are committed
   to a vision of making the world a better place.

4. **Champion information sharing and learning.** Recognize
   publicly those associates who model this imperative. This is part
   of sponsoring the dialogue. Everyone has opinions that they are
   going to express—somewhere. Present a forum in which opinions are welcomed. People learn when they are free to express
   feelings, question, challenge, argue, learn, and come to collectively accepted conclusions. The tension of the dialogue is stimulating, liberating, inviting, and compelling. Sooner or later,
   everyone will want in.

5. **Commit to building an exciting culture.** Everyone is running
   around spending great amounts of money to attract and retain

people. The most attractive thing an organization can offer is an exciting, supportive culture. Become an employer of choice. Lead by example. Show through your behavior and reward the behavior of others who provide examples of why this is a great place to spend a couple of thousand hours each year of one's life. People will flock to our door.

6. **Reward innovation and punish unreasonable resistance.** Make innovation a cultural artifact. This turns a culture's attention to the customer. Everyone has a customer inside and outside the enterprise. It is everyone's responsibility to know her customer and to constantly find new ways to make the customer's life better. Those who resist all this unreasonably must be punished. (We don't like to talk about punishment, yet we punish each other every day in subtle and not-so-subtle ways.) In time, the resisters will select themselves out of this culture, or we can help them find a way out.

7. **Focus on measurable results rather than processes.** Processes are work and expense. Results are fulfilling and valuable. The obsession with process in the past two decades—quality and reengineering—made a contribution to process improvement, but not always to business results. Now we have to dedicate ourselves to reinventing the enterprise and achieving strategic business goals rather than tweaking processes. Results must be stated in terms of gains in service, quality, or productivity that directly connect to corporate goals.

8. **Invest heavily in developing associates.** In a knowledge-driven economy, the organization with the best talent wins. Given the shortage of trained people, the only effective path to long-term competitiveness is through internal development. Education and training do more than improve knowledge and skills. They bond associates to the company by showing them that we care about them, we want them to learn and grow, and we will reward them handsomely when they do. It costs at least fifty times more to lose and rehire talent than it does to provide forty hours of training annually, and that doesn't even count the effects on customer service and retention.

9. **Develop a can-do attitude in the organization.** Make accountability a rule. People want to achieve, but Ed Deming

showed us how organizations get in the way of motivation. Let's not allow our organization to inhibit our associates' efforts. Let them know what we expect from them and that we believe they can accomplish it. Also let them know that we support their desire to achieve and find personal fulfillment in their work. Then, follow through and prove it.

10. **Listen to associates.** E-world is overwhelming us with data, the vast majority of which is superfluous. We spend time on things that make no difference, and as a result we have little time for the things that are most meaningful. Our associates are on the point. They know better than we do what is really happening. We must focus our limited time on the people who are going to make our organization a success or an also-ran. There is great value to be gained from listening attentively, from truly engaging with associates.

The literature is filled with lists and tips on how to be a leader. We could study forever and not find much more of basic value than what is encompassed in the short list above. If we can accomplish these ten things, we will have a competitive edge that few can approach.

REFERENCES

1. James Gleick, *Chaos: Making a New Science* (New York: Viking Press, 1987).
2. Marshall McLuhan, *Understanding Media* (New York: McGraw-Hill, 1964).
3. Margaret J. Wheatley, *Leadership and the New Science* (San Francisco: Berrett-Koehler, 1999).
4. Robert Rosen et al., *Global Literacies* (New York: Simon & Schuster, 2000).
5. James Kouzes and Barry Posner, *Encouraging the Heart* (San Francisco: Jossey-Bass, 1999), pp. 36–37.
6. Ibid., pp. 45–142.
7. Ikujiro Nonoka, "The Dynamics of Knowledge Creation," from Rudy Ruggles and Dan Holtshouse, *The Knowledge Advantage* (Dover, N.H.: Capstone, 1999).
8. Quoted in Warren Sussman, *Culture as History: The Transformation of*

American Society in the Twentieth Century (New York: Pantheon Books, 1973), p. 252.

9. Ibid.

10. Phillip Evans and Thomas Wurster, *Blown to Bits* (Cambridge, Mass.: Harvard Business School Press, 2000).

Chapter 6

E-Leadership Summary and Scorecard

LEADERSHIP IS A CONCEPT. IT is a term we have invented to describe a set of behaviors. To evaluate the effectiveness of a leader, we focus first on the behaviors that drive the subsequent responses of the followers and ultimately the results of those responses. This then presents the question, "What do leaders *do*?" In the simplest sense, they induce followers to behave in a certain way. In wartime, when the platoon leader yells "Charge!" and the troops leap at the enemy, we can see leadership in action. In business, leadership is less dramatic but no less important to the enterprise in terms of danger. The failure to lead can cause companies to lose market position, suffer diminished profits, and even file for bankruptcy.

There are as many lists of leader traits as there are books on the subject. Many traits overlap because people are complex, nonlinear beings. The more important issue is: What are the followers doing as a result of the leader's behavior?

Given the rapidly changing world and the expanding, volatile global marketplace, the e-world leader needs to be personally grounded. Two fundamental traits of an effective leader are competence and authenticity. Personal integrity and straightforward communication are more than ever essential. Organizations need to address the issue of leadership development and succession with a strategy. They need to establish a model and identify people who have the best chance of becoming leaders. Training, education, and work assignments should have an element of leadership development within them.

Leading others into e-world calls for a new, broader view of the task. The leader needs to understand the human condition as it functions within an organization and outside in one's personal life. The basic prerequisite today is to understand that people are assets, not expenses. When the leader recognizes and appreciates the many facets of the associates, he or she will learn how and when to call on them to help drive the organization toward its goals. Instead of trying to be all things to all people, the leader's most important task is to foster a leadership capacity within the enterprise. This means communicating that leadership can be anyone's job as conditions change and call for special insights. The leader sponsors an ongoing, enterprisewide dialogue inviting everyone to participate. This builds a culture of involvement and trust. Trust comes from listening to each other, responding authentically, and encouraging innovation and risk taking. Leaders are successful when they are able to generate a culture of open communication and collective support.

The "Leadership scorecard" assessment tool in Figure 6-1 can give us an idea of how effectively we are being led. When it is turned introspectively, it can also help us see how good we are at being a leader. The tool uses a performance rating method that provides a list of leadership actions, typical subsequent results, and a five-point rating scale. Think about how the items in the Leadership scorecard apply to your organization at the top and middle levels.

Figure 6-1. Leadership scorecard.

1. *Management of managers*   1   2   3   4   5
   Low   High

   How good is the leader at managing his or her direct reports? Is he or she missing or making market opportunities, investing in the wrong or right idea or technology, developing or not developing talent, and, most important, ignoring/violating or living the organization's values?

2. *Decisiveness*   1   2   3   4   5
   Low   High

   Are things getting done on time? Fear, analysis-paralysis, ignorance, and other deviant behaviors inhibit action. Are we taking advantage of windows of opportunity, making tough decisions, resolving conflicts positively, and executing the business plan?

3. *Consistency*   1   2   3   4   5
   Low   High

   Is there constant changing of mind and priorities, or is there constancy and reliability of focus? Do we see vacillation or steadfastness? Are associates of different levels or groups treated differently or the same?

4. *Openness*   1   2   3   4   5
   Low   High

   Is the leader closed or approachable? Is there an underlying feeling of lethargy or energy in his or her style? Does the leader's spirit bring people down or inspire enthusiasm, extra effort, and dedication? Do associates feel free to express themselves, be creative, and take responsibility?

5. *Sense of challenge*   1   2   3   4   5
   Low   High

   What expectation level is transmitted? Do associates feel that good enough is good enough, or are they stimulated to always do better? Is there a sense of indifference or a passion that draws out the best in the associates?

6. *Building*   1   2   3   4   5
   Low   High

   Does the leader try to act alone or build on the skills of others? Are associates stifled and controlled or offered the chance to learn and grow? Is organizational bench strength improving? Can we see people continually expanding their capabilities and performing at high levels?

(continues)

Figure 6-1. (Continued).

7. *Transformation*	1	2	3	4	5
	Low				High

Is the leader milking the organization for the short term or moving its culture toward e-world? Does the leader claim that "you can't argue with success," or is he or she showing awareness of the change forces? Are the associates picking up on the need to change?

8. *Balance*	1	2	3	4	5
	Low				High

Does the leader obsess on the numbers and ignore the human side or balance the need to grow both? Do priorities always lay in making the numbers at the expense of the associates, or is the leader's message that people are important and must be treated so?

9. *Collaboration*	1	2	3	4	5
	Low				High

Does the leader communicate a sense of isolation and arrogance or collaboration with outsiders? Are partnerships and alliances actively sought? Is teamwork given lip service or promoted and rewarded? As a result, do associates show an openness to working with and learning through others?

10. *Alignment*	1	2	3	4	5
	Low				High

Does the leader set the goals and leave the organization to achieve them or ensure that there is alignment from corporate goals through operating subjectives to resource management? Can the associates see how they contribute to the goals of the enterprise?

Part III

STRATEGY DRIVERS:

CONNECTIVITY, INNOVATION,

CUSTOMERS

Chapter 7

Building an E-World Strategy

ALONG WITH PROVIDING THE VISION and sponsoring a dialogue, the leader is responsible for outlining a compelling strategy, one that will place the company among the elite—the most talked about, the most emulated, the most successful. Cap Gemini Ernst & Young's Center for Business Innovation, the Wharton School of Business, and Forbes ASAP collaborated on an Internet survey to learn the extent to which company performance measurements were aligned with management decisions. As the researchers put it, the results showed "A glaring disparity between the information a manager needs to make strategic decisions and the actual performance data the company is able to generate."[1]

Eighty-one percent of respondents stated that their performance measurement system was not well aligned with their corporate strategies. Forty-five percent stated that the alignment between performance measurements and strategies was very poor. This is a chilling indictment of one of the most basic management tasks. A misaligned strategy is equivalent to an incorrect map. Following it can lead only to wrong turns and delays if not downright disasters. Given this profile, how can we determine the efficacy of our strategy? The answer lies clearly in feedback from the marketplace.

If we want to know how well-positioned, exciting, and wealth-creating our company is today, who do we ask? Do we survey top executives in our industry? Why ask them? Last year, 70 percent failed to perform at the mean of the S&P 500! They have shown by their performance that they are somewhere between mediocre and brain-dead. Would it be venture capitalists? Eighty percent of the companies they fund never fulfill the promise of their plan, and most collapse within five years. We can get better odds in Vegas. Would it be the media mavens? We're smarter than that.

BEGINNING WITH THE MARKETPLACE

If we want to know how promising our prospects are for the near future, we can get off to a good start by asking ourselves just one question: "Are the best and brightest talents beating on our door to come work with us?"

The smart people, both the kids and the experienced hands, can see through the press releases. They've heard all the platitudes about how important our people are . . . just before we lay off another thousand. They know that a company that has been buying back its stock is admitting it doesn't know how to invest its cash in opportunities that promise a return in excess of the cost of capital. The job seekers know enough to pick out the companies that are producing leading-edge versus bleeding-edge products. They know where the best price-performance buys are and where the wildly exciting new gadgets and deals are coming from. And they know from their friends what the best places are for people to excel.

In the late 1970s, I was with a young, fast-growing computer company in Silicon Valley. We had a novel idea for what was then called distributed data processing. For about six years after going public, we did very well. Then, to make a long story short, we started to fall behind the curve. I began to notice the type of people we were recruiting as we slid slowly down the curve. They weren't the best and brightest who had come to us in the early days. They were the burned out and the second-level talents. The job applicants were a parallel profile of our business. In a couple of years, we sold out to Motorola, which dropped a half-billion dollars in the company before giving up.

So it's an old idea with a new twist: When someone asked the automaker Mr. Packard how good his car was, he replied, "Ask a man who owns one!" Would we be brave enough to have Mike Wallace interview ten of our customers and associates on *60 Minutes* about our products, services, and employee management practices?

OK. Let's drop our defenses and get down to the truths of e-world strategies.

THE MARKET PLUNGE OF APRIL 14, 2000

April 14, 2000, is a day that has been recorded in the annals of the investment community alongside Black Tuesday, 1929. Literally overnight, over $1 trillion in market capitalization was wiped out. In one trading day, the market flipped 180 degrees from superheated hype to business fundamentals. Wall Street has always been and probably always will be about value investing. Wild ideas on the back of an envelope make great fodder for the media, but ultimately bad business. On April 15, the latest Great Idea that was going to disinter-mediate an industry suddenly became simply an alternative market-ing channel or a new product line. Everyone—not just the arrogant, adolescent, dot-com hypesters, but also i-world businesspeople, sea-soned investors, and social theorists—still believes that digital tech-nology will sweep aside every unwary enterprise and create enormous value for society and great wealth for insightful individu-als. The difference is that the notion of value creation as a result of supplier and customer interaction has been reinstalled as the bedrock of business. The good news is that there are still business managers who know how to see, appreciate, and deal with rapid change.

READY—SET—TRANSFORM

By now everyone agrees that innovation is an e-world impera-tive. There was a recent TV commercial in which people of several ages and obviously different races and countries posed the question, "Are you ready?" It is a compelling ad that draws us into the possibilities and probabilities of the new world before putting up the challenge. The thinking executive viewers must be asking themselves,

Innovation is not a liquid commodity; we can't just go to the faucet and turn it on.

"Are we ready?" Innovation is not a liquid commodity; we can't just go to the faucet and turn it on. Innovation is a result, not a prime cause. The prime cause is transformation. If we want competitive levels of innovation, we have to give our organization a makeover—and it had better be more than a facial.

How do we know if we are prepared to transform our company for the new marketplace? Before we leap off the cliff with the rest of the lemmings, it is useful to consider the evolution of our industry. We don't have to be in high tech to notice the bedrock shifting under our houses. Every industry is undergoing major change. Even public utilities, the staid bastions of i-world, look nothing like they did prior to 1990. E-world is obviously riding in on the digital rocket and smashing into everyone on the way. (At first I wrote "horse" instead of "rocket," which is a telling use of metaphors. I was born during the Great Depression, long before Neil Armstrong walked on the moon. Our language betrays our mental models. Anyone riding a metaphorical horse in today's market is on his or her way to becoming dog food.)

Electronic technology offers an excellent model for examining market evolution. The vacuum-tubed, room-size ENIAC ushered in the computer world at the end of World War II. For the next couple of decades, mainframe computers, largely sold and serviced by IBM, were the only choice. Then along came Digital Equipment Company and the minicomputer, which launched similar derivations. Throughout this period and for some time to come, the semiconductor industry drew everyone's attention. Semiconductors are the heart of electronic devices, hence a pivotal industry. By 1980, the personal computer had arrived. New types of peripheral equipment sprang up. Do you see the central theme here? Hardware! For thirty years, hardware ruled.

With the arrival of the PC, software rose in importance. As hardware moved out of the operations center and onto the desks of people, the possibilities of electronic data processing suddenly burst forth. Individuals with programming talent could start companies in their bedroom, and they did. No longer did you need several hundred million dollars to build a semiconductor facility or a computer assembly plant. As more people were able to take advantage of text and graphics programs, information emerged as an important market, leading to advances in printers and other peripherals such as scanners.

This led to the next phase: information. Research firms developed databases on everything from product development to management practices. In less than two decades, information became a commodity thanks to the latest Great Idea, connectivity through the Internet. The Internet is about *reach*. Not only are people connecting who never would have known each other before, but devices are connecting. Cell phones, pagers, video, PDAs, and tomorrow's gadgets are all converging on the Next Big Idea. The capability of the Internet is being stretched into another dimension thanks to tools like the Palm VII, with which I can now get my e-mail anywhere at any time—wireless—through cyberspace. This phase will in turn open new markets for new products, all coming faster than we can write about them. The point of this trip down memory lane is that we have evolved from hardware to software to information to the World Wide Web. Figure 7-1 illustrates the evolutionary track from ENIAC to connectivity.

Connectivity tends to turn niche markets into commodities. Companies that had a stronghold on a market sector suddenly find their space being invaded by companies they never heard of or anticipated having to compete against. As each business sector becomes commoditized, we have two innovation choices. We can either look for a specialty niche within the commodity, or we can look for the next phase in the evolution of our industry. Either way we innovate, stagnate, or disappear from the market. While it is fashionable to scream for innovation at all costs, let's look at what can happen to innovators.

DISRUPTIVE TECHNOLOGY

Clayton Christensen of the Harvard Business School has given us an insight into the process of innovation and disintermediation. He wanted to know what caused companies that were so good for so long to fall off the profitability trail. The common-sense theory is that profitable companies are led by smart leaders. So what happens when a long-term market leader suddenly loses its way? Christensen

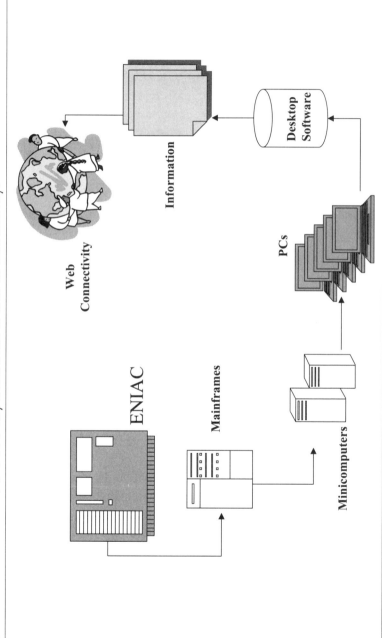

Figure 7-1. The electronic evolutionary track from ENIAC to connectivity.

studied both new economy companies (disk drives) and old economy institutions (steel mills) and found that the same force undermined both. He calls this force *disruptive technology*. Basically, the scenario goes like this.

Traditionally, profitable companies develop product lines based on steadily improving technology. That is, over time they learn how to make better-quality, high-margin products. In the steel industry the progression is from rebar, which is made from scrap metal and has low margins, to sheet steel, which is a high-quality, high-margin product made from refining iron ore. Given the choice, as a new technology comes into the market and takes on the low-end product, the leading big mill manager is actually happy. Now he can focus on the high end and maintain his margins. He sees no reason to try to compete for the low-end rebar business invaded by the mini-mill. Using scrap metal instead of iron ore and applying electric versus blast furnaces to the task, the mini-mills could make good money on rebars. In time, having mastered the rebar market, mini-mills developed newer, even more efficient applications of their technology for making bars and rods. This let them into a higher-margin product niche but still left the top end for the big mills.

We can see where this is leading. Over twenty years, the disruptive technology emerging from mini-mills has migrated all the way to the top of the business. The big mills cannot now match the margins because their technology is older and less efficient. Along the way the big mills could not defend a financial strategy of investing in mini-mill technology that was dedicated to making low-margin products. In time, this was like an infection that starts with a toe and gradually moves up until the foot and then the leg is gangrenous and permanently disables the person who failed to treat the toe.

DEFENDING THE LOW END

Many companies start with disruptive technologies that give them a foothold on a market niche that the giants don't care to defend. It happened with automobiles, personal computers, online trading, and electronic watches. In every case the giant scoffed at the "toys." In time, they found that they had to compete or suffer major disruptions in their earnings and market shares. However, when they did try to compete, the unsuccessful incumbents found that their bureaucratic systems could not move fast enough to deal with the invaders. By the time they pushed a new model through the risk-adverse corridors of Megacorp, the upstarts had leaped even farther ahead. The giants were used to taking a long time to thoroughly develop a new product, and the upstarts were introducing small changes continuously. I remember when the PC makers were offering enhancements every six months, while IBM was taking a year to come out with the next model. The only workable solution for IBM and others has been to set up a separate unit, far from HQ, that was virtually autonomous and staffed with radical thinkers who were happy to be doing something exciting for a change.

The disruptive technology factor needs to be considered in strategic planning. Can we identify upstarts who are using this technology as a wedge into our market? What is their strategy? What is the technology they are relying on to drive the wedge home? What happens to our margins if we decide to retool and compete? More important, how do we explain it to the financial analysts who hold us hostage? These are pragmatic questions that have to be posed and answered.

Before we leave the issue, there is another element that is often overlooked in strategic planning. We should give some thought to our associates. Very often the associates know more about the disruptive technologies than do the executives. The associates belong to a technological community that transcends the company. They have former school chums, neighbors, church friends, and bowling buddies who are working in the disruptive companies. They organize communities of practice on their own where they can share and play with new ideas inside their professional or technical field. Keep in mind that the multibillion-dollar personal computer industry was spawned by a bunch of bearded, outcast weirdos in the Home Brew Computer Club of Silicon Valley. At the time the club was meeting in the 1970s, the executives at IBM, DEC, and Amdahl were totally committed to big iron and couldn't be bothered listening to these kids with their crazy idea of computers for everyone. It makes sense to talk to the worker bees in our company, no matter the industry, to find out what they are playing with in their hobby shop or talking about in their community of practice.

GETTING OFF THE HYPE HORSE

We have to be genuine if we want to enlist the knowledge and hidden power of the people. We have to say what is on our minds. We have to admit when we don't know. We have to take some of the advice we ask for. We have to show that we care by our actions, not by memos or slogans, platitudes or rationalizations.

Don't think for a nanosecond that people can be fooled by corporate rhetoric. After being bombarded with fifty years of massive advertising, no one believes Megacorp. Recent polls chronicle the slow decline of American business credibility. The only way to regain credibility is to get off the hype horse, stand among the people, and talk like a human being. The smartest communications policy is the one built on total openness, honesty, and humility. We can't talk one day and clam up the next. Good news, bad news, all news has to be disseminated. We have to trust people to handle even the bad news. If there is a disrupter on

> *Don't think for a nanosecond that people can be fooled by corporate rhetoric. After being bombarded with fifty years of massive advertising, no one believes Megacorp.*

the horizon or in our tent, we have to acknowledge it. It is suicidal to play down a competitor's new initiative rather than acknowledge it and ask for ideas from our associates on how to combat it. We need to talk in the vernacular about the way things really are and encourage innovative ideas. There is tremendous energy, intelligence, and goodwill in the workforce, which, by the way, the workforce is more than willing to share. The only thing that gets in its way is a management team who believes people are stupid and not to be trusted. If anyone on our executive team ever says that about people, we should tell him or her to look in the mirror to see such a person.

Ed Deming proved that the principal barrier to high quality is not indifferent employees. It is micromanagers and faulty processes. People know more than management ever will about three things:

1. What customers want from the company
2. The problems that exist within the company
3. How to solve most of the problems in the most expeditious manner

People are irretrievably connected and communicating. If we want to build a compelling strategy and enlist the associates' support in a meaningful way, we have to communicate authentically.

THE E-WORLD STRATEGIC IMPERATIVE

The strategic imperative of e-world is not a new strategic plan or even innovation as a means of survival. These are by-products of something more basic. That something is capability. Top management's job is not to have all the answers and send the strategy down from the mountaintop carved in stone. That guarantees mediocrity. The boys and girls in the eagle's aerie have to build strategic capability into the organization. This is a corporate culture game, an extension of building leadership capacity. All associates must be offered—*and must take*—a piece of the action if we expect to move at e-world speeds. *Take* is the point. We can lead people to information, but we can't force them to use it for innovative pursuits.

Gary Hamel offers a list of questions in Figure 7-2 that we can use as criteria to assess our readiness for innovation.[2] I've personalized his list from the "your" to "our" company perspective. I started a company years ago and am still involved with it. Psychologically, it will always be my baby. I still search personally for the Next Big Idea while simultaneously urging my associates to find and champion new concepts. I am not smart enough to know where this wildly evolving market is going. When someone comes up with an idea, I have to say, "Let's give it a whirl," not "Write me a proposal."

Participation is explicit within Hamel's list. The background message is that if we want to attract and keep the best talent, we have to open up the strategy game to them. They are not like their parents and grandparents, who patiently and loyally waited for marching orders. The market is moving too fast for anyone to wait on someone else. Anyone who is not involved in thinking as well as doing is not adding value. Are we ready to encourage people to think, and are we prepared to listen and act forthrightly on what they have to say? Executives often ask, "If I do this, who is running the company?" The answer is that the inmates have already taken over the asylum, and they're not giving it back. The Web has provided an

Figure 7-2. Assessing our readiness for e-world.

1. Is our company ready to pump its aspirations to the point where anything less than radical innovation won't suffice?
2. Is our company ready to throw out its definition of "served market" and define its opportunity space more broadly?
3. Is our company ready to begin searching for a cause that will be so great, so totally righteous, that it will turn a bunch of apprehensive cubicle dwellers into crusaders?
4. Is top management ready to shut up for a while and start listening, really listening, to the young, the new hires, and those at the geographic periphery?
5. Is our company ready to throw open its strategy process to every great idea, no matter where it comes from?
6. Is our company ready to start funding ideas from the lunatic fringe even if 80 percent of them return precisely zilch?
7. Is our company ready to emancipate some of our best people so they can get to work on building tomorrow's business models?
8. Is our company ready to start paying attention to the tiny seeds of innovation that right now are struggling to break through the top soil?
9. Is our company ready to take on the imperialists who would rather preside over a big but slowly crumbling empire than give self-rule to eager young business builders?
10. Is our company ready to decouple compensation from hierarchy and experience and share wealth with the radical thinkers and courageous doers?

Derived from Gary Hamel, *Leading the Revolution* (Cambridge, Mass.: Harvard Business School Press, 2000).

extremely effective, informal communications channel for them. There is more potentially useful intelligence flowing through that channel daily than in most of the corporate communiqués. If we insist on fighting with our associates for control, the best and brightest will leave, and we'll have to entice another bunch of less talented and motivated people to manage. When we let this happen, the turnover is caused by our myopia and fear, not their ingratitude.

THE POWER OF DENIAL

In the Oscar-winning film *American Beauty*, Ricky Fitts, the son of the Marine living next door to Lester Burnham, is dealing drugs.

He is very successful and as a result can afford a large investment in electronic equipment and videotapes. When Lester asks him how his father fails to see the cost associated with these purchases and wonder where the money came from, the boy offers a memorable reply: "He thinks I earned it in the catering business. Never underestimate the power of denial."

Are we in denial about how profound a change is required to transform our company? The power shift of inviting associates into the strategy game is not going to be welcomed by many middle managers. If we are the CEO, we might not be concerned because we think we are still the biggest dog in the neighborhood. We can issue an edict and expect that most people will follow it, although possibly grudgingly. But if we are just one of the mutts in the local pack, we are not going to be too happy when new puppies come to eat out of our bowl or, worse yet, get to eat in the big dog's bowl. There are a lot of hungry hounds out there. Top management needs to recognize that the changes in the market are threatening to some of our associates who have earned their rank by past performance. Middle-level managers often impede any changes that come down from the top because they threaten the incumbent. Few people give power and position away willingly.

Executives have a nondelegatable responsibility to deal with the middle-level people who are threatened by the call for participation. We cannot go into denial and assume there is or will be no problem. People don't follow orders like they used to. It is easy to say, "Sign up or else," but we can't afford to lose people who have the knowledge and experience we need to compete in e-world. We taught them how the old organizational game was to be played. Now we are changing the rules. It is not only fair but good business to help them learn to play the new game.

WHITHER THE WEB?

Today every strategy has to include the Web as a channel for communication and sales. The Web has a unique characteristic. It strips away all pretense, whether or not we are directly involved in it. If we have a formal presence (i.e., a Web home page), everything we put on it is subject to scrutiny just like any internal or external communication we transmit. The difference with the Web is that everyone in the world can see it, not just a select few on a mailing list. This makes the content and format much more sensitive. Our competitors as well as our customers, prospects, and associates see it. How do you compose something that serves all eyes effectively? David Weinberger describes how communication is changing, regressing in a sense, because of the Web.[3] He calls it hyperlinking.

Weinberger states very pointedly that the traditional i-world business was constructed like a fort (Fort Business, if you will). The concept of the fort has these features:

- There are physically imposing buildings.
- Inside is everything we need.
- Outside is dangerous.
- The king rules.
- The king has a court.
- We have our role, our place.

He concludes the image by saying that if we succeed, we say *we* have won. And so, in this way the fort is a place apart—apart from the market.

But Fort Business's assumptions are being challenged by hyper linking, which connects one to many through the Web. Keep in mind that ultimately a business is about people and connection. That is where the Web is changing things back to the way we were in the village market. The Web both liberates and exposes an organization. It is important to understand the characteristics of the Web. Figure 7-3 is a summary of Weinberger's explication of the Web's character. It is both good and bad news depending on where you stand. But the inarguable point is that all us from the top to the bottom of the organization are in it, whether we like it or not. And we have to accommodate it in our strategy. So, what can we do—realistically?

Successful companies believe they can do anything. With success comes confidence, and with confidence sometimes comes arrogance. After all, who is to argue with our success? *We know!* It is only a matter of hard work, resource investment, and force fitting. To that attitude the market soon says, "Adios muchachos!"

Figure 7-3. Characteristics of the Web.

1. *Hyperlinked.* It consists of hundreds of millions of pages hyperlinked together by the author of each individual page. Anyone can plug in and any page can be linked to any other, without asking permission.
2. *Decentralized.* No one is in charge of the net. There is no central clearinghouse.
3. *Hyper Time.* Hyper time is supposedly seven times the velocity of normal time. The Web puts the control of my time into my hands.
4. *Open, Direct Access.* The net provides what feels like direct access to everyone else on the net and to every piece of information that's ever been posted. Nothing stands between any two individuals on the net.
5. *Rich Data.* The currency of the data is pages. The pages tell you as much about the author as about the topic.
6. *Broken.* Because the Web is the largest, most complex network ever built, it is always going to be a little bit broken.
7. *Borderless.* The Web is designed so you can make a link to a page without having to get the author's permission. It is often hard to tell exactly where the boundaries are.

If we know how to make big things but the customer is telling us he wants smaller versions, can we just downsize and keep him as a customer? Or do we make better big things to keep the customers who want big things? How does disruptive technology play here? I remember talking to a friend named Tubby Snodgrass who was a local political organizer years ago. What a guy. He was what his name sounded like—a savvy, outwardly simple guy who knew how to cut your heart out and smile while he was doing it. I asked Tubby how he went about winning over voters. He said, "Rule Number One is keep what you've got. First, you always make sure that the people who voted your way in the past are still loyal. Then, you figure out how you are going to take away voters from that other son of a bitch."

In business, we know that keeping a customer is less expensive than getting a new one. There are many companies that suffered after trying to change and losing old customers. Cadillac made a lot of money selling big cars, then lost a lot of money trying to sell small ones. Some stores that sell high fashion damaged their reputation by going downscale. On the other hand, Sears totally lost its way in the 1980s when it tried to change from America's clothing and hardware emporium to a set of boutiques. Who goes to a boutique to buy underwear, overalls, and a chain saw? While Sears was fiddling, Wal-Mart set fire to it.

The point is to do what we know how to do, *but* take into consideration how the new channel, the Web, is going to help us—and our competitors—serve our customers better. Sears closed its hundred-year-old catalog business just as the Web was about to offer a way to revitalize it. How can a business that was at the core of Sears's market position not be made profitable by being updated? We protect our brand by making it better, not by running after the latest fad and changing our products and focus. If we have to chase fads, I suggest we set up a separate company to do that and keep it as far away from our existing business as possible. Then our customers will not be confused as to who we are trying to be. Consider these strategic rules:

- **Strategy #1.** Do what we do, only do it better.
- **Strategy #2.** Watch out for competitors, inside but mostly outside the industry.
- **Strategy #3.** Look for extensions of what we do that will bring us new customers.

STRATEGY COMPONENTS

Strategies are based on the interlacing of four considerations:

1. **Our core:** What we are in terms of self-concept, our market identity
2. **Capabilities:** Our intellectual capital (associates) and physical resources
3. **The market:** Customers, suppliers, competitors, and technology
4. **The environment:** Economic, social, and political conditions

Let's look at each in turn.

- **Our Core.** This includes the mix of vision, mission, financial and market goals, and products or services that make us what we are. To the degree that we fully and objectively understand our strengths and weaknesses, we should be able to develop a winning strategy—provided we don't continue to revel in past glories. The barriers to achieving a winning strategy are corporate myopia, arrogance, unreasonable goals, and obsolescent products or services.

- **Capabilities.** The most important factors are our intellectual capital, the knowledge imbedded in our infrastructure, intellectual property and culture, the associates' capabilities, and external relations, principally customers. In addition, secondary relations are often downplayed but can be crucial forces. These include competitors, suppliers, and the various governments within whose jurisdictions we operate. Physical resources are the assets on the balance sheet: cash, receivables, real property, etc. These are inert commodities, which depend on intellectual capital for leverage.

- **The Market.** Besides our relations with customers, suppliers, and competitors, there are the realities. Customers have needs and service expectations as well as buying power, and these do not always coincide. Customers do not always appreciate the value of our service. Suppliers have certain levels of performance capability. Competitors have strengths and weaknesses just like we do. Today, technology is a major force with the arrival of connectivity. All of these factors are in constant motion, interacting to create and destroy markets—both local and global.

- **The Environment.** The environment affects business today more than ever in history. The sensitivity of groups to pollution, waste, and social desires combines with national and regional interests to inhibit the freewheeling of the past. No longer can monopolists operate unimpeded. Given the glacial pace of change typical of institutions such as government and education, industry is expected to take responsibility for more of the underpinnings of society such as health, safety, security, human development, and recreation.

The planning and execution of a strategy is much more complex today. The pace of change in all areas of life demands responsiveness of a level never imagined. Strategy has changed from a noun to a verb. Strategy is not a plan. It is a living, changing, evolving process in which all associates have a role, a stake, and a responsibility. Management's challenge is to weave this together and keep it whole and evolving as commerce is transformed.

REFERENCES

1. "Measuring the Future," (Cambridge, Mass.: Cap Gemini Ernst & Young, Center for Business Innovation, 2000), p. 4.
2. Gary Hamel, *Leading the Revolution* (Cambridge, Mass.: Harvard Business School Press, 2000).
3. David Weinberger, "The Hyperlinked Organization," from Doc Searls and David Weinberger, *The Cluetrain Manifesto* (Cambridge, Mass.: Perseus Publishing, 2000), pp. 115–160.

Chapter 8

Innovating and Setting the Standard

THE POLLYANNA FACTOR AND REALIZING THE RISKS

Innovation is an imperative in our strategic plan. With innovation naturally comes risk, yet risk management is seldom a topic in the e-business literature. The danger in this is that becoming overly stimulated by the unproven rewards of the new market and ignoring the risks in a radically new venture would make Pollyanna look like a raging reactionary. Several thousand wounded investors would testify to the folly of the lemming investment strategy. Before we take off into the heady world of innovation, it is useful to consider the management of the inevitable risks.

While we are being romanced about the fabulous potential of e-world, we have to keep in mind that it is largely still unknown and rapidly evolving. Risk is at the heart of e-world more than it ever was in i-world. We are entering an arena that is largely unknown and unknowable. The degree and rate of change in this economy is of an order of magnitude that surpasses the transition from the agricultural to the industrial era. Keep in mind it took several generations for that shift to take place. If you think that the industrial revolution was complete by the middle of the 19th century, think again. It wasn't until electricity replaced steam as the principal energy source in factories that we can say the new age had fulfilled its promise. That didn't come to pass until the 1920s, about one hundred years after the arrival of the first reliable steam engines.

This time around it will be more of a transformation than a transition, and it will probably be in full force within a decade. Having said that, I don't mean to imply that it will be over by 2010. I mean that by 2010 we will be fully into the new arena. The big difference will be that it will probably continue to evolve at light speed due to the constant and rapid advancement of technology. If you are old enough to remember how slowly products like home appliances changed, you know what I mean. If you bought the latest double toaster model with variable heat, you had the top of the line for years. Consider how much automobiles really changed over a decade. After automatic transmissions came in following World War II, when was the next major technological advance? Disk brakes? Front-wheel drive? Safety glass? How long did it take for those to become available?

Now, the risk is that on the one side only a few of today's wild-eyed predictions will materialize, while some others will exceed our imaginations. Knowing which will be which is the dilemma of i-world's leap to e-world. Senior executives have to look into the black hole that is sucking energy at record rates and decide how we are going to navigate before we get sucked in. How can we take our companies to the Promised Land before we are drawn into oblivion? This is a frightening question to a realist. It is this uncertainty that is contributing to our associates' unrest. Leadership is understandably confused. No one prepared us for e world.

The marketplace of the 19th century was less complex, more local, slower moving, and therefore more predictable than that of the last couple of decades of the 20th century. And the first truly global, technologically driven, information-rich marketplace of the 21st century is anything but simple or predictable. In the past, failure in one area or in one year seldom generated catastrophic results. Today, missing a quarter's financial expectations can wipe out a large percentage of a corporation's market capitalization within twenty-four hours. In extreme cases, short-term problems can drive a company into the hands of a predatory competitor or a corporate raider. The appetite for taking risk and the capacity for managing risk are key differentiators.

A few recent examples support my claims regarding the magnitude of risk facing executives. Intel is one of the more admired semiconductor companies, occupying the dominant position in its industry. One poor earnings announcement and its stock price dropped from $75 to $40. Apple Computer's market capitalization dropped 52 percent in one day after its September 29, 2000, announcement of a slowdown in future earnings. But the prize goes to Mattel. Management wanted to get in on the ground floor of the lifelong education market—one of the most predictable social changes. So Mattel bought the educational software company Learning Co. for $350 million in May 1999. In October 2000, they *sold* it for "no immediate payment" while taking a $430 million loss in the process.

THE INTERNAL STRUGGLE IN RISK MANAGEMENT

Risk management is defined by opposing views. On one side are those who look backward and rely on numbers to predict the future. Their mantra is, "You can't argue with success." I love to compete with these types because their eyeballs are glued to their backside. The opposing group argues that the past is no predictor of the future and you have to go with your intuition. Their slogan is, "No pain, no gain." They can be more sanguine since they are seldom risking their personal capital.

Looking at the numerists, we admit that without hard data from the past (there is no hard data on the future, only subjective estimates and extrapolations of probabilities), we rely totally on gut, the seat of the pants, or some other anatomical referent. These have nothing to do with the issue and everything to do with the issuer. Numbers can be fascinating in and of themselves, but for people who flunked high school algebra, they can be mystical and frightening at times. Numbers also have their limitations. They show what happened, but on their face they don't tell why it happened. In a search for those insights, a discipline as old as the ancients, *copying*, has been resurrected under a new moniker, *benchmarking*. Studying effective practices of others is helpful and can lessen risk, provided what we see meets these criteria:

1. The driving variables in the subject group are similar to ours.
2. The reported outcomes were sustained over a long period.
3. The results are generalizable outside of the subject group.
4. The report is accurate.

So-called *best practice* reports are fraught with problems. Many of them are slapped together based on hearsay and self-reporting with no effort to verify the data. Saratoga Institute's study of current best practice reporting has shown that in well over half the cases, the report details are sketchy and the results are questionable. Basing resource allocations on such foundations is highly risky. Nevertheless, many projects have been launched from them. An A. T. Kearney study of change projects found that only one in five, or 20 percent, achieved lasting improvements. Earlier studies by a number of the major consulting firms claimed that less than one-third of such projects achieved lasting gains, and in a very high percentage of times, not only was there no value added but the result was wasted resources and frustrated associates. This problem is so endemic that McKinsey and Company has launched a long-term research program to locate the underpinnings of change in organizations.

Given that it is natural to take the path of least resistance, it is easier to copy what someone else reports as a success than it is to check out the statement before acting on it. There are several downsides to this behavior. At the least, we are apt to learn that the report was less than accurate and that we have wasted our time in trying to emulate the reporter's practice. In the worst case, we might find that the practice not only did not transfer easily to our environment but was actually harmful to us. This "viral effect" can introduce elements into our culture or operation that are hard to cure. The lesson is that when looking at so-called best practices, look carefully and be skeptical. Forewarned is forearmed.

THE BEGINNING OF RISK MANAGEMENT

The Greeks were probably the first we know who displayed a trait often overlooked by modern best practice mavens. It is called proof, or, at least strong demonstrable evidence. The Greeks accepted only those ideas that were substantiated, generalizable, and transportable. They learned well and carried the concepts along as they conquered.

The formal search for understanding risk also goes back several centuries. Current insurance premiums are based on actuarial tables, a process first developed by John Graunt in a 1662 study of mortality in London. To thinking beings, it has always been clear that more things can happen than will happen. The desire is to know as clearly as possible what is most likely to happen. In more recent times, this desire is pursued through sampling. We can seldom see all of what we want to know, so we take as large a sample as possible and rely on statistical procedures and tables to yield a degree of probability. Business risk is also subject to statistical studies. The risk of introducing a new style in clothes, automobiles, or consumables is mitigated by samplings of potential buyers. So while statistics have a key role to play in risk management, there is another overriding force that often cancels the most logical, demonstrable course of action. It is called human nature.

PEOPLE ARE PECULIAR: THE IMPORTANCE OF HUMAN NATURE

Anyone who has been in an organization for any length of time has seen how human nature overcomes the most reliable data. I led a study of plant location for a computer company in the early 1980s. We applied a set of about a dozen desirable criteria, such as geographic centrality, quality of life, cost of living, proximity to higher education facilities, and government concessions. We identified three sites that met most of the criteria. However, the decision was made to locate north of Dallas, which was not one of the choices based on the criteria. Instead, that was where the key executive wanted to live!

Human nature can be recognized by its powers of evaluation and decision making. The decision to buy or not is seldom based solely on price. It is driven by perceived utility or value balanced against cost. If we are dying of thirst in the desert, we'll pay everything we have for a gallon of water. If one suit costs $100 more than another but we believe that the more expensive one makes us look better (whatever that means to us), we might spend the extra C-note. If we have to make a decision about launching an e-business venture, we consider not only the cost to our company and the profit margin of the product or service but also the likelihood that the customers will want to do business over the Web. Our risk decision therefore takes into consideration the quantifiable data, gained through a sampling of the prospective customers; an intuitive assessment, based on our experience, our personal needs, and corporate goals; and the actions of competitors. The confounding factor is the capricious behavior of human beings. They don't always do what they say they will in the market research. Therein lies the greatest risk.

In addition to unforeseeable human response, if the decision requires a significant investment, the question of incremental value comes into play. In short, how much more market share or profit margin will this represent if it works? Is that a large percentage or a small one? Mathematician Daniel Bernoulli claimed that "the utility resulting from any small increase in wealth will be inversely proportionate to the quantity of goods previously possessed."[1] In other words, are we approaching the point of diminishing return? Is the investment worth the gain, even if the gain is almost assured? Would it be better to put money into traditional methods at this time or into a Web-based program? We don't have to abandon past success totally. The Web will still be here tomorrow. But can we wait until tomorrow to jump in? Executives get paid to make that decision and make it right more often than wrong.

> *The Web will still be here tomorrow. But can we wait until tomorrow to jump in? Executives get paid to make that decision and make it right more often than wrong.*

ROOTS OF INNOVATION

Successful innovation does not come as a flash of lightning. More often, it is the result of one of two sources. First, if we are really lucky, we might find something new through serendipity. In the course of studying one thing, we come across a by-product or a modification that yields an unanticipated but useful result. When this happens, we simply thank "The Force" and carry on. The second case is more common. Here, a good idea is the direct result of a good question. As someone once said, the answer to every problem lies within the question. So how do we learn to ask the right question?

Americans are not known for our analytic tendencies. We are a people of action, not contemplation. We are a nation of pioneers and cowboys. All of our old west morality plays exemplify this behavior. From the Lone Ranger to Shane, right is reinforced with a pistol, not a Socratic debate. This does have its advantages in that we do tend to get things done more quickly than some other cultures. The problem lies in that sometimes we shoot the wrong guy.

Although we are all stressed to the gills trying to be responsive to the customer and beat the competition to market, there is value in taking time to understand the problem before firing our gun. It is not a coincidence that the Ready—Fire—Aim Syndrome is an American phenomenon. And lest you think it is a recent development, let me assure you that we were exhibiting the same behavior in the slower-paced 1960s. The solution is to ask, "What is the underlying issue here?" For the moment, let current circumstances rest undisturbed and think about what is behind them. When you think you have that answer, ask the same question again: "What's behind this?" Then ask it again and again, being skeptical of every answer until we feel very confident that we are as close as possible to first cause. The final question is the *coincidence test*. Just because two or more things are moving in parallel does not prove that they are interrelated. They might just be coincidences. To test that, look for evidence of effect. What is there about "A" that might be affecting "B" and vice versa? What makes us think there is a relationship beyond parallelism?

Skipping a Step

Sometimes solutions come from skipping a step. I don't mean to go back to the shoot-em-up model at all. On the contrary, I'm suggesting that we consider each step in a process and ask ourselves why we do it, how it adds value, and what could happen if we stopped doing it and went more directly to the objective of the process. In short, what's the risk of dropping the whole thing and going at it differently? This is a suggestion that we shift from focusing on incremental improvements to a redefinition of the issue. Quality programs work on incremental improvements. Reengineering looked for radical solutions by redefining the problem and not accepting past assumptions without checking. Although reengineering foundered by ignoring the human element, the thought process has merit. But it is still not as big a jump as might be required by the market.

Take a case of how to be timelier in responding to customer problems. The Charles Schwab Corporation provided a good example of this redefinition approach.[2] At one time it was taking the company two weeks to resolve a customer complaint. The process started with an acknowledgment letter, then a tracing of the complaint back to the business unit under question, investigating the customer's allegations, reaching a decision, and finally writing back to the customer. Someone suggested the company make complaints a priority, but that did not offer a significantly faster response. Just paying attention to something might improve it but seldom yields a quantum leap. Then someone suggested skipping the letter-writing step and calling the customer directly, which would save several days in the mail. However, another person believed that regulations required a written response. When this belief was checked out, it was found to be not true. Still, the quantum leap had to wait until the problem was redefined as "customer retention" rather than "complaint response." This put the issue in a whole new light, turning it from a negative situation to a positive opportunity. This opened up the imagination and changed the metric from response time to retention rate. What would you rather have: faster response or a retained customer? The staff began to look at their work differently and have continued to find ways to improve the process and retain the customers.

RULES OF INNOVATION

Lee Davenport has a long career in research starting during World War II, when he worked at the MIT Radiation Laboratory on fire-control radar. Over the course of his decades of work in corporate research, he developed seven rules of innovation, which were reported in *Upside*.[3] Many of them apply to business innovation.

1. Realize that success is based on schedules and results, not effort.
2. Since most projects last a long time, break them into measurable short segments.

3. Never allow general goals. Make them all measurable.
4. Look for idea people. Encourage the few individuals who have unique, harebrained ideas.
5. Find internal product champions, who understand the technology and can push ideas through.
6. Keep a little money on the side. Sometimes it's the only way to pursue great ideas.
7. Hire young blood, and balance it with experience.

One of the major barriers to innovation is being the leader in a field. The most successful company is the most vulnerable. Overconfidence is often a by-product of success. *Not invented here* and *you can't argue with success* are two of the most stultifying statements that a company must eradicate. There are ways to avoid paying the price of success. One is to set revenue targets for new products. Establish an annual goal that X percent of revenue must be generated by products that have come to market within the past year. What that figure should be depends on the nature of the product or service line. A second and more dramatic play could involve a means for shifting the business from a reliance on hard goods to soft goods. I'm suggesting the adoption of an entirely different model. IBM, among others, has shifted its business dramatically from hardware to services. Then, by setting stretch goals for service revenue without trading product revenue for it, it can literally change the nature of the company. A third method is to set up a "skunk works." This is a new venture located away from the core of the business, geographically distant if possible, funded separately and charged with coming to market with a radically new product within a short time frame. It is possible to incorporate all three alternatives into our strategic possibilities. They are not mutually incompatible. But in every case, funds have to be made available to bolster the innovation. We can't have a major breakthrough without the resources to drive it. Stretching is good—breaking is bad.

CONNECTIVITY BREEDS INNOVATION

Now that it is here, the Web has forced collaboration. Not joining the worldwide conversation is total stupidity. No one can hide, so why not jump in?

Metcalf's Law, that the value of a network squares with the addition of each new participant, implies a geometric growth of opportunity through connectivity. Doc Searls and Dave Weinberger expanded that in *The Cluetrain Manifesto* with their Cluetrain Corollary: "The level of knowledge on a network increases as a square of the number of users times the volume of conversation."[4]

> *The Web has forced collaboration. Not joining the worldwide conversation is total stupidity.*

Every time a new Web site comes up and attracts attention (and they are appearing in the thousands per day worldwide), the value of every other Web site increases not by one, but by the new total number of connections made on the Web. The mathematics are mind numbing and not important. It's about the prospect and the opportunity. If we were physically capable of seeing the exponentially expanded possibilities, they would be beyond human comprehension. But while we can't see the Web, in effect, we can imagine its magnitude—somewhat. Let me try to illustrate the prospect.

Let us assume there are 1 million Web sites, of which 500 deal with our special interest, e.g., golf. When we add one new golf-based Web site, all 500 golf sites now can connect not only directly with new golf site (NGS), but also can reconnect with all other old golf sites (OGSs) as new combinations. Assume NGS is focused on golf history and memorabilia. Every golfer is interested to some degree in golf history and memorabilia; we're a sentimental group deeply in love with the world's greatest game. Now, every one of the 500 OGSs can look at NGS as it relates to and compares with the other OGSs. This is not just 501. It is 501^2. If any of the other 999,500 Web sites gets interested and puts out a message about NGS to their contacts, the numbers go still farther than imagination can handle. Now substitute your message for NGS and imagine what can happen!

BUSINESS CONCEPT INNOVATION AND THE WEB

Gary Hamel claims that only by what he terms *business concept innovation* can someone create a competitive advantage. He offers a model of innovation based on four approaches.

The starting point is continuous, incremental improvement. It deals with components of the system. As improvement moves from incremental to radical, we are into the range of nonlinear innovation (Hamel's second approach). This implies greater gains from action. As we move from component-level to system-level improvement, we embed new processes in the business (the third approach, business process innovation). But Hamel argues we need to combine radical innovation with system-level improvement, in what he labels business concept innovation.

Continuous improvement, nonlinear innovation, and business process innovation all have their place in the past. They are artifacts of i-world, where tinkering with processes was a proven method for incremental improvement. Now, in e-world, only by creating a new business model is a company truly innovative. Dell Computer, Starbucks, Virgin Atlantic, Charles Schwab, and Monster.com are all examples of new business concepts applied within established industries. In every case they shook the industry at its base and stimulated others to match and try to compete with the lead they set. Also, in every case they severely wounded the established companies while excavating new marketing channels for their industry. Finally, in every case they are making excellent use of the Web to either drive the business (Monster.com and Charles Schwab) or enhance the business (Dell and Virgin). When we take a new business concept and we drive it onto the Web, we create a juggernaut. This is because of the unique connective and multiplicative properties of the Web.

Like the authors of *The Cluetrain Manifesto*, Kevin Kelly, the executive editor of *Wired* magazine, talks about how the Web opens up an organization. It affects innovation, the associates, and our customers. Kelly states: "When given the choice between closed or open systems, consumers show a fierce enthusiasm for open architectures. They choose the open again and again because an open system has more potential upside than a closed one."[5]

Take that thought and apply it in your company, to your associates, and to innovation. People in an open system are free to express themselves, share ideas, debate, and argue positively. This is the stuff on which innovation thrives. The more we open our corporate communication, the more people enter and participate. In a closed system all good ideas must flow from the top, and I don't know about you, but I don't have enough good ideas to keep my company ahead of the collective imagination of the competition.

If we apply the open system claim to the Web, we see it confirmed in spades. How many million people joined the Web in its first five years? Why? Because they could. The Web is open to all and everyone is there. My grandma Emma used to say, "It takes all kinds of people to make a world and they are all here." Grandma must have been anticipating the Web because they are all truly *here*—here via the Web. When companies move toward the Web as a major channel of communication and sales, they have to become innovative in their use of the new medium. As pointed out above, by its nature, the value of the Web increases exponentially as each new person joins it. So it behooves our organization to maximize the Web as an indirect means of maximizing ourselves. As the Web itself grows, its potential as a channel for us grows exponentially. If the Web closes down, we face not only current but future losses of value. Behind the Web is the network of players and technology that makes up the infrastructure. Whenever any of the players innovates, it affects all other players. So the Web and the underlying network are connected synergistically, for better or worse. As others innovate, they stimulate us to do the same. As we innovate, we turn the challenges back into the net toward others. Thus it goes around and around, ever increasing and ever adding value to those who play.

Figure 8-1 represents the upward movement of innovation through the Web. Of course, while this is going on, Web technology is also evolving. Nothing is static in this game. The bottom line is that innovation is a basic requirement in every strategic plan.

MAKING STANDARDS

Whenever innovation disrupts a market, by definition, some of the old standards no longer apply. The market seeks new standards because it naturally wants to find a framework that offers some degree of equilibrium. Today, equilibrium is somewhere between a dream and a false hope. Nevertheless, standards have value because they accelerate innovation by providing a common, reliable pathway.

Intangibles such as various forms of information need standards

Figure 8-1. The upward movement of innovation through the Web.

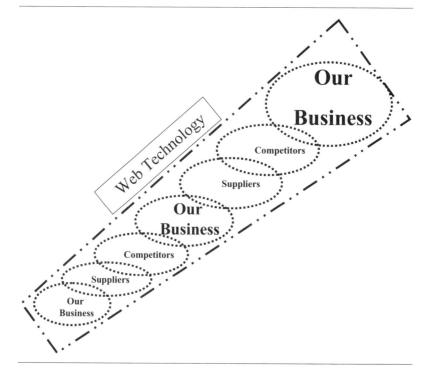

(e.g., Generally Accepted Accounting Practices) as much or more than tangibles. We can't pick up intangibles, weigh them, or measure their reflectivity or hardness. As standards solidify, they become imbedded in hardware and software and are there forever (almost). Information is a good example of the need for standard methodology. When information is published, consumers need to know if it is reliable and valid. If we say that the average cost of a given process is $XXX, how have we defined the process? What have we included and excluded as steps in the process? Unless there is a standard formula for the calculation, with all variables unequivocally defined, we don't know what we are looking at.

When I started the Saratoga Institute in 1978, I had one great concern: the fear of being wiped out by one of the big consulting or information firms. So the first imperative I set for myself was to become the standard source for human capital performance measurement and benchmark metrics. To do this, I allied my Institute with the Society for Human Resource Management, the national human resources professional society, and with several national trade associations. Their sponsorship and imprimatur immediately made Saratoga the accepted standard for the thousands of companies participating in those groups. After sixteen years of publishing data using the Saratoga Institute's standard methodology, we are clearly the global referent that everyone looks to as "the source."

This is an example of success in finding a community of potential customers who have a common interest and then marketing directly to them. When enough customers respond, you can set the standard. Being the standard is a competitive advantage that is extremely difficult to overcome. But by controlling the standard, we can influence customer needs, develop offerings before others even know there is a perceived need, and move on to the next product enhancement while the competition is trying to catch up to the last one.

Today, your company is moving into a new market: the e-biz business. In a sense it is as vulnerable as I was, even though yours might be a multibillion-dollar enterprise. You can be selling the same products today as yesterday, but you have new competitors and a new channel of communication and distribution. In a new market all players are equal initially. If you sell a product such as steel, which is made to ASTM standards, you have neither the problem nor the opportunity to change that chemical standard. But you can add specialty items to your product line (which we will discuss shortly). If you are marketing an intangible, a service, a nonstandard commodity, or a new specialty, you have the opening to set the standard.

For years I have advised individuals starting businesses and managers looking for a competitive advantage to find a way to create the standard. In my opinion there is nothing nearly as powerful as being the standard setter. Have you ever heard of Microsoft?

MOVING THE STANDARD

A traditional way of setting standards is to bring together as many companies as possible within a given industry for the purpose of tying them to the technical standards agreed to by their peers.

This works for the benefit of all by providing a common language or methodology for sharing, comparing, and advancing the state of the art of all. But from a competitive standpoint, this does not help one establish an advantage over others in its industry. The way to jump the fence yet maintain the standard is to pick up the standard and move it to a new territory.

> **The way to jump the fence yet maintain the standard is to pick up the standard and move it to a new territory.**

What standard methods can we pick up from our product line and carry over with some slight variation into a new product line for a new batch of customers? Alvin Toffler warned us over twenty years ago that the era of mass production was disappearing.[6] Basically, his theory was that mass society was fast giving way to niches, communities, and interest groups. His prediction has come true in that we are now a society of special interests. There has been a tremendous proliferation of focused interest groups, large and small, some quite powerful. The American Association of Retired Persons is a very strong force today, and the National Rifle Association and the NAACP wield substantial political power. Below that level there are literally thousands of groups. Each one of them is a market for something from collectible comic books to antique thimbles. Today, they are all reachable through the Web. They are all conversing among themselves over the Web. They all talk about their experiences with their suppliers as well, so one slip can become a topic for national discussion overnight.

Figure 8-2 represents how the market has changed as it has begun to move from i-world dynamics to e-world dynamics. I-world was a closed, slow moving, linear system of simple mass production and mass consumption. There was very little room for niches to emerge. The most visible example of that was the automobile industry shortly after World War II. The Big Three had pretty much locked up the market, and people as powerful as Henry John Kaiser and as innovative as Preston Tucker failed to break the Detroit stranglehold. One of the Big Three could have bought Tucker with lunch money and used his innovations to gain competitive advantage, but linear thinking doesn't allow for that. It wasn't until Volkswagen redefined the automobile from status symbol to basic transportation that the first crack appeared in the fortress. Japan saw it and Honda followed

Figure 8-2. The changing market dynamics of i-world and e-world.

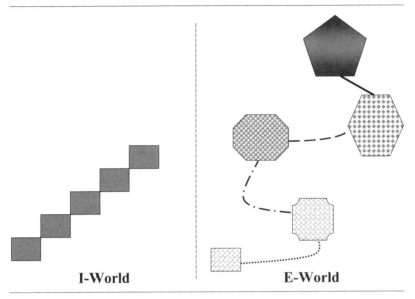

I-World   E-World

with the Civic. The rest is history. In the past thirty years, trillions of dollars have turned from Detroit and headed for Stuttgart and Tokyo.

CREATING AND EXPANDING NICHES

In e-world, people and businesses are communicating again. The market has reopened and the possibilities abound. The e-world market is more diversified because it is already serving the many interest groups with variations on a central product or service. It is much easier for a niche market to emerge and grow. Look at how Sony has taken its technology and created an electronic games market that could hardly be called a niche today. See how simple Post-it Notes have evolved into a multiproduct line for 3M. Consider what Swatch did to the watch business by thinking of timepieces as fashion items rather than chronometers. 3Com created a very lucrative spin-off market with its Palm Pilot. Now others are carving niches within the Palm market for specialized software and integrated communication.

In time it is predictable that this software will migrate into other products.

Regis McKenna established himself as an original thinker by helping to market some of the great success stories of Silicon Valley, the most notable being Apple Computer. He talks about market creation as opposed to market sharing. The notion is that applying a differentiation strategy can create new markets: "The emphasis is on applying technology, educating the market, developing relationships with the industry infrastructure, and creating new *standards* [my italics]. The company with the greatest innovation and creativity is likely to differentiate itself and win the desired market."[7]

He illustrates his thesis with the story of Apple and Tandy, which looked at the nascent personal computer business with a market-creation viewpoint. Through the mid-1970s, many large companies looked at the market for inexpensive computers and decided it was a hobbyists' market—too small to bother with. But Apple and Tandy, rather than focusing on what was, dreamed up what could be. They transferred a hobby tool to a business setting. In doing this they invented the new small-computer market, which is now a several hundred billion dollar market.

FROM COMMODITY TO SPECIALTY

Another way to create new markets is to turn commodities into specialties. There are very few commodities that cannot be transformed into specialties. It is true that a supertanker loaded with oil or a one hundred–car freight train filled with coal are bulk commodities. That is not the point. The concept is that the company that extracts crude oil and the mining company that digs coal can come up with ways to specialize. The simplest way has been to expand downstream into processed derivatives of the bulk material. Oil becomes gasoline, solvents, heating oil, plastics, or even fertilizer and can be sold at wholesale or retail. Plastics are a massive industry on their own, and specialty petrochemicals are another. At the retail level, gas stations are becoming convenience stores. Over time, the stores can take on more items or branch into drive-throughs or even home deliveries. And if we start delivering, why not add a small automated bakery and bring fresh bread and pastries? Why not: Is there a law against it? No, because there is at least one gas station I know of that has a small bakery attached to it. Now local bakeries have to compete with a gas station. Who would have predicted that?

The same principle applies to coal. It is processed into many products and wholesaled by the coal company, but the company could go into manufacturing the derivatives or into transportation since it uses railroads so extensively. Rail transport has already expanded into trucking and trucking into air cargo. Flying flowers from South America is a far cry from hauling coal from Montana, but the lack of imagination or the fear of failure is the only limitation of commodity businesses.

One might argue that telephone service (information) is a commodity. Hundreds of millions of calls are made every day. Telephone service per se is approaching the point of essentially being free. As customers are drawn to more of this nearly free service, human nature kicks in. When we like something, we ask what else is available. The instrument is extremely cheap, so cheap it can be thrown into a service offering telephone lines. Kevin Kelly provided an insight into how this has worked for telephone companies.

First, we get one phone for every room. Then, how about one for when we are traveling so we won't be tied to one location? Solution: the mobile line. Then the kids want mobile phones, so what the heck; it is only a couple of dollars a month more per line and the phone is free, isn't it? It's part of the service. Next come refinements of the service itself: call forwarding, answering service, call waiting, caller ID, fax and modem lines. The possibilities are limited only by our imagination, which itself has no limits. The initial information product, the cell phone, is *apparently* free if you sign up for services. The cost of the hardware is buried in the service charge, and the retailer hopes for renewals of the subscription. When renewals come, margins leap and we have a real business. It is a sure bet. That is the nature of a subscription business. Now, instead of selling a telephone, we are selling a service.[8]

The interesting thing about information and connectivity is that the more people get of it, the more they want it. Connectivity is such a basic human need that it generates an unlimited market for information-related products and services. Each time we learn something, we are stimulated to know more. There is no boundary to human desires since our imagination is practically limitless. If imagination and thereby desire were not intriguing and nearly infinite, there would have been very few inventions. Once we got fire and food, why would we need anything else if our imagination had not asked, "I wonder what it would be like if . . ."?

There is a caution amid this trip through innovative euphoria. That is, it takes time and commitment to find a niche, nurture it to a new standard, and defend it against attack. In the past it often took five years before the market accepted a new standard. Even Microsoft's DOS did not overwhelm the market overnight. There was an operating system called C/PM that competed for several years before IBM and Microsoft hooked up and made DOS the preferred system. Even in today's cyclonic market, most new standards do not explode into megabusinesses overnight. The lesson is, we must expect rejection at first, competition for a while, and finally an acceptance of our idea as the standard. Only when that arrives will an exceptional ROI be achieved. But from then on the sky is the limit!

REFERENCES

1. Peter Bernstein, *Against the Gods* (New York: John Wiley & Sons, 1996), p. 105.
2. David Pottruck and Terry Pearce, *Clicks and Mortar* (San Francisco: Jossey-Bass, 2000), pp. 143–145.
3. "Seven Rules for Innovation," *Upside,* June 2000, p. 290.
4. Doc Searls and David Weinberger, *The Cluetrain Manifesto* (Cambridge, Mass.: Perseus Publishing, 2000), p. 83.
5. Kevin Kelly, *New Rules for the New Economy* (New York: Penguin Putnam, 1998), p. 65.
6. Alvin Toffler, *The Third Wave* (New York: William Morrow, 1980).
7. Regis McKenna, *Relationship Marketing* (Reading, Mass.: Addison-Wesley, 1991), p. 29.
8. Kelly, p. 54.

Selling and Servicing E-Customers

WHEN DO CUSTOMERS BECOME COMPETITORS? In some industries, a company can be a customer one day and a competitor the next. The arrival of the Web has allowed people with very local businesses to sell worldwide. This capacity has muddied marketing channels and made relationships more sensitive than ever before.

Electronic shopping is definitely going to be a major channel in the near future. As technology improves and merchants learn how to employ it, more buyers will try it. The more that try it, the more merchants will be driven to respond with better service, and even more buyers will try it. Progress is inevitable. Already, nearly one in five shoppers claims to prefer e-shopping over in-store shopping. This is demanding that merchants respond or become fragile enterprises hovering over the chasm of extinction. Just as the individual store was marginalized by the mall, so too can the Web marginalize the mall.

Merchants are also threatened from the supplier side. Manufacturers can put up Web sites and sell direct. This is happening in apparel, recreational goods, and insurance and other financial services. What is to stop any major manufacturer or service business from selling direct? Why couldn't automobile manufacturers sell direct and turn dealers into pick-up and service centers? Who would object to not having to deal with a high-pressure car salesman? Channel conflict is a rapidly approaching dilemma for both sides.

The bottom line is that marketing and selling are about to undergo a major face-lift. New skills in information gathering, prospecting, selling, and servicing are imperatives. The basic truth of the new market is that there is only one certain way to differentiate ourselves. There is just one way that is the hardest for our competitors to emulate. It isn't product, because product features can be reverse-engineered or knocked off and improved upon. It isn't price, because scale is not a compelling factor in the mass customization market. The only sustainable differentiator is service. Retail stores with their nonexistent to atrocious service are most at risk. Those who don't understand this and don't learn to shift their focus from merchandising to customer service will be out of business in less than a decade. Those who master the new interaction between buyer and seller will be the winners.

SELLING INTO E-WORLD

The first year that computers outsold TVs was 1995. Although it had been creeping in for a couple of decades, 1995 could rightfully be labeled the first full year of the Information Age. It was only years earlier that the Rural Electrification Act began to push electricity vigorously beyond city limits. At that time, no one could foresee what electrification meant and what it would do to consumerism. New methods of communication, entertainment, and life in general came with turning the sun on twenty-four hours a day. Now, as we lurch into the 21st century, we are beginning to see the next step in the offering and consumption of goods and services. With it, the relationship between the supplier and the customer is profoundly changing. One point is becoming exquisitely clear: *The e-world customer is not the i-world customer.*

THE E-WORLD CUSTOMER

The e-world buyer profile is no longer predominantly white, male, Christian, Baby Boomer. Father doesn't always know best anymore. The new profile looks like this: multiethnic, older, and most important, female. This has a profound implication for e-world marketers. Paul Saffo, director of the Institute for the Future, nailed it when he said: "What excites me most about the new economy is that we're in the middle of a fundamental change in the nature of commerce, in the nature of capitalism. Commerce isn't about buying stuff—it's about interacting with people in different ways. And that's happening everywhere."[1]

The e-world customer is likely to be female, older, and busier than the typical customer of the past.

Gender

Anyone who doesn't know that women feel, think, and act differently than men has never met a woman. Men tend to be narrowly focused. Males see this piece here and that piece there. Men compartmentalize. Women have more acute and broader peripheral vision than men. They see the big picture. Women see the whole and make decisions based on their instincts or intuition after all the data are in. I believe that perceptual acuity is responsible in large part for what we call feminine intuition. Basically, women live life deeper than men do.

My metaphor is that men float on the surface of life's ocean and women are the scuba divers. They want to feel they know what is going on underneath the waves. They care about relationships. They want to know something about the company with whom they do business. They like to know how we treat our employees. They care about how clean and orderly our stores are, how late we stay open, and how well lit and safe our parking lots are. They would like to have a deeper level of relationship with their supplier than men do. It matters what a company does to maintain the relationship—how we show we care about the customer. When dealing with female customers, companies have to think deeper and longer-term than just this sale. Beyond the basics, merchants can't buy women's loyalty with discount coupons alone or ignore them when they walk into the store with their male companion.

Another story illustrates this last point. In 1999, my wife and I decided that she should trade in her minivan for a newer model. We drove to auto row and entered the first dealer's lot. I purposely stayed several steps behind my wife. The ever-smiling salesman, coming out to greet us, walked right past my wife and came to me. I told him my wife was interested in a new minivan. He started his pitch to me, completely ignoring her. My wife was rightfully insulted at his lack of sensitivity and civility. Needless to say, he didn't get the sale. C'mon guys. Wake up.

Age

Every day in the United States, over 10,000 Baby Boomers turn fifty. By 2020, 35 percent of the U.S. population will be over 50. Simultaneously, almost all other categories will decline as a percent of the population.

What is the older, more mature buyer like? At age 65, my grandfather was worn down from fifty years of heavy manual labor. Today, most 60-something men are still physically vital, yet stereotypes maintain a picture of paunchy, balding couch potatoes. The facts say something else. Research and consulting firm AgeWave IMPACT describes six myths about customers age 50-plus. Being well into that group myself, I can confirm their findings.

MYTH	FACT
1. **Today's mature adults are similar to their parents.**	Using the same celebrities, music, and slang with a new generation doesn't work.
2. **The mature audience is homogeneous.**	We become less alike and more ourselves as we age and as our lives take different courses.
3. **Mature adults are brand loyal.**	Nearly 70 percent of adults are willing to switch brands if they see something that better suits their needs.

4. **Mature adults have consistent and predictable behaviors.**	Midlife often causes us to reevaluate what we've done and what we want to do in the future.
5. **Mature adults are inflexible and resistant to change.**	We act more on information than impulse, but we feel less restrained than ever before.
6. **Marketing models that have worked in the past will work in the future.**	The media blitz of the last fifty years has oversold us. We want to do business with a company we can trust.[2]

Time

Never before in history have consumers felt so rushed, and it isn't going to let up in the foreseeable future. We can see many new services coming on the market that are aimed at helping us save time, making it easier and faster to do business. There is also room for things such as a reminder service. Have you ever forgotten an important date like an anniversary or birthday? Wouldn't it be useful to have an automatic reminder service beyond a note on your computer or Palm Pilot?

iVillage Square is a wireless service that notifies people about an impending personal event for which they have asked to be reminded. As an anniversary, birthday, or other event approaches, a signal comes through their telephone or pager, and a message appears reminding the customer of the occasion. Busy women like it, and men need it because they are somewhat absent-minded when it comes to anniversaries and birthdays. If the reminder comes with an easy way to buy something, the service will be a winner.

FREE INFORMATION OR JUNK?

About a hundred years ago, inventor and manufacturer King Gillette gave us a lesson that is coming home to many people: Give the razor away and sell consumable blades forever. Now, technology has advanced to the point that it has made some razors so cheap they can be combined with the blades and both are thrown away! Is this a great country or what?

This supposedly free concept has moved into the information business big time. The Web is loaded with free information. We can find answers to all types of questions and can research everything from alpacas to zoos. There has never been such a resource, and it is growing faster than anyone can keep up.

In the service businesses, *free* is a marketer's dream. Newspaper and magazine subscriptions, initially obtained as free offerings or loss leaders, are later sold, resold, or morphed into online services. The hunger for information knows no boundaries. Initially we can give away information. The more people get of something they like, the more they want. This is because each learning and fulfillment of a need stimulates a desire to know or have more. There is a subconscious feeling with a credit card that we don't even have to pay for what we want—at least for thirty days.

From the provider side, eventually, the revenue-generating business will depend on the content as well as the speed of service. If the base product or service does not meet people's needs or is no good, they will not re-up and the cost of marketing will sink the product and maybe the company. Free junk is still junk.

E-tailing has already seen some of the irrationality burn out with the April 14, 2000, sell-off of the dot-com market. We can only give something away and lose money for so long. The traditional fight for brand identity, market share, and share of spend resurfaced on April 15, 2000. In the end, operational excellence and exceptional service will always prevail.

CUSTOMERS AS ASSETS

The key to sustainable profits is not eyeballs on a Web site, since more than half the people who browse a Web site do not buy. The key to success is identifying, acquiring, and retaining profitable customers. There is very little margin on the front end of many sales. It is only by retaining a customer that we obtain an acceptable return on the marketing investment. Yet in e-world's hypercompetitive market, retention is the problem. Companies typically lose two out of three of their new customers by the end of the third year. Customer needs are not fixed and change over time. Their needs are fulfilled or found not to be so important any more. If we can't keep up with the changes in the customer's life, we lose him or her. Many of the dot-coms act

> *The key to sustainable profits is not eyeballs on a Web site, since more than half the people who browse a Web site do not buy.*

as though the customer is just one facet of the business along with technology, employees, and finance. They seem to miss the point that *the customer is the business.*

Marketing's contribution has to be its ability to identify future customer service opportunities. That comes not from sending out mass mailings but from wide-ranging research, both formal and informal.

- We have to learn customers' needs, desires, and idiosyncrasies.
- We have to let them know we think about them in everything we do.
- We have to be in touch with them before and after the point of a sale.

It's called *building a relationship.*

When we know our customers better than our competitors do, we can offer them something that the competitors can't and we can almost name the price. Figure 9-1 lays out the pathway to the customer and profits through managing a relationship that leads to repeat sales. The key is to make each contact with the customer positive from the customer's viewpoint. To achieve this, the prime imperative is to get marketing and sales to talk to each other.

GETTING TO KNOW OUR CUSTOMERS

There are many paths to customer knowledge. These are the most obvious low-tech methods:

Figure 9-1. The pathway to repeat business.

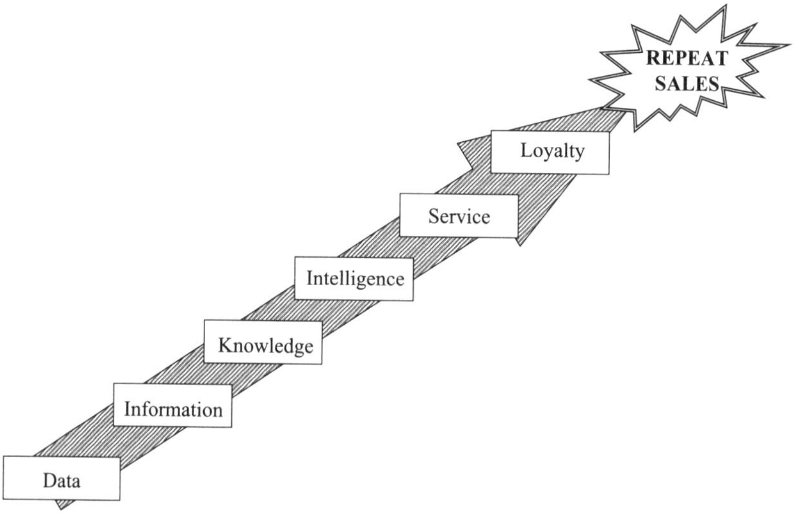

- **Individuals.** We can survey our customers in several ways, including face-to-face interviews and mail surveys regarding what they like, don't like, and would like. In addition, toll-free hot lines let people reach us with problems, compliments, and ideas for new services.
- **Groups.** Focus groups, customer panels, and user groups can be organized or approached for reactions to our current products and services as well as new ideas we have.
- **Visits.** We can send out mystery shoppers or employees to talk with users and prospects at their site. Visits of peers such as engineers with engineers can yield the type of data that a salesperson would never get.

Besides learning about product and service, we can dig into the perceptual realm by asking a target population what they think of our brand. This can tell us the position that our product occupies in the market of the mind. Ultimately, action is a function of thought and thought is a result of a perception. The way people *feel* about us is critical. It is extremely difficult to overcome negative perceptions. We need to know our mindspace early and often. Just as it is cheaper to keep an old customer than it is to get a new customer, it is easier to maintain a positive perception than it is to overcome a negative assessment of us. Figure 9-2 is a list of questions suggested by Michael de Kare-Silver to gauge how customers view your brand.[3]

SALES VS. MARKETING

Breaking through Internal Barriers

There is a history of antipathy between sales and marketing folk. Sales has an element of disdain for the marketing folk, who spend their time on communications pieces but never get face to face with the customer in a selling situation. Sales types believe, and rightfully so, that they are the shock troops. They are the ones who experience daily rejection from sometimes not-so-nice prospects and customers. They are the ones who have to explain why the product is late or why it doesn't work the way the marketing piece said it would. Marketing people often see sales as a group of promise-anything hawkers who live by their wits. They believe that the sales force puts the company in a position that is unrealistic and impossible to support.

Figure 9-2. Testing how customers view your brand.

1. Do customers, without prompting, name the brand as the leader in its category sector?
2. Is the lead versus the next-mentioned brand name significant?
3. Have a high proportion of target cusumers purchased the product at least once?
4. Is there a high proportion who would count as regular users?
5. Is usage of the product typically highly satisfactory?
6. Would target consumers say they trust the product?
7. Would target consumers agree there is no need to check the product out before purchasing it again?
8. Are intentions to repurchase at high levels?
9. Do consumers see a clear difference in value versus other competing products?
10. Is the ongoing brand investment by the company higher than that put in by competition?

We are not going to be as successful as we could be until we bring these two forces together with a common goal. The common goal is knowledge of the customer. One way to do this is to put marketing people in the field with sales so they gain firsthand experience.

Sales Retraining and Incentives

Sales training today needs a face-lift. We have trained our sales forces to sell, not to cultivate relationships. When I was a salesman in i-world, I was trained to get the customer's attention, elicit his interest in the product, describe the features and benefits, and close him. No one told me to learn as much as I could about the customer, and this product-first orientation is the way many salespeople still work. In e-world, we have to retrain our sales force. Now, their job goes beyond selling a product to keeping a customer. This requires continually talking to the customers about their needs and wish lists.

The e-world sales process really starts with understanding as much as possible about the customer. Salespeople need to know not only the immediate needs but also the dreams and future desires of the customer. They have to spend time with the customer, building a relationship that opens up a personal conversation. That conversation yields information that, if put together with other data, can lead to building a knowledge bank. The knowledge evolves into competitor as well as customer intelligence because the customer tells you what she likes and dislikes about your competition. Bringing home that information helps us develop new offerings. Customer and market intelligence helps the salesperson select the product or service that will best fulfill the customer's needs and desires. This fosters customer trust and loyalty, which is the foundation of repeat sales in e-world markets. This is quite a bit different from trying to make an immediate sale by describing features and benefits.

> *Most people in sales love the immediate gratification that comes from closing a sale. We are going to have to change that behavior . . .*

To gain this shift in mindset, we might have to redesign our sales incentive programs. Most people in sales love the immediate gratification that comes from closing a sale. We are going to have to change that behavior, which is not easy with commission salespeople. To convince them to delay the immediate sale in favor of learning about the customer will not be easy. Every salesperson will tell you he knows his customers. However, that knowledge is usually very thin, seldom getting below the surface to anything that requires interpretation. I doubt that 99 percent of the sales force in retailing knows as much about their regular customers as Amazon.com knows about me. How could they remember all the information that Amazon.com captures about my buying habits? This is understandable because we have paid our salespeople to make sales, not to know the soul of the customer. This has to change, and the compensation system must reflect the value of the information or it is not going to happen. As an old salesman, I guarantee you that I would go where the money is.

Customers don't want to be treated equally. They want to be treated individually, to feel special or exclusive. Salespeople must be given the tools they need to help the customer create her own barrier to exit. They need skills and tools to help the customer give us information that we can use to give her value, which further binds her to us. Prices are transparent. Products are commodities. What is left? The answer is relationships.

CUSTOMER EXPECTATIONS

Message Factors Inc. is a company specializing in value analysis. Over the years, it has run its processes for hundreds of client companies. As a result, it has formulated what it believes are the four basics that customers want to communicate to their suppliers. The four basics are:[4]

1. I expect you to have mastered the basics of what you are in business to do—design, build, sell, service, account for, and so on.
2. I expect you to go beyond the basics and provide me with what I value. Loyalty is based on giving me what I value.
3. I don't like some things you do, but they are not important enough to drive me away. Delivering on time as promised

would help, as would making it more convenient for me to shop with you.

4. I don't care about some things you do, so don't waste resources telling me about them. Newsletters often fall into this category.

Before World War II, when life was more localized, people depended on each other more. This included their suppliers as well as their extended family and neighbors. Life moved more slowly, and long-distance travel was unknown to most. We tended to do business with people we could see and talk with directly. Now, as the world has opened up, family relations are geographically extended, social institutions have weakened, and life has become more impersonal. Technology has extended this impersonality. For the first time in history, the average person has his hands on powerful Web technology every day in every aspect of his personal and business life. As a result, e-world customers are less tolerant and more demanding than at any time within living memory. But they've lost the personal contact of the past. They yearn for the closeness of that time. Young people ask, "What was it like? How did it feel?" Instinctively, human beings are social animals who want relationships. The company that can give it to them will be rewarded with a long, profitable association.

CUSTOMER RELATIONS MANAGEMENT

Customer relations management (CRM) is not about buying software. It is about garnering customer intelligence. The critical differentiator is that CRM is not an exclusively marketing department program. It is a companywide imperative that starts with top management support and should involve everyone:

- R&D (future products)
- Manufacturing (unit costs)
- Accounting (best customers)
- Customer service (additional customer information and opportunity to serve and sell)
- Human resources (selection of relations-oriented associates)

Customer intelligence does not exist in isolation but is the currency of the relationship between the supplier and the consumer. It is built through affinity and mutual trust. Associates love sharing their personal customer knowledge. It makes them feel important to show how well they know the customer. At Saratoga Institute, we hold monthly employee lunches where our associates are encouraged to tell about their experiences with customers and prospects who call in. This confirms that they are an important part of our enterprise and gives management special information that it can get from no other place.

Top management needs to learn about CRM data and how they can be used. This requires a long-term vision and a relations strategy since the customer knowledge base is cumulative and changing. It also takes an act of faith. It takes time to build a customer database. Conservatively, we estimate it is a minimum of eighteen months, depending on the sales frequency and cycle, before we see the effects of the use of the information. It may be another annual cycle before we can realize its full effectiveness and ROI.

The problem with this long-term payback is that management is under the gun to produce short-term results. For the past thirty years, the model has been to offer all kinds of bribes and discounts to make current sales and to build loyalty. Consumers tell you that without quality products and personal service, each new inducement is as meaningless as the last. Most discount programs are imitative and uninspired. Sixty percent of supermarkets have loyalty programs based on discounts, yet they receive only half of their customers' grocery spend. People who can afford it shop at the store they like the best. Those who have to watch their pennies organize their shopping plan to buy only discounted items.

Me-too programs are always losers because they offer nothing that can't be found across the street. The best example is frequent flier miles, which every major airline gives out. You can also get them from a growing list of nonflying activities, so what is the advantage to the airline? If everyone has the same offer, there is no advantage and no customer loyalty associated with it. I'm probably like you in that I belong to a half-dozen programs and fly with whichever has the best service, the most convenient schedule, and the best price. Frequent flier miles is about fourth on the priority list.

WHITHER PROFITS?

E-world demands a refocusing of our marketing from push to pull, changing from a focus on us to a focus on the customer. We need to stop selling/promoting features that don't grab customers and start selling benefits that they value. We have to ask ourselves, "How does the customer benefit from this in *her* terms?" The benefit is almost always something other than savings. Research shows that price buyers have no loyalty.

Offering discounts only strips dollars from your top line. Things that are given away free are perceived to be of little value. People know there is no free lunch.

Price Buyers vs. Relationship Buyers

As a past salesman and a company owner, I can tell you it is very hard to let go of a customer, even a marginally profitable one. There is always the hope that we can move her up to a better margin relationship. Unfortunately, that is a fool's errand. There are two types of buyers: price and relationship. They have distinctly different profiles.

PRICE BUYERS
- Nothing but cost matters.
- No loyalty.
- Not very profitable.

Price buyers are deal-seekers. They don't want a relationship and will never be loyal. They know how badly we want to sell to them and they take every advantage they can of us. We have to find the courage to close these accounts and leave these buyers to our competition, so other companies can lose money on them. Meanwhile, relationship buyers have a different profile.

RELATIONSHIP BUYERS
- Look for someone who is reliable, honest, and therefore trustworthy.

- Want to be recognized and remembered.
- Appreciate special consideration when we bend the rules for them.
- Are profitable and loyal.

Relationship buyers do not value price-sensitive promotions. They want us to concentrate on recognition, helpfulness, service, true value, and occasional surprises to bond with them.

Involving Customers

Relationship buyers often respond to requests for information on their needs and interests. Some suppliers ask customers to go beyond filling out questionnaires to actually volunteering time and opinions regarding current or future products. Focus groups are used to review products or ideas for products. Beyond that, individuals are sometimes engaged in helping to redesign a product or create a new service. The more time and effort that a customer applies to the supplier, the more involved he feels. As the level of involvement increases, so does customer satisfaction. Getting information from customers takes time, but the payoff is great.

D. M. Rousseau and K. A. Wade-Benzoni studied the involvement issue and found an interesting but somewhat predictable answer.[5] They wanted to know if there was risk involved in building close supplier-customer relationships. Specifically, their question was: "Do highly involved customers who become more dissatisfied with the core factor of their relationship with a supplier express greater overall dissatisfaction than customers who are less involved?"

Core factor is their term for the central product or service relationship. As something in that involvement becomes dissatisfying, does it expand or flow over to general dissatisfaction with the supplier? The simple answer is "yes." This is not a surprise. It reinforces the notion that the closer we get to our customers, the more risk we take in dissatisfying them. Relationships are always like that. The more we like another person, the more disappointed we are with her if she does something we don't like.

So what is the conclusion of this common-sense finding? It is a good idea to become as close as practically possible with our custom-

> **If we can't provide great customer service, we shouldn't try to draw customers too close.**

ers. Closeness leads to loyalty and greater lifetime value. But we have to be careful that we don't create a bond that we cannot support. If we can't provide great customer service, we shouldn't try to draw customers too close. For example, bank advertising that touts "your personal banker" is often a sham. A call to my "personal banker" may reveal someone in a service center who knows nothing about me beyond some statistics regarding my account. It goes back to the old saying, "Be careful what you pray for. You might get it." If you can't take care of it, don't ask for it.

ACTIVE VS. PASSIVE RELATIONS

I do a lot of business with two companies that I like, Lands' End and Amazon.com. Both provide a good product at a good price and exceptional service. Yet their relationship approaches are different. Lands' End pursues what I call a passive relationship program. They send me catalogs almost weekly highlighting something special. It might be seasonal clothing, end-of-season specials, overstocks, or whatever. The catalog is the only medium they use to contact me, and they send out a million of them, so I know I am nothing special to them.

On the other side is Amazon. Almost every week I receive an e-mail message focused on something that they think interests me. I know that they have a profile of me and people like me, and we probably all get the same message. However, mine opens with a personal salutation and refers to past purchases. Both companies spend a lot of money soliciting my interest, yet I "feel" like Amazon knows me and cares about me a little more than Lands' End.

According to marketing consultant Seklemian/Newell, in all the businesses it has studied over the years, 30 percent to 50 percent of sales came from 10 percent of the clients' customers.[6] An even more eye-popping statistic is that 1 percent of customers account for 10 percent of sales, with an even smaller percentage accounting for 10 percent of total profit.

In banking, the top 20 percent of a bank's customers contribute

140–150 percent of overall income. The bottom 20 percent eats up 50 percent of it. Why do you choose one bank over another? They all have the same product at about the same rates. Presumably, the answer is service. I've banked with my friend Alex for over twenty years as he has moved across three banks. I will stay with Alex until he retires because somehow he takes care of me personally. If I am overdrawn, he calls me. If I have money coming in, as I did when my wife and I sold our company, he calls and talks to us about how to invest it. It's interesting how two banks dealing with the same customer in the same situation can act so differently. At the time of our sale, half of the proceeds went to Alex's bank, where my wife has her account. Half went into my secondary account at Citibank to save any initial confusion. Within a couple of hours after Ellen's wire transfer arrived, Alex—who didn't know it was coming—called to let her know it was in. Two days later, Citibank had not notified me. They were quite upset when I closed the account later and transferred all my funds to Alex. They were too little, too late, despite what their ads were saying about how personal their service was.

CUSTOMER LOYALTY

The Thin Edge

Customer loyalty is not a function of satisfaction. Companies have believed for decades that if their customer satisfaction survey scores were above the middle of the scale, they were acceptable. However, acceptable is no longer acceptable. If customer loyalty is the most important goal in today's market, and it is, then midrange scores are not acceptable. Loyalty is obtained only when customers report consistent high satisfaction in their relationship with the provider. At the risk of using the "customer delight" cliché (a phrase worn out by the customer service satisfaction movement), let me point out research that has shown how much difference there is between the two points.

Many marketing and customer service studies have demonstrated that the relationship between satisfaction and loyalty is nonlinear. That is, they do not move in parallel. As we improve our service and satisfaction, we don't see a dramatic rise in customer loyalty until we reach the top end of the scale. Ron Zemke and Tom Connellan suggest a dual scale for testing satisfaction and loyalty.[7] I paraphrase their two basic questions below:

1. How satisfactory was my transaction?

Not Satisfied	Somewhat Satisfied	Satisfied	Very Satisfied	Completely Satisfied
1	2	3	4	5

2. What is the probability that I will do business here again?

Definitely Not	Probably Not	Maybe/ Maybe Not	Probably	Definitely
1	2	3	4	5

From *E-Service: 24 Ways to Keep Your Customers—When the Competition Is Just a Click Away.* Copyright © 2001 Ron Zemke and Tom Connellan. Published by AMACOM, a division of American Management Association International, New York, N.Y. Used with the permission of the publisher. All rights reserved.

Their research confirms earlier work that claims loyalty increases significantly only when the scores are both 5s.

So, how do we win our 5s? The principles of customer satisfaction have not changed. However, they have taken on some additional nuances that separate the "Satisfied" from the "Completely Satisfied" and the "Maybe" from the "Definitely."

Winning Customer Loyalty

As I said in the Preface, people are still people, not numbers on a piece of paper. Their loyalty can be gained by treating them as intelligent human beings who have needs that they bring to the enterprise to be satisfied. Customers are not interested in our product; they are interested in satisfying their need. We have been accorded the courtesy of an opportunity to serve that need. If we can't, someone else surely will. If we can, we will

> **Customers are not interested in our product; they are interested in satisfying their need.**

have not only a customer but a friend, and friends are precious in this alienating world. This is what we have to do to gain and hold customers/friends:

- **Act like we care more about them more than ourselves.** Make them honestly feel that their convenience and happiness are more important than ours. When we do that, most people reciprocate.
- **Make it easy to do business with us.** Put the policy manual aside and serve the customer. Answer the phone or e-mail quickly, and make our Web site easy to navigate. Build an infrastructure that supports the total transaction from initial contact to delivery, payment, and refund, if necessary.
- **Personalize our service.** Greet them as individually as possible. Keep information on them so that when we meet them again, we can recognize them as a friend we are happy to see.
- **Go all the way in taking care of each aspect of the transaction.** Empower our associates with information and authority to make decisions and handle problems on the spot.
- **If there is a problem, fix it fully and fast.** Admit it when we make a mistake. People appreciate others who don't try to cover up with corporate double-talk. It might be necessary and is always a good idea to give recovered customers something extra as payment for their inconvenience. This can be a discount, a credit against future purchases, or a tangible item. The cost is neglible, but the value to us can be great.
- **Think relationship.** Make retention of customers the target that everyone supports. As in the case at Charles Schwab described in Chapter 8, turn customer complaints into a customer retention opportunity.

I've been rather personal throughout this book because I believe business is a personal issue. I've offered my experiences as examples not because I am special but because I am just like you. So let me close this chapter with one of my most recent experiences in customer relations.

In November 2000, Saratoga Institute held its national conference that is conducted every eighteen months. About two weeks afterward, I received an e-mail from a long-standing customer who had taken the time to comment on his experience. He opened with some complimentary remarks and then proceeded to unload how upset he was with certain aspects of our program. I responded *immediately*. In my reply, I thanked him for attending and giving us an opportunity to continue to serve him. Then I agreed with him that we had made a couple of mistakes. I didn't try to alibi; I just admitted it. I told him that I had passed his comments on to our conference team and had called a meeting for the following week to do something about it next time. Within an hour, I received his response. It was short and to the point. He said: "Thanks for your frankness. I'll see you at the next conference."

I believe I've kept a friend as well as a customer.

REFERENCES

1. Paul Saffo, "State of the New Economy," *Fast Company,* September 2000, p. 128.
2. Reported in Frederick Newell, *loyalty.com* (New York: McGraw-Hill, 2000), pp. 67–68.
3. Michael de Kare-Silver, *e-shock* (New York: AMACOM, 1999), p. 80.
4. Frederick Newell, *loyalty.com* (New York: McGraw-Hill, 2000), p. 31.
5. D. M. Rousseau and K. A. Wade-Benzoni, "Changing Individual-Organization Attachments: A Two Way Street." In A. Howard (ed.), *The Changing Nature of Work* (San Francisco: Jossey-Bass, 1995), pp. 290–333.
6. Newell.
7. Ron Zemke and Tom Connellan, *e-service* (New York: AMACOM, 2001), pp. 49–50.

Chapter 10

E-Strategy Summary and Scorecard

STRATEGY DEPENDS ON VALID, RELIABLE data and on the involvement of the best thinking available. In many cases, neither of these are the exclusive province of senior management. Associates often have more accurate data on daily operations than ever filters up to the executive floor. Since the associates are in the face of the customer daily, they often know how the customer really sees the company. And we know that supervisors and managers block and manipulate the data that get through to the top. These two points support the notion of involving lower-level personnel in strategy more now than we have historically.

The emerging e-world wants new strategy models and new strategic methods. Strategies ride on four considerations: our core, our capability, our market, and the environment in which we intend to operate. As we remake our strategy to deal with the new marketplace, we have to keep cool: Overheating on the promise of the Internet is dangerous. The power of the Web has to be an integral factor and force within our plan, but it is not the sum and substance of our enterprise. Business is more than a Web site. Nevertheless, the Web's connective power affects people, technology, customers, allies, and competitors. A tool with such strength must be a central element in our planning. The key to the new strategy model is not to work harder or do more. Rather, it is to introduce the capability of the Web to leverage the intelligence of our associates. Let me repeat that: *Use the capability of the Web to leverage the intelligence of our associates.*

Given the need for data on which to base our strategic deliberations, we often turn to benchmarking and to studies of so-called best practices. This can be both useful and dangerous. The utility is that we can learn from others and save ourselves time and resources. The danger is that the data we find in benchmarking and best practice studies may be flawed. It is wise to check out the methods, assumptions, and interpretations in those studies before we accept the findings.

Innovative advantage can be achieved best by becoming the standard for the market. The first consideration is finding a niche that exists or for which there is an opportunity. If we can occupy that product or service niche better than others, we can manipulate it in our direction. When we have enough customers accepting our version, we are on the verge of becoming the standard. The standard-bearer comes as close to controlling a market as is possible. In extreme cases, it becomes a monopoly. By owning the standard, we can mold it, move it, and expand it in ways and at speeds that the competition cannot match. Owning the standard allows us to take commodities and create specialties. Spin-offs and knock-offs always follow the standard. By controlling the standard, we stay ahead of the "offs" and achieve the greater margins.

EVALUATING THE PLAN

There is an inherent problem with assessing the utility or value of a strategy or a strategic plan. Since strategy deals with the future, the results are yet to be known. We cannot say on the day our strategic plan is completed that it is effective or not. Only time will tell.

Measurement or scoring of strategic plans is obviously subjective because the evidence will not be forthcoming for some time. Yet, one way to know how clear and comprehensive our plan is is to have a diagonal slice of managers and supervisors look at the plan and score its various aspects. The basics of any plan are its guiding principles: Do the managers and supervisors see the foundation for the plan? Along with these come the elements: products and services, suppliers, customers, competition, and environmental factors. Then we need to discuss the forces: current and future capabilities and our infrastructure. Finally comes the clarity of the explication. Are we communicating our intent effectively? There are factors around the development of strategies and the building of plans that can be used as criteria for determining how good a job we have done. The set of questions in Figure 10-1 can be used as criteria for self-testing our plan. Managers can score these and other elements along a continuum from "Totally Unclear" to "Totally Clear." As the scores move to the left, the respondent is telling us that there are unresolved questions or perhaps even contradictions inherent in the plan.

It is very difficult for senior executives to have their work scored by junior personnel. But on the other hand, would it be better to go into the game with inadequate systems or confused players? Worse yet, would it be better to have outsiders comment negatively on a poorly designed plan or the competition beat up on us because we had not planned well?

E-RELATIONS

There is no secret to profits in e-world. Making profits starts with identifying the types of customers who are right for us. This requires data that can be turned into information, knowledge, and intelligence about the customer. Everyone in the company who has any direct or indirect contact with the customer should be generating and sharing data for that purpose.

As we plan our innovations, we need to keep the focus on the actual needs of the customers—not the desires of the designers. Many products are overfeatured today. They confuse the customer, who does not have the technical background to use the advanced features, and they also make troubleshooting impossible. This leads to an excessive dependence on the customer service function. Delays and poor support lead to dissatisfied customers. We have to keep in mind that the 21st century is an information and communications market. The more information people get and the more they are able to communicate easily with each other, the more they want to do it. This gives them the courage to challenge and demand service. Strate-

(text continues on page 136)

Figure 10-1. Strategy scorecard.

1. *Scope*

1	2	3	4	5
Totally Unclear	Rather Vague	Basically Understandable	Rather Clear	Totally Clear

How well does the plan cover all relevant issues, including current and future products and services, the consideration of known and possible competitor plans, governmental and environmental conditions, community relations, associates' capability, and financial capacity of the company to support the plan?

2. *Market Analysis*

1	2	3	4	5
No		Somewhat		Yes

Is the plan based on a thorough analysis of the current and near-term market dynamics? Is it focused on increasing current market share or on finding new markets for current capabilities?

3. *Imagination*

1	2	3	4	5
No		Somewhat		Yes

Does the plan represent out-of-the-box thinking? Is there evidence of new perspectives? Will this plan excite the associates, or will they see it as simply an update of past plans?

4. *Alignment*

1	2	3	4	5
Totally Unclear	Rather Vague	Basically Understandable	Rather Clear	Totally Clear

Is there a clear line of sight from the corporate imperatives and initiatives through the operating objectives of the business units to the support base of resource management?

5. *Flexibility*

1	2	3	4	5
No		Somewhat		Yes

Are there backup plans with alternatives listed in case unforeseeable events occur?

6. Infrastructure

1	2	3	4	5
No		Somewhat		Yes

Has consideration been given to the technology and process capability of the company to support the plan?

7. Resource Allocation

1	2	3	4	5
Totally Unclear	Rather Vague	Basically Understandable	Rather Clear	Totally Clear

Is it clear how resources will be allocated in support of each of the major initiatives of the plan?

8. Assumptions

1	2	3	4	5
No		Somewhat		Yes

Are there unexplained assumptive leaps that leave questions?

9. Responsibility and Accountability

1	2	3	4	5
Totally Unclear	Rather Vague	Basically Understandable	Rather Clear	Totally Clear

Are clear lines of responsibility and accountability laid out in the plan, along with schedules and time lines?

10. E-Business

1	2	3	4	5
No		Somewhat		Yes

Are the forces and potentials of e-world represented, with the listing of e-business initiatives and assumptions regarding risks and potential returns on the investment?

gic business plans have to incorporate that need and behavior. By combining *bricks with clicks,* we can build the infrastructure to support those requirements.

In the e-world market, we will concentrate on building a strong, binding relationship with customers through a customer relations management (CRM) program. We will think of our customers as human beings—not as consumers of our products or services. When we treat them as friends, they will decide for us which of our services they need. Once we have won them, we will do everything possible to actively rather than passively connect with them. Finally, we will find the courage to drop the high-cost customers who are a drain on profits.

Measuring the return on investment of a customer relations program requires patience and a mindset shift to include qualitative as well as the more familiar quantitative data. Since it often takes two to three years to determine how effective a CRM program has been, it is unreasonable to expect a definitive answer in less than eighteen months, and even that is stretching it. In the near term, there should be some signs that indicate possible movement as a result of a customer relations program. Keep in mind that the longer the period of review, the more the results of the effort can be confounded by any number of intervening variables. We can measure a true ROI only after a program has run its full length, the data derived from it have been used in customer contacts, and the returns are complete in terms of market share and customer knowledge (for future programs).

Despite these forces and factors, there are standard indices that can be monitored on an ongoing basis for signs of improvement in customer relations. A list of common ones is shown in Figure 10-2. They are as follows:

1. **Acquisition.** How fast are we growing new customers? This is a very positive motivating metric, provided it meets the objective.
2. **Loyalty or Losses.** I suggest that instead of customer retention, we use an index of customers lost involuntarily. It has a greater psychological effect to think of losing 10 percent versus retaining 90 percent. More important, what does it cost us to lose a customer?
3. **Mix.** There are many ways to look at this, and they can be inter-

Figure 10-2. Customer relations scorecard.

	This Period	Last Period	Percentage of Change +/−
1. *Acquisition.* Number of new customers acquired as a percent of total customers.	____	____	____
2. *Loyalty (losses).* Percent of customer base lost this period; determined by customers who bought from a competitor in a formal bidding case. Can also calculate the cost of a lost customer.	____	____	____
3. *Mix.* Product profile by type, number sold, gross margins, and total dollars in revenue.	____	____	____
4. *Recency.* Percentage of customers who made a purchase during this period.	____	____	____
5. *Volume.* Number of sales made and gross dollars in sales.	____	____	____
6. *Share of spend.* Estimate of sales as a percent of total customer spend.	____	____	____
7. *Advertising/Marketing expense.* Total advertising and marketing dollars spent in the period.	____	____	____
8. *Sales costs.* Average cost per sale as recorded in various channels.	____	____	____

sorted. For example, product/service type and profitability can be viewed interactively.

4. **Recency.** This gives us an idea of the amount of activity per account, which can be compared to carrying costs, lifetime value, etc.

5. **Volume.** Another look at account activity and penetration.

6. **Share of Spend.** Account maintenance is only slightly more important than account penetration.

7. **Advertising/Marketing Expense.** Compare to sales to see what it costs us to support a sale on the front end. Customer service costs can also be tracked to see what it takes to support

an account. All these are factored into a calculation of lifetime value.

8. **Sales Costs.** From this we learn what it costs in terms of a sales force to make a sale. This can be viewed by channel: inside and outside sales force, Web site staff, independent sales reps, etc.

In addition to the above, most companies track macro measures such as market share and carry out surveys of brand awareness. Frankly, I am wary of brand awareness surveys in that the questions and resulting statistics can be manipulated easily to tell a skewed story.

Part IV

HUMAN CAPITAL:

THE E-WORLD LEVER

Chapter 11

Power to the People

LABOR SHORTAGE SMOKESCREEN

Everyone is talking about the recent labor shortage as though it is the most important human capital problem of the day. It is not! It is only a by-product of something more important and fundamental in the long term.

The most important issue today is the relationship of the organization and all that implies—management, policy and procedure, culture, structure, systems, and resources—with its employee, our associate. Organization is nothing more than an abstract term we have invented to encompass the above. When we speak of relationship, we are actually talking about two interconnected behaviors. One is the decisions and behavior of the people who reside at the top of the enterprise. The other is the reaction to those decisions and actions by the associates who occupy and give life to the enterprise.

Effective management can draw greater loyalty and productivity out of a lean staff than ineffective management can out of a bloated one. Granted, there are not enough people trained in the new technologies and organizational dynamics as are needed. Yet a few companies are rolling along at a much faster pace than 90 percent of their competitors. Have they found a bottomless well of talent, or are they just paying people so well that once in the company no one leaves voluntarily? The answers are *no* and *no*. What separates the best from the rest is that the best have found a way to become what some call an *employer of choice*. This means that people want to work in those organizations because they fit the culture, are treated with respect, have an opportunity to achieve and grow, are paid competitively (among other things), and most important, have leaders at the top and effective managers throughout. Chapter 12 details how to be an employer of choice. In this chapter, we look at the nature of the human elements of the enterprise.

SAME AND DIFFERENT

What is it about the associates today that is the same as their parents and also different from their parents? Let's count the ways, beginning with the differences.

Differences

*   **Number 1.** The biggest difference is that there are relatively fewer associates today in terms of the size of the national economy than there were forty years ago. The labor shortage is well documented. After the Baby Boom of 1946 to 1964, the birth rate dropped over the next dozen years. This produced a 13 percent drop in the number of 20- to 24-year-olds during the 1980s. The industries that hire young people—retailing, high tech, and the military—were the first to be affected. By the mid 1990s, while the U.S. economy was exploding, the number of people needed to staff professional and managerial ranks began to shrink. From 1996 through 2006, the percentage of workers ages 25–34 will decline by 9 percent, and those 35–44 will shrink by 3 percent.

    Exacerbating the shortfall is the increase in new technologies. Employers have to share the blame here because they did not foresee the need and were not investing in technical training at a rate required to meet the needs of their staff. Some of them still aren't, preferring to raid other companies for their talent—a bankrupt strategy. The number of technically literate people in the 30 + ranges is not sufficient to support the growth of both old and new industries. The good news is that no one company is trying to hire the whole of North America. We only need to get our share. Good attraction, development, and especially retention practices mitigate much of the talent shortage for smart companies.

- **Number 2.** Today's world is not the same as yesterday's. Life today is more technically driven, with semiconductors in everything and telecommunications rampant. This has caused a level of stress that hasn't been felt since the Great Depression. Even World War II did not generate today's tension. Of course, during the war many families lost their young men and women in combat. In addition, many people moved or were displaced as a by-product of military service and the rise of jobs in the defense industries. But the explosive growth of the economy in the 1990s and the increase in the pace of life through telecommunications has changed daily life for everyone. Even for those not directly affected, the constant bombardment of stressful news subconsciously affects all of us. If every day we hear, see, and read about the stress of life for others, sooner or later we internalize it for ourselves.

- **Number 3.** Support systems are breaking down. High divorce rates, physical distance from our extended family, disaffection with religious and governmental institutions, and neighbors who are too busy to bond with each other have pulled the metaphorical rug out from under most of us. Very few people today feel as secure as they did thirty years ago, even though they have more creature comforts now than they did then. Automatic dishwashers, CD players, television sets, home computers, and SUVs are not huggable.

- **Number 4.** There is constant pressure to learn and adapt. The invasion of technology has created unprecedented opportunity for anyone who is willing and able to take it on. But the majority of people reach a point in midlife when they would rather level off their growth rate and begin to enjoy the fruits of their labor.

Now that is not possible. Ambition is no longer a matter of choice. For those who are not willing to continually raise their level of skill and knowledge, the world has become a threatening place. The forty-year employment and gold-watch paradigm has been shattered. It's grow, step aside, or get out!

- **Number 5.** Needs are changing as a result of life changes. Alienation is more than sociological jargon. By its nature, technology alienates. Every step up the technology ladder is a step away from the solid ground of nature. In the past, people who had to walk or ride a horse were very much in touch with nature. First, their feet were literally on the ground and not on concrete most of the time. Second, walking and riding a horse or buggy averages from two to ten miles per hour on a road and a good deal less on a rutted trail. When the pioneers crossed the continent from Missouri to California and Oregon in the 1850s and 1860s, a good day's travel was ten to fourteen miles. Many of them *walked* 2,000 miles, some pushing or pulling handcarts.

    The retro movement is an attempt to feel back in touch with nature. We saw it in the 1970s with the western clothes fashion boom. Everyone wanted to dress like an urban cowboy or girl because that is part of our national mythology. Now we are seeing it again with the revival of the Volkswagen Bug, the introduction of the Chrysler Cruiser, and the popularity of SUVs. How many urbanites spend any amount of time off-road so that they need high road clearance and four-wheel drive? Nature trip vacations and the movement toward golf instead of tennis are attempts to get our feet off concrete and onto grass. The teens and college kids are wearing clothes reminiscent of the 1960s, an era they've only heard about. Arts and crafts and mission-style furnishings are a return to the 19th century. The cigar boom was a visit to the days when "men were men and women were women." We are driven by a deep need to get out of the whirlwind and go home psychologically.

- **Number 6.** Self-determination is the new bedrock supporting the demand for a piece of the action. People are better educated in some ways—at least, they have more years of formal schooling—and they won't be told what to do. They want to participate in issues that affect their work lives. With the dissolution of our support systems and our resulting disillusion about being cared for, we want and need to take more control of our lives. It is the only way we can regain some sense and degree of security. Industry, religion, and government have shown themselves to be self-centered, so we have to fend for ourselves.

Similarities

- **Number 1.** We have not changed in the most fundamental areas of ourselves. We still need love, security, socialization, and opportunity. In fact, because of all the differences listed above, our most basic needs are more important today than in the past. In a frightening environment, the need for safety expands. In a workplace where security has disappeared, we need to grab some power from management. Given the shortage of skilled labor, power naturally shifts from the buyer of talent (the company) to the seller of talent (the person).

- **Number 2.** People are social animals who need to communicate. Again, in this high-anxiety world, we need more than ever to be in touch. Why the popularity of the Web? Is it just the latest toy, or is it a way to get in touch with others and thereby with ourselves? Need we ask? What is the logic behind chat rooms? Why do we want to communicate with and share some of our most secret desires with strangers thousands of miles away? Part of it is safety. We can join and quit, remain anonymous, and assume fantasy identities, all from the safety of our homes. The larger part is the sharing. Whom else do we have to share our thoughts with, and where else can we find sympathetic ears? Single people as well as many married ones live much of their lives in isolation. This is a way to let our feelings out and connect with other human beings, and it is a lot cheaper than going to a shrink.

- **Number 3.** We want material goods just like our parents did. We want enough to feel that we have our fair share. This means we need a good and increasing income. We need benefits to provide security, free time, and certain types of support. Because we are moving faster than ever before, we have less time for maintenance activities like shopping, cleaning, and keeping in touch with friends and family, so we need the income to pay someone to do that for us or to buy the gadgets that make it easier and faster.

SHOW ME THE DATA

Where do these conclusions come from? Are they just the meanderings of a middle-aged man trying to understand his world, or do data support them? Fortunately, there are plenty of data. If we turn off the hype machines and stop focusing on the latest electronic gizmos for a few minutes, we find both current and past research that speaks to these ideas.

Since 1996, Saratoga Institute has been interviewing and surveying people who have turned down job offers, accepted job offers, gone to work for a company, and finally became upset with the company and quit. The facts are overwhelming. People join, stay, and enjoy companies that have strong, positive, caring leadership. There are exceptions to every rule, but it is unequivocally clear that leadership is the differentiating factor. It is true that inadequate or improperly administered pay drives people out of the best-led company, but that is seldom the prime reason for bailing out. Departing associates claim that they reached a point where they "weren't being paid enough to put up with" their treatment. Does this mean that they were dissatisfied with pay? No. It means that the working conditions, supervisory relationships, and/or company expectations became so onerous that they felt the money wasn't worth the trouble.

> *People join, stay, and enjoy companies that have strong, positive, caring leadership.*

The top four reasons for people leaving companies at the end of the 1990s have been found to be, in order:

1. Ineffective top-level leadership
2. Incompetent, uncaring supervisors
3. Little opportunity for achievement and growth
4. Compensation (first pay, with benefits a distant second)

LEADERSHIP COMMUNICATIONS AND THE EMERGENT WORKER

As discussed in Chapters 5 and 6, leadership skills are changing. The command and control environment is eroding in most but not all companies. Research conducted by Lou Harris for Spherion over a two-year period split the values of the workforce into what was identified as "emergent" and "traditional." The traditional worker is principally a conformist who will work in either an emergent (participative) organization or a traditional (controlling) organization. All we have to do is explain the rules and expectations, and this type agrees to play along. The emergent worker, whose profile is not confined to the younger worker, will not tolerate the culture of a traditional organization. Emergents are less rule-oriented and process-focused and more communicative, assertive, and results-focused.

The workforce overall is moving inexorably toward the emergent profile just as customers are moving inexorably to a high-service profile. This is no surprise. Between 8 A.M. and 5 P.M., the person is a worker. After that, she changes hats and becomes a customer. It is the same human being playing a different role. The projection is that as the emergent model becomes more common, traditional organizations are going to find themselves trying to recruit from a diminishing labor pool. These organizations are the ones that will feel the talent shortage the most.

Leadership is synonymous with communication. Every effective leader in any business, political, or religious organization has been a good communicator. Assuming a positive value system and vision, the person who knows how to communicate that vision will win the hearts of people. Associates who "buy" the vision of the leader are emotionally committed. That is a much stronger bond than intellectual commitment. Pay and perks are intellectual factors; values and relationships are emotional factors. Given the power of the Web to connect people inside and outside the organization, executive communication has become a much more dicey task. There is only one simple rule to start with: Be honest.

> **Leadership is synonymous with communication.**

Past and Future

In the past, corporate communication was largely a one-way game. For most organizations it still is, no matter what the boss's platitudes about having an open door policy. Only the bravest, most secure associates venture to communicate up more than one level. The evidence for such reluctance is clear. Many companies run employee surveys, but most executives do not respond to the concerns of the associates voiced in the surveys in a way that can be seen or felt. In fact, at Saratoga Institute we have had instances where the data from exit interviews that we conducted for clients were explicitly thrown out because of fear of how the leaders would respond. Other consultant friends of mine echo our experience. An all too common reaction is a strong negative response to the data and an attempt to denigrate the information. Many managers absolutely do not buy into the two-way communication myth. Douglas McGregor's Theory X managers still inhabit companies.

Before the Web, management could get away with ignoring the workforce, which was fragmented and disconnected. Most associates had only a small circle of direct contacts within the company and no easy way to voice their gripes beyond their immediate circle of family and neighbors or to union representatives if they were present. Those days are gone forever. The Web has enabled everyone with a computer and a modem to join the worldwide conversation. Whether or not the corporation formally joins the conversation is a moot point. It is already immersed in it.

In olden days, before 1995, voices inside organizations got lost or were squelched. Today, no more. Employees tell friends within the company as well as total strangers in chat rooms about their company. Suppliers share their Megacorp experiences with other suppliers. Communication is insidious. All corporate warts are visible. E-world has taken muted people off the sidelines and made them first-team communicators. The Web implicitly asks everyone to play just by its open, inviting nature. When the corporation tells people they have to have personal Web pages approved or that a particular community of practice will be monitored, people simply abandon that page or community and set up another hidden one. In the worst case, when management claims that it wants to hear the voice of the people and then does not listen to it, the voice not only does not go mute—it hollers with all its might, and it is heard.

The Power of Compound Communication

It used to be that no matter what policy the company came up with, someone could figure out how to get around it. Now, not only can the path around be found, but it can and is communicated to everyone through a series of address extensions. You tell me, I e-mail my friends, and they e-mail their contacts. Again, each does the same. How many iterations does it take for one message to reach a million people? Assume the average person has twenty people on his e-mail list. In just four iterations of a message ($20 \times 20 \times 20 \times 20$), 3.2 million people can receive a message about our company. If that message is negative, it will more than likely hit a chat room or bulletin board. Now how many people know about our warts? Likewise, if the message is positive, think how many people now know we have a great place to work. It is just like compounding interest. The good news explodes across the market.

It is so easy with the Web for anyone to communicate that attempts to constrain the conversation are laughable. The i-world mass production, stovepipe, bureaucratic, stultifying culture is as anachronistic as Big Brother and The Organization Man. Do we get the idea?

We no longer control the conversation. Here's a quick example: For decades many companies had a rule against discussing salaries. The system was not even published, and termination was the penalty for discussing pay. If we tried to enforce that prohibition today, the associates would fall over laughing before they had time to become resentful.

We have to face it: The inmates have taken over the asylum and we will never regain control.

We have to face it: The inmates have taken over the asylum and we will never regain control. We can order them around, we can threaten them, we can incent them, or we can expel them, but the next group will be just as unruly. A better way to deal with this universal conversation is to get involved. If we leave the room and pout, they'll just talk about us anyway. I was in a client's meeting recently where two executives made a pitch to the group about a new project, how important it was, and the roles they expected people to play. After the group left, the execs congratulated themselves on what a wonderful job they had done in motivating the attendees. Later, I was walking through the building and passed the cubicle of one of the attendees. She was furiously typing and clearly was in a high state of "motivation." I stopped and inquired as to her agitated state. She proceeded to tell me what a couple of dumbasses the two execs were and how she was passing her irritation on to friends on her e-mail list. If she was doing it, the odds are that other attendees were as well.

Infinite Connectivity

People today are irretrievably connected and conversing. Figure 11-1 illustrates the notion of infinite connection. People, information, and technology combine inside the organization, enabling people to communicate, learn, share, grow, and work. But they are also connected via the Web to other people, information sources, and technology platforms around the world and indeed into outer space. There is literally no limit to communication other than the energy it takes to transmit a bit of information as small as a photon. Every day we shoot information out into the universe and take in data from the universe without being conscious of 99.9 percent of what is passing through us. To assume that we can control even that tiny bit of which we are conscious is an act of unparalleled naïveté. Since there is this humongous conversation going on constantly, it's better to join it purposefully than fight it. So let's jump in and tell our side of the story in believable terms.

In spite of and because of this gee-whiz technology, we have to keep in mind the needs and values of the audience when we communicate. Management communication is neither more nor less than a selling opportunity. Management is the seller and associates are the buyers. The lesson is that besides always being truthful, the communiqué needs to be framed in the right medium and transmitted by the right person so that the associate will respond positively.

Figure 11-1. Infinite connectivity.

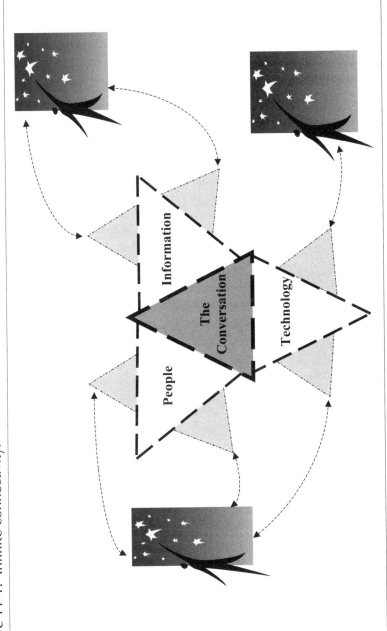

NOW TO THE PROCESS

There are five rules in the process of communicating to associates. The first rule in selling is to get the buyer's (the associate's) attention. This means we have to open with something that is meaningful to the associate. If the communication is about the financial performance of the company, it is a waste of time to send the same press release to associates that we send to the financial analysts. Different audiences need different approaches. Many employees don't know or care about the market capitalization of the company. They care about their jobs and don't connect stock price with job security. So we need to frame the financial communiqué in terms of how this information describes the financial health (read: associate security) of the company.

The second rule is obtaining interest. What can we say that will peak the interest of the unsophisticated employee who wants to know what this means to her? Perhaps we open with a short story about how one business unit did something that positively affected the financials of the company. Associates can relate to that because they see things like that daily in their workplace and because we are talking about their peers.

Third, describe the features of the issue. We are going to talk about the current trend in our income and expense levels and their effect on the assets and liabilities of the company. We use small, common words and very briefly explain their relationship. We have to do this only once because people are smarter than we give them credit for being. Once we explain it, they know why the financials are important to them in the trenches.

Fourth, give them the benefits: the good news. There is usually something good even in the worst periods that we can refer to before and after we lay out the problem. We put a positive face on press releases, but we must tell the naked truth to the employees. If there is no good news, then we tell them what we *all* need to do to make it better. Ask for their help and mean it. When subsequently they offer advice or information, we *listen* and *respond* and communicate to everyone how a group of their peers is helping change things.

Last, describe how together the changes that they will help bring about will be good news for them. The cardinal rule is always to focus everything on what this means to the associate.

THE POWER OF THE SUPERVISOR

An unpublished study of communications preferences carried out with 2,000 people throughout North America identified one's immediate supervisor as the first choice for communication from people at all levels. (I did the study twenty-five years ago, and current research at the Saratoga Institute confirms it today.) Associates depend on their supervisor for a great deal of information. This ranges from personal data on pay and performance to corporate data on organizational changes and financial condition. On a day-to-day basis, people lower in the system need the supervisor to explain, train, counsel, schedule their projects, and be available to help solve problems. Farther up the system, technical and professional associates need their boss to interpret strategy, facilitate communication, and support partnerships with other units.

Saratoga Institute's research with current and past employees shows a clear set of needs and expectations from the supervisor. The most important are:

1. Telling me what is expected of me
2. Providing the resources I need to do my job
3. Facilitating communication within and outside our group
4. Translating organizational communication in terms of impact on me
5. Helping me solve problems
6. Recognizing me for my successes
7. Helping me learn, develop, and advance in the company

The Gallup Organization conducted a long-term study of managerial behavior. Their work was the topic of the book *First, Break All the Rules*.[1] They found essentially the same set of factors. Effective supervisors perceive the unique needs of each individual and find ways to communicate that stimulate high performance.

Between the Rock and the Hard Place

I am empathetic toward supervisors, particularly those in the lower half of the hierarchy. They are the people who get the work done every day. They receive the marching orders from the top and have to carry them out. They have to produce daily because the outputs of their units are very visible. The farther up one moves in the organization, the more room there is to blame failures on some other person or unit. The first-line supervisor receives less training and more garbage with less room to hide it than anyone else in the company.

Supervisors need to know a few things well. The basic skills every supervisor must have are how to:

*   Induct a new employee into his/her group.
*   Describe the way things work (culture) to get understanding and buy-in.
*   Explain pay and performance systems in a way that motivates people.
*   Coach, counsel, and discipline in a respectful, team-building manner.
*   Gain cooperation from other peer units as well as from people up the chain.
*   Recognize and celebrate exceptional performance.
*   Terminate someone in a humane manner and deal with the survivors.

Theirs is a very direct, simple world. So why do supervisors have a difficult time with it? The answer is that many in management have been raised with the notion that people are a troublesome expense. Because accounting has treated pay and training dollars as an expense instead of an investment, associates are seldom managed as a value-adding asset. As evidence of this belief, we lay off thousands at the first sign of a business slowdown. Again, accounting is the culprit. Since people costs cannot be amortized, they negatively affect earnings and therefore stock price. If we spend money to retrain associates, we are penalized rather than lauded. The financial markets drive executives because if they miss one quarter's earnings, the stock is blasted and their options submerged. It is a circuitous and systemic problem that is not easily solved. Nevertheless, at the ground floor it can be mitigated. The leader can proclaim the vision, but the supervisor has to translate it, support it, and make it happen. Supervisors can improve productivity if senior executives support them.

ACHIEVEMENT AND PRODUCTIVITY

It has become fashionable to talk about helping people grow. This is good because the emergent worker wants to grow. But it seems that achievement is lost in the hyperbole. Human beings have an inherent need to achieve. Not everyone wants to be CEO someday, but everyone wants to accomplish something while at work. When people do not have an opportunity to obtain a sense of accomplishment in their job, they find it outside in hobbies, community work, or other personal endeavors. Through all the hysteria and hype of the 21st century marketplace, the basic question remains: What drives people to be productive and achieve today? The corollary to that is: What builds loyalty, commitment, and retention?

> *Human beings have an inherent need to achieve. Not everyone wants to be CEO someday, but everyone wants to accomplish something while at work.*

Employee productivity has been studied for decades, and a myriad of hypotheses have emerged on how to make people more productive. Frederick Herzberg's seminal study of motivation was once well known but of late has been forgotten by some.[2] His findings fit today's workforce as much or more than the original study population. Herzberg replicated his initial study many times and consistently found the five factors that caused people to be satisfied and motivated in their work. They are:

1. Achievement
2. Recognition
3. The work itself
4. Responsibility
5. Advancement

Pay was not a motivator; it was an expectation. It came into play only when it was not perceived as competitive and fairly administered. This is similar to our findings in studying the effects of pay and its administration on retention.

Think about those five factors for you, today. Do they resonate with you? Would they make your job satisfying? Would they stimulate you to do your best? Are they particularly important given today's high-anxiety work world?

Herzberg's findings have been confirmed many times over past decades in one way or another. Twenty years ago, I commissioned a study of motivation and productivity for the computer company where I worked. The consultants carried out a large-scale review of the literature on productivity before developing a survey instrument. They built a list of several dozen variables that might affect productivity. From these, factor analysis yielded twenty-two items that described the interaction of the associate with the company. A questionnaire was then administered to most of the employees of the company. Figure 11-2 lists and defines the twenty-two items. Of the twenty-two, self-esteem turned up as strongly and more closely correlated with employee productivity than did any of the other factors. Responsibility was a close second. Self-esteem is based on a person's perception of his worth and the confirmation of his worth from others. If people feel good about themselves and their supervisor treats them with respect and recognizes their accomplishments, motivation and productivity are enhanced. Further confirmation from coworkers helps. Responsibility, both given and desired, implies a measure of control, accountability, and a chance to show what a person can do. Together these factors seem so simple as to fall into the common-sense category. Do they apply to this generation of associates?

At the end of the day, can we see that the fundamental needs that people had a generation ago still apply? Don't most of our associates still want interesting work; want to be responsible, achieve, and be recognized; and need to feel good about themselves and have this confirmed through advancement? Who would argue that they don't? Despite what we have heard about Generation X or other current groups, the basics of human nature still apply. What is different is that in today's marketplace, these basic human needs are stronger and more desirable than ever. They have to be played out in ways

Figure 11-2. Factors affecting employee productivity.

1. *Capability:* Associate's skill, knowledge, experience, and education related to the work
2. *Company:* General attitude toward the company, its style of operation, and its stability
3. *Coworker personalities:* Level of respect and liking among members of the work group
4. *Coworker work behavior:* Cooperation and support of peers
5. *Delegation:* How the supervisor delegates responsibility and accountability
6. *Economic needs:* Degree to which the job satisfies associate's need for food, clothing, and shelter
7. *Equipment:* Design and ease of operation of tools and equipment
8. *External environment:* Effect of outside social, political, and economic forces
9. *Job satisfaction:* Associate's general attitude and satisfaction with the job
10. *Job stress:* Internal conditions and feelings about job security.
11. *Leader behavior:* Supervisor's support and availability.
12. *National scene:* Effect of country's economic and social forces on the company
13. *Pay and conditions of work:* Salary, performance reviews, advancement, and work scheduling
14. *Personal problems:* Effect of work and overtime on personal life, plus personal problems
15. *Resources:* Availability of tools, material, and people needed for the job
16. *Responsibility accepted:* Desired workload and responsibility versus actual levels
17. *Safety:* Company's actions to provide a safe and healthy work environment
18. *Self-esteem:* Associate's sense of self-respect and respect from others regarding performance.
19. *Self-responsibility:* Associate's commitment to high performance
20. *Strictness:* Fair and equitable enforcement of company policies and procedures
21. *Structure and practices:* Availability of training, work layout, and organization
22. *Work problems:* Physical and psychological fatigue resulting from the work

that fit the new environment. From management's perspective, we have to support those needs in a more authentic and understanding way than we might have in the past. The need is the same, but the expression—the communication—has to be updated.

REFERENCES

1. Marcus Buckingham and Curt Coffman, *First, Break All the Rules* (New York: Simon & Schuster, 1999).
2. Frederick Herzberg, Bernard Mauser, and Barbara Snyderman, *The Motivation to Work* (New York: John Wiley & Sons, 1959).

Chapter 12

How to Become the Employer of Choice

MANAGEMENT BY IMITATION

One of the most consistent business behaviors is management by imitation. Executives and managers at all levels often don't know what to do to make their enterprises more competitive. Rather than step back and analyze what their organization is all about and what they should commit resources to, they look outside to see what can be adopted from other organizations. Imitation may be the sincerest form of flattery, as Oscar Wilde said, or it could be an admission of creative deficiency. The main problem with imitation is that it takes away competitive advantage by putting us behind those we are copying. By the time we find out what others have done and adapt that to our situation, the top performers have moved to the next level. In the end, we are as far behind as we have always been. Imitation breeds mediocrity.

Consulting firms and publishers have found this phenomenon of imitation to be a lucrative source of income. One of the best examples is *Fortune*. Every year this popular business magazine runs a number of "Best Company" features. Probably the most widely read is the annual issue entitled "The 100 Best Companies to Work For."

It is popular because people like to read positive stories. In addition, managers want to know what other companies are doing so they can copy it or reject it as "impossible here." When we studied the most recent issue, we found a remarkable similarity across the one hundred best. Most of the hundred are doing what most of the hundred are doing. It is almost like they all read the same book or went to the same seminar. We don't find radically different values, approaches, or programs among the group. Yes, there are a few unique employee support programs. But in most every case, those were designed to meet a special need within that company. If we look for a pattern, we find four approaches that underpin the employers of choice. Imitating specific programs is not a practice that drives competitive advantage. On the other hand, if we uncover the rationale behind successful effects, we can use that to design our programs to suit our unique needs. Following are the factors driving successful programs:

1. **Money.** Frederick Herzberg told us forty years ago that money is not a motivator, but these people don't believe it. The most common programs are various forms of wealth building. Profit sharing, 401(k)s, stock options, and good old-fashioned retirement programs come up time after time. Cash bonuses are also popular. Along with that are a large number of employer-paid benefit programs. My interpretation is that the hundred are providing financial security in the short run with fully paid, generous benefit plans and in the long run with some form of retirement income. None of the companies could be described as "flips" (venture capital looking for quick in and out situations).

2. **Time.** Many companies offer some form of sabbaticals (extended leaves for various purposes including volunteer programs) and flex time. Besides the recharging of personal batteries that sabbaticals offer, there is recognition that time is as valuable as money in some cases. People have many obligations outside of work, and the hundred best understand this.

3. **Personal Support.** Related to the time issue is the need to support associates in other ways. This takes several forms, with child care centers or subsidies of some type for child care. We believe that with the high rate of dual-career families and single-

parent situations, the employers see it is necessary as well as a recruitment and retention inducement to offer this type of support.

4. **Lifestyle.** The companies offer a number of programs related to physical well-being. These include fitness centers, on-site health centers, and, increasingly, free massages at the worksite to help people who are hunched over computers all day loosen up and freshen up. In the long term, these programs positively impact health care benefits. By concentrating on prevention, companies find associates are healthier and have fewer medical claims and time off for illness.

MANAGEMENT MOTIVATION TO CARE ABOUT ASSOCIATES

Our interpretation of these company policies and programs is that the hundred best think about and, more importantly, care about associates differently than do many other organizations. My opinion is that those top executives have a more mature attitude toward associates. They see associates as more than economic units. They understand that it is not only good economic policy to support the humanity of associates: It is the right thing to do. This comes through in the cultures they build. They know that associates have a life outside the office that is more important to them than their work. Although their career is central to their life for professionals and executives, their family is at least as important. And within the lower ranks, the outside life is usually much more important than the job.

People have to spend at least eight hours a day within the corporate culture. It only makes sense to have this be a nurturing, fun, and exciting place to be. Many executives outside the hundred best apparently do not acknowledge or understand this. They are so focused on meeting the expectations of Wall Street or on adding to their personal scorecard of success that their actions are driven solely by financial considerations. They adopt some popular benefit programs, but that is the

> People have to spend at least eight hours a day within the corporate culture. It only makes sense to have this be a nurturing, fun, and exciting place to be.

extent of it. They have not accepted the truth that human effort is the most powerful lever of profitability. On the other hand, in many of the hundred best we can see evidence of the humanity school. For instance, how many top people believe as Jim Goodnight, founder of SAS Institute, does that people's personal life is as important as their work—and *act* on that belief? At SAS, the building is locked at 5 P.M. and employees have to go home to families or other personal pursuits. It is easy to say "people are out most valuable asset," but when economic considerations give way to that statement, we can believe it is sincere. This is a perfect example of what I described in *The 8 Practices of Exceptional Companies* (AMACOM, 1997). Practice Number One was a balancing of human and financial considerations.

THE PANACEA APPROACH AND BENCHMARKING

In addition to *Fortune's* list, we can find a wider range of imitation opportunities by perusing the flood of journal articles and books on managing organizations and human capital. A week doesn't go past wherein we aren't offered another study of so-called best practices, company histories, or recent applied research. Figure 12-1 shows the plethora of management panaceas that have come and

Figure 12-1. Fifty years of management panaceas.

	? ? ? ?
2000	Intellectual Capital - Knowledge Management
	Balanced Scorecard - Rightsizing - EVA
1990	TQM - Reengineering - 7 Habits - Learning
	Downsizing - Customer Service - Benchmarking
1980	Kaizen - Empowerment - Continuous Improvement
	Corporate Culture - Change Management - MBWA
	Intrapreneuring - Relationship Marketing - Excellence
1970	Quality Circles - Diversification - One Minute Managing
	Work Simplification - Hierarchy of Needs - Productivity
1960	Organization Renewal - Value Chain - Portfolio Management
	Managerial Grid - Matrix - Hygienes and Motivators - Theory Z
1950	Theory X & Y - Plan—Organize—Direct—Control - Human Relations
	Management by Objectives - Management Science - Decision Tree

gone over the past fifty years. I've used this chart many times in seminars, talks, and previous books. It speaks to two idiosyncrasies of American management. First, we are always looking for better ways to do something; we are not a nation that thrives on the status quo. Second, it is a telling picture of how we continually follow new, unproven ideas. We have a tradition of choosing the path of least resistance and acting rather than taking the time to diagnose the root cause of our problems. Although the themes of human capital management may vary in terms of their perspective, we find an underlying consistency across the publications. People are to be valued, allowed to participate, and recognized for their contributions. It's all good stuff, but it leaves one question: If most people agree about effective management of human capital, why aren't more companies doing it?

My experience, and that of most consultants, is that as we roll out a set of findings and implications before almost every client or audience, one reaction is predictable. It happens so much that it has a name—the "Yes, but" response. No sooner do we put our data and recommendations on the table than we hear, "We can't do that because . . . ." This is not a new phenomenon or a product of e-market. It has been around longer than anyone reading this book. (I brought it up in 1984 in my first book.[1]) There is always a reason why not to do something. If there is not enough energy or courage to make a change, why do we want to know what others are doing?

We could write this peculiarity off as human nature or laziness if it weren't for the benchmarking syndrome. Since 1985, Saratoga Institute has been publishing metrics on human capital management. Invariably, as soon as people have the data in their hands, they ask us how the best performers were able to achieve those results. People most often want to know *how* someone did something. This desire has reached such levels that it has borrowed the word from surveying: benchmark. A benchmark is a stake in the ground that is a reference point for other measurements. Untold millions of dollars have been spent on business benchmarking trips, books, and seminars, mostly since Robert Camp's book on benchmarking came out in 1989.[2] Individuals and teams have made trips across oceans to learn about how other companies manage certain processes. These range across manufacturing, marketing, R&D, accounting, IT, and human resources. After spending sometimes thousands of dollars, an overwhelming percentage of cases end with the "Yes, but" response killing any subsequent action.

The Awful Truth

There are two basic issues behind the "Yes, but" syndrome. One is fear and the other is ignorance. Fear takes two forms: active and passive. Active fear is driven by the belief that the change is going to harm me. I stand to lose power, position, competence, reputation, or another asset that means a lot to me. Passive fear is fear that the change will not bring me anything of additional value, so why spend my time and energy doing it? It's easier to continue the status quo than it is to try something new. This is where WIIFM ("what's in it for me?") comes up.

Ignorance is the second stumbling block. People simply don't know how to do something. Everyone can understand the models, but few know how to choose the one that will work for them or how to implement the suggestions. Herein lies the greatest opportunity for a company to make a quantum leap ahead of its competition.

There are a number of ways that people respond to their own ignorance. Those with low self-esteem or intelligence back off. They hide out, do nothing, and wait for the latest fad to pass. Those with high self-esteem and ambition usually attack their ignorance and overcome it. That takes care of the 16.6 percent on each end of the bell curve. The remaining 66.8 percent who make up the bulk of the workforce deal with ignorance in both ways as well as in other ways. Some toward the bottom end of the scale go for the *not invented here* or the *we tried that in 1965 and it didn't work* responses. Those toward the upper end of the scale ask for help in learning how to do it. These last are the people who can be partnered with the high-end chargers to carry the day. Someone once said, "This country does not suffer from a deficiency of ideas. It suffers from a deficiency in execution." The differences brought on by e-world exacerbate that deficiency.

While management by imitation is the preferred mode of many, we seldom know how to execute someone else's process. This leads us down an endless trail of looking, kicking the tires, and thinking of reasons why it won't work. Have faith. We will solve this problem in Part V.

FIFTY HUMAN CAPITAL MANAGEMENT AGENDAS

In early 2000, *HR World* magazine interviewed fifty human resources executives from top multinational companies.[3] The objective was to learn the key issues that were on the executives' minds. We reviewed the findings and discovered five themes that ran across most of the respondents' agendas. These are:

1. **Values.** Everyone mentioned integrity and ethics as no-debate fundamentals. The other major value issues were a strong emphasis on respect for individuals and individual differences, dedication to customer service, a pronounced requirement for teamwork, and a strong achievement drive. Because all these companies operated in many countries, there was also great sensitivity for cultural differences.

2. **Culture.** Being multinational operators, all the executives mentioned having a global mindset as the base for associate relations, daily operations, decision making, and program development. This led to encouraging and sponsoring diversity for creating shared values and meanings. Many respondents recognized technology as a communications tool and as a unifying factor through facilitating networking.

3. **Associate Profiles.** As a general condition of employment and as targets for associate development, there was near consensus around five factors that make for exceptional associates. They are flexibility, adaptability, emotional stability, open-mindedness, and being effective communicators. Hiring strategies should be organized around hiring for "fit." The first priority should be to seek aptitudes. When these personality characteristics are found and developed, the operational skills can be taught.

4. **Talent Infrastructure.** In one way or another, everyone talked about what I would call building a talent infrastructure. This is being operationalized by a number of activities. Companies are

identifying key competencies and success characteristics and linking hiring and training to them, as well as identifying high-potential personnel as early as possible and guiding their development. Several companies assign mentors or monitors to ensure that the high-potential people are receiving the training and experience they need. Some companies centralize part of the recruiting process by putting all resumés online and making them accessible to managers.

5. **Knowledge Management.** The focus was on building a knowledge infrastructure. There was a very strong emphasis on integration and alignment of knowledge initiatives with the strategic plan of the business. Several executives spoke of creating communities of interest or practice to facilitate dissemination of information and knowledge. Others mentioned using quickly organized teams to solve specific problems or launch ventures. The results are presented to senior management and, most important, the experience and learning is broadcast for others to learn from. Finally, there was mention of pushing everything possible onto the intranet, so that associates can get answers to personal issues such as benefits or training opportunities and learn about corporate systems such as performance reviews and the pay program.

Under the Rainbow

Close review and contemplation of the five themes above reveals superordinate themes that underlie and drive the visible initiatives. The first is clearly a determination to live by a set of values. Values are part of every person's personality. Because an organization is an extension of the people who create it, it too has values whether or not they are articulated. I believe that we have come to learn over the past two decades that there is more to business than a business plan and operating systems. As the world began to spin out of its familiar orbit, people naturally felt a need for a foundation—something that would support them, something to hold on to. Values will continue to grow

Values will continue to grow in importance as we continue our transformation from i-world through e-world to new-world.

in importance as we continue our transformation from i-world through e-world to new-world. The CEOs of these fifty top companies apparently believe this as well and have committed to laying out a clear value path to guide associates and managers.

The second dominant theme is recognition of the complexity of the current and future global market. There are few simple, one-sided problems or solutions today. Respondents' organizations see the world shrinking in terms of distance and expanding in terms of contacts. Many of the subject organizations derive 50 percent or more of their revenue from markets outside the United States. Domestic and foreign markets contain a multitude of unique human capital needs differentiated by level, gender, ethnicity, nationality, and culture. Provincial management attitudes clearly are no longer functional. Ideas that work very well in some countries create problems in others. Companies must learn more about the labor force, the culture, and the customers in foreign markets in order to be competitive.

Complexity and its characteristics are driving collaboration as the third key theme. No one, and no small group, can know or keep up with everything that is exploding in e-world. There is a need to tap the talent of the entire organization as well as learn how to build external relationships. Internally, teams of all types are being organized. They are for the most part temporary groups brought together to focus on a given opportunity. Many of them, such as communities of interest or practice, are voluntary. People join when it suits them and leave of their own volition. Externally, companies are learning how to bring customers into strategy and product-design sessions. They are also becoming more adept at building alliances and partnerships with other organizations, even with competitors.

All the themes rest on the one most common function of human life inside and outside of organizations: communication. Many problems are created by naïve or untimely communication. Many more problems can and are avoided or resolved by communication rooted in a thorough understanding of the people and situation. Check these off and think *communication*:

• Values that are not communicated verbally *and* nonverbally cannot be supported. Associates who have heard the values and then seen them communicated through consistent management behaviors have no problem understanding and committing to them.

- Complexity can be overcome only through communication. The more forces and factors there are to a situation, the more people need to discuss and debate it. As change continues to pound organizations, communication is increasingly critical.
- Collaboration does not exist without communication. Effective collaboration is built on a discussion of mutual needs, preferences, methods, constraints, and goals. Management's role is to sponsor and underwrite collaborative efforts.

BRINGING IT HOME

Now that we have seen what is driving fifty of the more successful multinational corporations, it is appropriate to turn inward and ask ourselves what is driving us. How can we take this and use it to help us become an employer of choice? Typically, we would answer this by having a group of top-level executives discuss the question, which would give us an idea of what the senior people perceive. Yet if we restrict the discussion to a small group of senior personnel, we make the same mistake that GM, Ford, and Chrysler did in the 1950s. Their conversations were so incestuous that they could not accept any model of the automobile marketplace other than their own. Volkswagen and Honda forced them to see another perspective. The problem is that by the time Detroit had a strong response, Nissan, Toyota, BMW, Mercedes, and Volvo had taken major bites out of market share. The lesson is that when we really, really want to know something, rather than just talk to ourselves, we need to expand the pool of discussants. If we asked a cross-section of associates what they see as the most prominent and consistent factors affecting our customers, would they agree with the executives? If they did, it would be the first time in recorded history.

In every case that I know of from my personal experience as well as that of colleagues and other researchers, the perceptions of the rank and file are markedly different from those of senior management. The CEO talks to other CEOs. He listens to the advertising and public relations folk, who owe their living to him and accordingly would seldom tell him something he doesn't want to hear. Contrarily, the CEO seldom walks the street and talks to a consumer or goes into a customer's shop and talks to an engineer. When he does take the hike, it usually is as part of a formal event accompanied by an imposing entourage set to pounce on anyone who dares to speak frankly. Meanwhile, associates talk to their neighbors who are consumers and talk to customers every day. They hear the good and the bad, unfiltered by self-serving constraints. (Then, they broadcast it over the Web.) Do we want to feel good, or do we have the courage to hear the truth? It's probably better than we fear, so let's give it a go, mate.

ATTRIBUTES OF EMPLOYERS OF CHOICE

What have we learned from the companies profiled above? Are they living in another labor market where there is an abundance of talent readily available? Do they have a monopoly in their marketplace? Is their world stable and unchanging?

Of course, the answers to the above are all a resounding *no*! They are in the same world as we are. They too face a great deal of competition for talent and market share. Technology and accelerating customer expectations keep them awake at night as well. So, what do they do to calm their nerves and gain competitive advantage? They work very hard at becoming an employer of choice.

There is no secret to becoming one of the "best companies to work for," an employer of choice. Anyone can do it. The requirements include a humanitarian value system, consistent executive behavior, a commitment of resources to people who are the great productivity levers, and an opportunity to learn and advance. Figure 12-2 shows how each attribute of an employer of choice builds shareholder value.

Enterprise Values

Most CEOs have led the development of a values and vision statement. This is the foundation for all things to come. It is broad-

Figure 12-2. The value path of employers of choice.

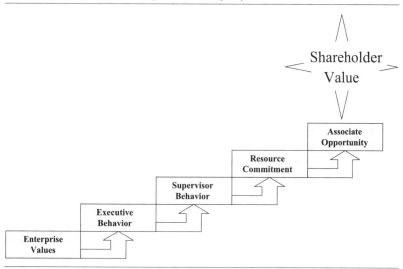

cast to all employees and often distributed in the form of plaques and wallet cards. Yet very often we find that clients cannot recite the value statement of the organization, which is strange given the time and money spent on the PR effort. The first reason why values cannot be remembered is that the list is usually too long. Psychological and educational testing has shown that most human beings cannot hold and commit to long-term memory more than seven items in a list. (There are exceptions, but we are talking about the masses.) The second reason is that different people learn in different ways—some by sight, others by touch, others by hearing, others only through direct and repeated physical experience. If we want to communicate, we have to understand the various ways in which people comprehend what comes at them. Developmental psychologist Howard Gardner claims that there are what he calls *multiple intelligences.*[4] These are:

1. **Linguistic.** A sensitivity to the meanings of words, their order, inflections, and rhythm; the syntax and semantics of the language. Socially oriented people are usually strong in this.
2. **Musical.** A capability to learn and communicate through musical sounds and forms; pitch, rhythm, and tone. Computer programmers are often skilled musicians.

3. **Logical-Mathematical.** A skill derived from confronting the physical world; usually learned through attempts at ordering objects. Later in life this is applied to philosophical, mathematical, and scientific problems.

4. **Spatial.** An ability usually begun through contact with physical objects that leads to being capable of understanding patterns and trajectories. This is a visual skill that sees and interprets movements and designs.

5. **Bodily-Kinesthetic.** A motor ability that uses one's body in differentiated ways developed through contact with objects. Athletes and mechanics exhibit this ability through the use of their major muscles or fingers and hands.

6. **Personal.** A knowledge of the self, derived from reflection on personal experience and from the interaction with others. Leaders will increasingly have to have a keen sense of self in order to guide others in the nuances of e-world.

Why is it useful to know this? The lesson is that not everyone possesses each of the six intelligences. Most of us learn and are adept at only two or three of them. This is the basis of the stereotyping jokes about computer geeks, dumb jocks, and bleeding heart social workers. When we find someone who is adept at more than three, we think of Leonardo da Vinci. Unfortunately, he is not in the labor market today, so we have to construct our value messages and reinforce them through a variety of methods for us common folk.

Each of those archetypes is an exaggeration based on its dominant type of intelligence and the value system that flows from it. That is the point. We know there are exceptions to all generalizations. Nevertheless, on average, what values tend to go with each of the intelligences? How do we communicate with them? What do linguistics-oriented people tend to value? For the most part, aren't they thoughtful types who value discussion over rash action? They usually want to talk about the topic before accepting and acting on it. What about the logical-mathematical types? Wouldn't we agree that they like structure over ambiguity? They tend to be skeptical and want to see the evidence behind our assertions. On the other side, the bodily-kinesthetic ones are usually competitive and more willing to go for it, trusting to their ability and physical skills to win out in the end.

Now we can see why it is useful to know what types of associates we are talking to. If we are trying to sell the scientific and engineering types, the thrust of our presentation on our enterprise values is going to be different from when we are talking to the human resources, sales, or accounting staffs. It makes the job more difficult, but when we're talking about values, it is worth it to make sure everyone "gets it." The first stepping-stone on the path to shareholder value has been laid. This sets us up for the second requirement of becoming an employer of choice.

Executive Behavior

Often this topic is entitled "management" behavior. I have purposely used *executive* rather than *management* because the top executive team has more impact on an organization's being an employer of choice than does any other group. The executives' actions are under a constant, intensely focused employee microscope. Executives must always show by word and action that they are living and supporting the values and vision required to make the company an employer of choice. Given the pressures and constant violent swings of e-world, this is not easy. If we say that we are a company that believes in respect for the individual, then the top team cannot ever violate that, actively or passively. At a personal level, they must treat all associates, in private and in public, with the respect due a decent human being. In addition, they must not allow others to disrespect associates.

Are there exceptions wherein disrespectful executives have still drawn people to their company? Of course, there are always exceptions. One is Steve Jobs, who is known for his temper tantrums. I remember talking to an executive years ago at Apple who said, "We are trying to help him grow up." Others who were notably disrespectful did not draw people to the company. An example is Robert Crandall, the retired executive of American Airlines, who left behind him a legacy of very negative union relations that is still costing AA a lot.

> *The list of rude, boorish executives is very long. Yet despite these exceptions, more than nine out of ten exceptional executives have been known for their respectful treatment of employees.*

The list of rude, boorish executives is very long. Yet despite these exceptions, more than nine out of ten exceptional executives have been known for their respectful treatment of employees. Their behavior confirms the values and sends the message to managers and supervisors that the executives are serious about the values.

Superior Behavior

Behind the executive behavior is middle management and supervisory behavior. Even if the top team is respectful, supervisors and middle-level managers who are not can undermine executive behavior. I've mentioned earlier how the negative behavior of one's supervisor drives associates out the door. The lesson is that executives have to constantly show all levels of management by action—reward and punishment—that the values of the company must be upheld. When disrespectful behavior is allowed by anyone, the message is clear: Management is not walking its talk.

Besides being respectful of associates, supervisors need to be available in times of stress. The supervisor earns her pay when an associate is having a problem. Finally, supervisors have to be certain that they are consistent in their treatment of associates. There can be no favorites. Everyone has to be treated the same in terms of work. Still, supervisors have to be able to deal with individual situations and needs in a way that does not engender resentment on the part of other associates. One more time, remember that associates have access to the Web and vengefully share their negative experiences with e-world.

Resource Commitment

The fourth leg on the employer-of-choice stool is a commitment from management to putting the necessary resources into the hands of the people. Associate commitment is the most precious asset a company can obtain. It is the force that lifts the lever of skill and drives productivity, and also helps associates weather storms and stay through the tough times. But their commitment cannot be greater than the commitment of the company to provide necessary resources. Budgets must be drawn that contain funding for the tools the associates need. There are examples of unusual resource commitments coming out regularly. Recently, we learned that Ford and Delta Airlines were putting computers into the hands of all employees, not only at work but also at home. The commitment to training is much higher in *Fortune*'s "100 Best" than in the average company because they believe in the value and integrity of people. Some executives have the attitude that training people just prepares them for the next employer. That is true. But we have to ask what we are doing that drives our associates to consider leaving us. They joined us freely, so why would they want to leave? If we treat them well, they will stay and the training will be used here.

Employers of choice create an environment that draws and holds talent. One of the best ways they do this is by making work as easy as pragmatically possible. When tools, training, mentoring, problem-solving support, and cooperative and talented coworkers are available, why would a person want to leave? Ask yourself: If you found a company that made this commitment, would you be looking actively to go somewhere else? I believe the answer is no, unless this next and last requirement is missing.

Associate Opportunity

Someone once said that Americans are bound to be disappointed for they are the only people in the world who believe that tomorrow will be better. We are people seeking opportunity. Our forefathers came here because this is truly the land of opportunity. Most Americans want to and expect to progress in life and in their careers. Most organizations pay a living wage and provide security through benefits. Although there is little employment security in e-world, almost everyone who is up to speed on technology, and capable of working and learning, can find a job in this economy.

Aptitude is the base of opportunity. Employers of choice usually make available tools that associates can use to uncover their aptitudes and interests. They develop career paths and provide self-directed career-interest tools. Mentoring programs are increasingly evident. Job postings tell what is available. Employers of choice focus on being learning organizations. Job experience is captured and disseminated so that the company and the associate learn how to grow together. Associates who show potential for growth are often given extra help in fulfilling that. In many ways, employers of choice constantly help people learn and advance because there is a good economic as well as humanitarian advantage for it.

PAYBACK: SHAREHOLDER VALUE

When the employer lives by a humanitarian value system; has executives, managers, and supervisors who consistently support it; commits resources to make the job easier; and gives associates the opportunity to learn, grow, and advance, it will find itself to be an employer of choice. Both academic and field studies have demonstrated that employers of choice are paid back with less costly and faster recruitment, more productive associates, lower turnover, and, at the end of the day, higher profitability and returns to shareholders. This fulfills the mandate under which every top executive must perform.

REFERENCES

1. Jac Fitz-enz, *How to Measure Human Resources Management* (New York: McGraw-Hill, 1984), pp. 8–10, 13–14.
2. Robert Camp, *Benchmarking: The Search for Industry Best Practices That Lead to Superior Performance* (Milwaukee: American Society for Quality Control Press, 1989).
3. "The Top 50—Revealed and Analyzed," *HR World,* March/April 2000, pp. 12–39.
4. Howard Gardner, *Frames of Mind* (New York: Perseus, 1983).

Chapter 13

Integrating Knowledge Management and Learning

THE REALLY BIG DIFFERENCE

The most elemental shift that I have witnessed in forty years in business has been the attitude toward alliances: collaboration versus competition. It has been brought about partly because the world is shrinking and everyone everywhere is communicating with everyone else.

Attitudes weren't the same in the olden days. Back in 1960, we viewed almost every other company with a degree of suspicion. We had a guarded reticence regarding fraternizing or even communicating. Of course, we had our few close business friends from other companies. Most often, they were from within our supplier-customer chain, but almost never from competing organizations. If you happened to have a personal friend at a competitor, you never mentioned it for fear of being under suspicion yourself. We were living with the postwar paranoia of the Communist menace and on the remnants of the robber baron's *"crush* the competition" ethic.

In 1991, Regis McKenna attracted our attention to the idea of collaboration in his seminal work *Relationship Marketing.*[1] His premise was that selling and marketing were taking on new looks, the result

of the increasing complexity of products spawned by electronic technology as well as the customers' desire to form a personal bond with
the supplier. He told us it was imperative that sellers go beyond
pushing product to building relationships with customers. Concurrently, Saratoga Institute was finding in a five-year study of 1,000
companies that collaboration was already a hallmark of the top-per-
forming enterprises.[2] The example set by those early leaders gradually invaded business practice until today almost every company
seeks partnerships and alliances with other enterprises.

The fact that we are collaborating openly and actively with customers, suppliers, and competitors has an effect on our psyche.
Thirty years ago, social psychology researchers established the fact
that frequent contact with others induces more favorable attitudes
toward them. That flies in the face of the old adage that "Familiarity
breeds contempt." Now we are seeing this new view functioning on
a grand scale. This does not mean that we are not competing fiercely
with each other. Nevertheless, while battling for market share on
one hand, we are simultaneously discovering ways to ally with our
competitors for mutual benefit.

COLLABORATING WITH CUSTOMERS

Alvin Toffler coined the term *prosumer* in his 1980 masterpiece
The Third Wave. He speculated that: ". . . Third Wave civilization
begins to heal the historic breach between producer and consumer,
giving rise to the 'prosumer' economics of tomorrow. For this reason, among many, it could—with some intelligent help from us—
turn out to be the first truly humane civilization in recorded
history."[3]

The first phase of his optimistic prediction has come true as
providers have opened the tent and invited customers to join in the
creation of the product or service. The provider supplies the raw
material in terms of data or product components, and the customer
molds the product from the parts supplied. It is the modern version
of kit building but with design shifting from the provider to the customer. Today, we can design a suit or an entire wardrobe online from
Lands' End. We can make deposits and withdrawals, transfer funds,

and apply for loans through an ATM or from our home with an online connection to the bank. Technology is truly now in the hands of the people.

After a period of distrust and fear, consumers have come to enjoy the personal satisfaction they gain from creating their own solution. The Web is like a buffet where we fill our plates with whatever we want to consume. When we are free to choose for ourselves, we enjoy the meal more than the *prix fixe* menu. This is because of the creative process, which we dictated and in which we participated. As a result, we begin to have a more tolerant and perhaps even a benevolent attitude toward the provider. What some call mass customization has more to do with attitude than product.

COLLABORATIVE CULTURES AND CHANGE

The place that collaboration is most needed and can generate the greatest value is within our enterprise. It is much easier to implement change and grow an organization where people are cooperating across business units. Collaboration is an enterprise value and a corporate culture trait. It starts with the actions of top management. When the CEO and the executive team speak and practice it, gradually everyone catches on, and it has a chance of becoming a cultural artifact. The objective of collaboration is to create a place where skills and knowledge are shared for the purpose of positive change.

In e-world, change has evolved from an occasional project to a way of life. As such, it is a topic that attracts almost as much energy as leadership. Change manifests itself both as a constant occurrence and as a project. On a daily basis, there is always some small change taking place. We call it evolution. Often change is wrought through a focused, concerted, corporatewide effort. We call this revolution. While evolution is inexorable, revolution often fails. Rather than repeat failure statistics and dwell on the negative, let's look at how to make planned change work.

KNOWLEDGE, LEARNING, AND CHANGE

Successful change is dependent on a few key factors. The two that are seldom mentioned in the change literature are learning and knowledge. Learning is the process by which we acquire knowledge to manage change and serve customers. To my way of thinking, if we are looking to change something, we need learning and knowledge as initial enablers. Formal and informal learning processes empower change processes with the

> **Learning is the process by which we acquire knowledge to manage change and serve customers.**

knowledge of which skills and resources are needed to make the change. Data tell us the current state of the process. Benchmark metrics from outside show us where we stand within our comparison group, be it industry or geography. Our knowledge of our business and the market converts the data into information and eventually into practical intelligence. This shows us what needs to change and how much change we want to and can effect. These activities must be linked. The fact that people talk about knowledge management (KM) and organizational learning as a single entity and have gone so far as to put an acronym on it—KMOL—does not make it a reality. Knowledge management programs and learning as an organizational capability are not often connected and communicating.

Knowledge management and the learning organization are both outgrowths of the intellectual capital movement. The organization that aspires to manage its intellectual capital does so through learning and knowledge activities, not through manufacturing. To manage intellectual capital, we have to collect, organize, disseminate, and evaluate information about the company and its internal and external stakeholders. When we do this consciously, we are learning and managing knowledge. Obviously, the two factors are interdependent.

While knowledge and learning are management processes, a third factor in this scenario is a practice. That practice is collaboration. Effective change requires collaboration across units, functions, and levels. We cannot change one unit of a business organization without affecting other tangential units. Involving related parties in a change project increases its odds of being successful in terms of serving the larger goals of the enterprise. Historically, many change projects have failed to produce expected results. This is usually because we didn't fully understand what we wanted to affect and what would be affected by the change. Since change is a complex activity, it is more successful when it deliberately brings learning, knowledge, and collaboration into the equation.

Figure 13-1 shows how the management processes of change, learning, and knowledge should be embedded in a collaborative culture. The logic of this diagram is that for change to occur in a managed way, the first step is to gather information on past and current conditions. To keep the effort from being locked in the past, it must be focused on future goals. Then, the information needs to be converted into knowledge of the state of the function undergoing change. This knowledge is matched with individual and organizational learning and skill development regarding how to manage a change process. Most important, the interchange of knowledge and learning is supported by a collaborative culture that reduces friction and inefficiency, speeds the process, promotes effective action, and achieves the desired change. To understand how to make this complex operation work, we have to understand the characteristics or nature of each of the factors. This is still a dream for most organizations that have not linked knowledge management with organizational learning beyond a project level. In a recent Saratoga Institute survey of eighty-two companies, only nine reported that they attempt to link knowledge management with organizational learning. The same survey asked the companies to rate how collaborative their

Figure 13-1. Change, learning, and knowledge embedded in a collaborative culture.

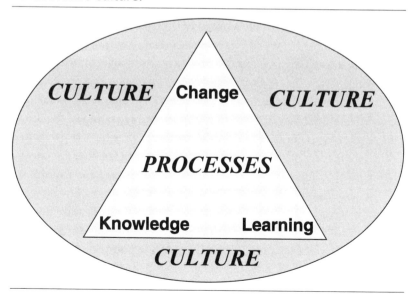

culture was. On a ten-point scale, with one being highly collaborative, forty-eight rated themselves below five.

PATHWAY TO INTEGRATION

Arguably there are many questions to answer in solving the integration puzzle. There are enough to fill another book. Nevertheless, the solution is going to be found within two basic questions. The key to integrating knowledge organization and human development is that it is not about data and training. First, it must be addressed in higher-order terms. The starting point is this seminal question: *How do we accelerate the capacity of the organization to compete on the basis of human capability and commitment?*

Once we are clear that this is the real purpose behind the issue, we can ask the follow-up operating question: *How do we integrate organizational knowledge and human development?*

The answers to both these questions are different for every enterprise. The best we can do within the format of this book is to provide principles and models of both success and failure. Here is a model of success.

A $5 BILLION SUCCESS STORY

CSC is a major technology consultancy headquartered in northern Virginia. It has a knowledge/learning system that it claimed to be a "critical factor in closing over $5 billion" in business in the past year. CSC's Knowledge Program Products and Services is organized around a three-part model. The parts are:

1. Knowledge communities that develop and share knowledge as a natural step in delivering services to clients
2. A knowledge database that preserves CSC's core methodology and serves as a guide to the company's expertise
3. A collaborative environment strongly supporting the use and operation of the knowledge base and encouraging formation of the knowledge communities

The key element in any knowledge program is the sharing of experience. CSC's knowledge communities are formed to connect people of common interests and expertise. People are comfortable talking to professional colleagues to exchange experience and leverage innovation. An expert group offers thought leadership, guidance, and coaching. People can tap into expert networks and participate in communities of interest. The company has nurtured this knowledge-sharing culture that encourages and rewards collabo-

> **There needs to be a formal program for rewarding knowledge sharing.**

ration. The key word is *rewards*, the missing ingredient in most knowledge programs. There needs to be a formal program for rewarding knowledge sharing. It is natural for people to hoard knowledge, because knowledge is truly power. Various reward methods have been used in the CSC program. Some organizations go so far as to require associates to make contributions to the system and have them scored by an expert group for value. Performance ratings take into consideration those scores along with the person's work outputs.

CSC's system encourages associates to access the knowledge base that houses tools and work products useful in their client assignments. Associates can download over 1,500 computer-based training courses to grow their theoretical knowledge and practical skills. Also, they can tap into the work of other associates as another means of accelerating their learning. The company believes that there is a critical difference between practitioners and knowledge workers, summarized in Figure 13-2. Practitioners are self-centered and closed; knowledge workers are enterprise-centered and open. E-world will not be a hospitable place for companies or individuals who subscribe to the practitioner beliefs and behaviors.

At the core of the CSC system is a business change methodology that puts key skills, ideas, and practices within easy reach. The system is called the Six Domains of Change. The six are:

1. **Business processes** address what the enterprise does and how it does it. Change in this domain drives change in all other domains.

Figure 13-2. Practitioners versus knowledge workers.

Beliefs	Practitioner	Knowledge Worker
	Knowledge that one has is critical to personal success.	Knowledge that one has and shares is critical to personal success.
	Reuse destroys creativity.	Reuse can fuel innovation.
	Value is derived only from personal creativity.	Better ideas can be generated from interaction and collaboration.

Behaviors	Practitioner	Knowledge Worker
	Occasionally captures and shares knowledge with personal network.	Routinely captures and shares knowledge with global network.
	Occasionally seeks knowledge to fill gaps.	Routinely seeks knowledge to increase effectiveness.
	Leverages personal network.	Leverages institutional networks.

2. **Organization** deals with the people in the enterprise: culture, capabilities, roles, team structures, and support systems.

3. **Location** focuses on the physical facilities and delivery capabilities needed to perform.

4. **Application** deals with technical structure, design, and software capabilities along with the human factors required for effective use.

5. **Data** addresses the content, structure, relationships, and rules regarding the information the company requires.

6. **Technology** covers the hardware, system software, and network components needed to support the enterprise.

Collectively, these domains provide a common intellectual framework for approaching client assignments. They are interactive forces that create a holistic way of doing business that gives CSC a competitive advantage. The company assesses the value of the knowledge program from six angles: employee retention, employee productivity, profitability, return on investments, organizational agility, and win rate on business. It is the most comprehensive and verifiable system I have had the pleasure of studying.

ORGANIZING KNOWLEDGE

Learning is the process by which we acquire knowledge. Usually, learning in organizations is driven by the training or human resources function. This is what Tom Stewart, author of *Intellectual Capital* and member of the board of editors at *Fortune,* calls the "sentimental model." Often learning is a list of loosely connected training experiences and perhaps improvement programs. On the other side, knowledge management is typically centered in the IT function—as Stewart calls it, the "mechanical model." Projects are run and databases are developed within the project unit, again without dissemination. As organizations attempt to become learning centers and to manage knowledge, they must bring the functions together. Having learning managed in one area and knowledge in another is inefficient, to say the least. Separation suboptimizes both. Only in rare cases such as the CSC example does the training ever get with the knowledge exchange and vice versa.

> Having learning managed in one area and knowledge in another is inefficient, to say the least. Separation suboptimizes both.

In the spring of 2000, I spent time at one of the World 100 companies that had nearly twenty "knowledge" projects underway across its many divisions. There was no plan to share the learning from those projects or knowledge gained in them outside the unit that was sponsoring them. The CEO who had funded this effort did not seem to be concerned about it. He thinks he has a knowledge program that he can talk about.

Knowledge, learning, and intellectual capital are interdependent. Knowledge management depends on the ability of an organization to learn and to share knowledge. The content of both learning and knowledge management is intellectual capital. Human beings consciously and unconsciously absorb information every second of their existence. Probably more than 99 percent of the sensory stimuli that impinge on us are not perceived or are consciously noted and ignored. The remaining fraction of information is processed and utilized. It might be stored for future use, or it might be applied immediately. The information we use in our organizations is what has come to be called intellectual capital. As we saw in Chapter 3, IC is knowledge of organizational factors, associate characteristics, and external groups such as customers, suppliers, and competitors. This is the knowledge that we try to expand, disseminate, and apply for competitive advantage.

DEVELOPING A KNOWLEDGE STRATEGY

Logic tells us that before there can be knowledge management, there must be a knowledge strategy. That is to say, before we invest, there must be an understanding of the business need. I recognize that this is not a novel statement, but I make it based on studying the knowledge movement since its inception. KM started as an IT activity with the funding of knowledge exchanges. Initially these were elaborate Lotus Notes programs. Although some of the programs have migrated, many are still managed by the IT function with its professional viewpoint.

The missing point in these cases is that knowledge is not a technology issue. It is a human issue. Until we implant ROMs behind people's ears, learning will not be a technology-driven business. Technology is only an enabler. Notwithstanding HAL from the movie *2001*, databases do not learn, at least not yet. They are little more than repositories of 1s and 0s. Knowledge is not about building databases. It is about pushing useful information into the hands of the people who can apply it. Beyond that, people have to be taught how to use it, why to use it, and why they should contribute to it. In many cases today, knowledge is still predominately a technology game. One large-scale study revealed that only 10 percent of the respondents had access to lessons learned elsewhere. In all the factors studied—generating, applying, leveraging, and sharing—the highest success rate was reported in less than 40 percent of the cases. Finding the lessons learned across the company reportedly occurred in only 13 percent of the cases.[4] I doubt that this is much better than in the days before we ever heard of knowledge management.

Famous failures include companies that have spent millions on databases that don't get used, skills inventories whose access is so restricted that they never reach the units needing them, communities of practices in which people don't care to participate, and cultures where knowledge hoarding is the norm. The most common reasons behind failures have been well documented. They are:

- No sustaining support is received from a management champion.
- Resource commitment is insufficient or is withdrawn too early.
- KM initiatives are not connected to a business goal.
- Cultural/behavioral changes are ignored in favor of technology.
- The information system is difficult to access and navigate.
- No measurable impact on the business can be found.

There are lots of ways to spend money. Since KM technology is expensive, we need to ensure that there is an alignment between it and a basic business priority. Knowledge and learning have to be aligned with the business strategy. Unfortunately, experience shows there is often a very thin line connecting, but not binding, knowledge and learning beyond the nice-to-do stage.

Repeated surveys have shown that knowledge and learning are recognized by CEOs as keys to future competitiveness. The Gartner Group predicts that companies that don't make KMOL a priority will seriously lag behind their competitors in offering new products and services.

We also have abundant evidence about the best way to launch and expand KM. The first is through the formation of communities around a common issue. There are two kinds of communities: communities of practice and communities of purpose. Ann Noles at Capital One has provided a graphic example of the differences as shown in Figure 13-3. Communities of practice involve people who perform the same types of activities, are located in disparate locations, have a common interest in their work topic, and endure over time. Communities of purpose come together to work on a project, perform dissimilar activities, share interest only in the project, and disband when the project is complete. Thus, to build KM, you should form communities of practice.

The second step in KM is to ensure distribution of the learning.

Figure 13-3. Communities of practice versus communities of purpose.

	Communities of Practice	Communities of Purpose
Type of Work	Similar	Dissimilar
Time Frame	Continuous	Beginning/Ending
Interest	Subject	Project
Reason to Meet	Interest in the Topic	Project

This is less a problem in communities of practice because interested and needy parties are often directly or secondarily involved. A person might be in the group or a colleague of someone in the group. In the second case, the colleagues naturally talk about what they are involved with, thereby passing the learning outside the immediate group to the larger community. Contrarily, KM will not be built on communities of purpose unless—and this is the big unless—the knowledge gained in the project is disseminated to other units or individuals who could learn from it. This is where most break down, and this is where technology and culture meet. Where management has taken an active role encouraging sharing and putting technology and recognition in place, knowledge often flows beyond the transient communities.

ACCELERATING TIME TO COMPETENCY

The seminal question remaining is how to make knowledge and learning work together smoothly. The objective is what is coming to be called *time to competency*. Given that there are not enough qualified people to fill existing and projected jobs, companies need to accelerate the skills of their current staff. By combining knowledge with learning and taking advantage of the connectivity of the Web, companies can build a competency system that outperforms the competition.

Since knowledge management is viewed as a technology matter while learning is a human resources initiative, there needs to be a basic reexamination of the issue. The CSC case described above is the beginning of the integration movement. However, I believe that the training function needs a major overhaul in order to contribute to e-world. A few of the problems with a traditional training function are:

- Too much learning is focused on traditional classroom experiences.
- Distance-learning technology is not used to its fullest.
- Much of training content is out of date or disconnected.
- More human development needs to take place in the "real world."
- Learning and knowledge management are not connected.

If we can solve the last, it will carry the others with it.

The basic question is, how can associate and organizational learning be accelerated by integrating it with knowledge organization and vice versa? Let's examine the principles involved. Knowledge starts with data emanating from the organization's experience and position within its marketplace and community. Data are constant and overwhelming to the point of being impossible to absorb and organize in their totality. Hence, the first task is to establish the rules of engagement with data. These are the basic data questions:

- What is out there (in e-world) and what is in here (inside the enterprise)?
- What types of information would be useful for us now and in the near future?
- When do we need it and how often do we need it?
- How do we convert data into information and practical intelligence?
- When we have it, who (which jobs and people) should be able to access it and who should have it pushed out to them on a regular basis?
- How do we get them to use it and ask for what they need?
- Finally, how do we encourage the associates to push data back into the center so that the data can be organized for use by others?

Keep in mind that collecting data is a useless expense until the information is acquired and converted into meaningful information. That leads us in the direction of learning.

Now we are ready to address learning. Here are the basic human development questions:

- What do people at various positions and at various points in their career need to know?
- What are the most effective media for facilitating the learning at those positions and points?
- How do we convince supervisors at all levels to focus on advancing organizational learning as an integral and important part of their job?

There is one basic answer to the human questions above. If we want someone to do something, we have to show them what's in it for them. I don't mean to imply that people are totally egocentric, but they are human beings whose first instinct is *survival*. The second is *comfort,* and the third is *growth*. If we keep these three simple, basic criteria in mind when dealing with people anywhere, we will be successful more often than not.

ORGANIZATIONAL LEARNING

Ever since Peter Senge published *The Fifth Discipline* in 1990, management has been playing with building what he called a "learning organization."[5] I use the word *playing* deliberately. Learning is one of the many management solutions that have come along in the past fifty years. Some companies jumped on the bandwagon and have seriously attempted to transform their organization into a learning center. Many others are simply playing with the idea. They assign responsibility for the transformation to the training director and go back to doing business as usual. The more earnest ones have appointed a chief learning officer and allocated resources to this new idea. In very, very few cases has there been a top-down dedicated attack on this goal. For the most part, after the big splash produced by Senge's book, learning has been pushed gradually back onto the long list of things we do. It is replaced with knowledge management or abandoned in pursuit of a dot-com makeover. If you ask companies if they are a learning organization, you get a mix of reactions from a smirk to a "we're working on it."

Judy Rosenblum was brought into Coca-Cola in the mid 1990s to build a learning organization. Despite her great talent and energy, she left five years later with the following statement: "Introducing learning into a large, diverse, global organization is a struggle."[6]

We don't have to read very deeply between the lines to understand what she is saying. She goes on to describe what it is like to drive this central idea through a large i-world corporation. Without her saying it in so many words, you can feel her frustration. People who worked with Judy at Coca-Cola have told me of several examples of how her staff supported major business initiatives. They were much more than detached central service. Still, when a shuffle occurred at the top of the organization, support for learning diminished.

Judy shared her experience in an interview in *Fast Company* in which she told what was necessary to make learning a cultural hallmark. Her points are simple, direct, and not surprising. In response to the question of how one creates a learning organization, Rosenblum provides us with a primer on what it takes. The article states:

> *It depends on the culture of the company and on what the leaders* will stand for. *Learning has got to be connected directly to the business. We must stay away from offering a "learning program." We have to find people who are ready and willing to join us. If those people add value to the business, others will come. Rosenblum says that one thing she accomplished was to teach leaders that learning is a strategic choice. It doesn't just happen. It is a capability that depends on skills, processes and leaders who value it. People are learning all the time as a result of their work. But someone has to decide that learning is not just an individual experience, but also a collective practice. Market forces and organizational structures get in the way of learning. First, because organizations have to respond to financial markets there is a sense of urgency to make the numbers. This can prevent an organization from taking the time to learn. Second, if we want people to take time to think and learn we have to reward that. A learning organiza-*

tion asks people to consider why whatever is happening is happening. Organizations don't pay for learning.[7]

TRAINING VS. LEARNING

Many companies have approached the learning idea through an increase in the corporate training budget. Ironically, training can be an impediment to learning. A strong dedication to training, such as Motorola is famous for, can replace learning in the minds of leaders and managers. It is a fallacy to believe that establishing an in-house university and sending everyone to class will produce a learning organization. Bob Galvin, former chairman of Motorola, believed that training and learning are noble things to support, and he was right. Unfortunately, training as a *good thing* often produces a growing list of expensive training programs. It does not ensure that a company will be learning and maintaining a competitive position in the market. Despite its massive commitment to training in the last two decades of the 20th century, Motorola discovered that it had missed the analog-to-digital transition in telecommunications. Falling behind the competition in a core business is not a good idea.

> *Training can be an impediment to learning. A strong dedication to training, such as Motorola is famous for, can replace learning in the minds of leaders and managers. It is a fallacy to believe that establishing an in-house university and sending everyone to class will produce a learning organization.*

Other organizations, such as General Electric, have also established internal universities or development centers that do support true learning because of the companies' dedication to development. GE is famous for its Crotonville development center, and the company has always been known for its ability to develop business managers. It is dedicated to total talent development as a systemic business activity that has learning as its foundation. At GE, people know they can develop as far as their talent and ambition will take them. But personal development is not the whole point. Development is constantly learning as a business as well as a personal imperative. Michelin has its unique system of womb to tomb development of people, based on the principle that an employee is an asset of the corporation, not of any one business unit. Michelin puts associate development very high on the list of business imperatives. It is a living example of what Judy Rosenblum said: "Learning is not a program, it is a capability."

BUSINESS-DRIVEN ACTION LEARNING (BDAL)

Another method that has gained credibility without being drawn into the fad camp is what some call business-driven action learning. This is slightly different from straight experiential programs that are often labeled "action learning." Action learning revolves around some type of physical and mental involvement in an issue. However, the topic is not always important. The focus is on learning by doing versus learning by listening. BDAL is different in that it has at its core a business issue of strategic-level importance. BDAL is a topic of some complexity and subtlety, but I will summarize the key issues. For those who wish to go deeper into it, I recommend Yury Boshyk's *Business Driven Action Learning.*[8] It is a collection of cases of BDAL from companies such as DaimlerChrysler, Dow Chemical, DuPont, General Electric, Heineken, IBM, Johnson & Johnson, Motorola, Phillips, Siemens, and Volkswagen.

In discussing his work on BDAL, Boshyk stated that five conditions are necessary for action learning to work. They are:

1. Active involvement and support of senior executives
2. Focus on real business issues and strategic opportunities
3. Research devoted to company experiences and attention dedicated to solving business issues
4. Leadership development through teamwork and coaching
5. Implementation of recommendations and follow-up examination of business results and the learning that comes from the analysis

The goal behind BDAL is that the organization should learn faster than its competition. This is what makes it particularly appropriate for e-world. Traditional classroom training is often too theoretical. Outdoor exercises such as survival programs don't transfer the learning from field and stream to corporate bunkers. BDAL can be very effective because it is not process-bound. That is, it does not rely on one or two methods of learning. It can draw from cognitive methods such as lectures, self-paced instruments, consulting methods, benchmarking and effective practice analysis, team learning, project management, and information technology methods.

BDAL is being used by a number of the major multinationals to accelerate development of executives. By working on strategic problems that are real, the individual is necessarily focused on learning by doing—the best method. The project also gives the organization an opportunity to assess its high-potential people engaged in real work versus simulations. Management can see who has the ability to advance and how far. It can also see who would be good at senior staff work versus line management. When carried out properly, BDAL can speed the development of learning for the purpose of improving profitability as well as groom the next generation of executives. Anything that helps us leap ahead of the normal time frames is worth looking into.

SUCCESS AND MEASUREMENT

Linkage Inc. recently carried out an intensive study of KMOL in ten organizations: Ernst & Young, Hewlett Packard, AT&T, Microsoft, The World Bank, Buckman Labs, Shell Oil, InFocus, Massachusetts General Hospital, and Norske Skog Flooring.[9] The companies identified the most critical success factors for their KMOL program, shown in Figure 13-4. A community of practice was the most often mentioned factor for a successful program. Top management support (senior buy-in) and making a convincing supporting business case were the next two that ranked in the top half in terms of importance.

Participants were asked also to rank order the steps taken to reinforce and sustain the initial successes in their KMOL system. These are shown in Figure 13-5. They were in agreement that culture and employee behaviors cannot adjust to the change without ongoing nurturing. They agreed further that it was important to track the involvement of employees through metrics of usage. These included hits on the intranet and tracking of submissions to virtual communi-

Figure 13-4. Critical success factors for KMOL programs.

Success Factor	Median Rank
Communities of Practice	2.50
Senior Buy-In	3.14
Creating a Convincing Business Case	3.28
Overcoming Resistance to Change	4.28
Enabling Leadership Development	4.42
Technology Implementation	4.85

Scale: 1 = most often.
        5 = least often.

Figure 13-5. Factors for sustaining success in KMOL systems.

1. Feedback sessions/focus groups
2. Metrics in measuring employee use and involvement
3. Empowerment of workforce in access to knowledge sharing
4. Rewarding employees for providing and increasing enterprise intellectual capital
5. Recognizing employees for adding value to intellectual capital
6. Developing communities of practice
7. Development of different applications in managing tacit and explicit knowledge
8. Coaching and mentoring

ties. However, in the foreword of the report, Hubert Saint Onge, a pioneer in knowledge management and organizational learning systems, stated, "We have yet to see the emergence of a robust measurement approach to support a comprehensive KMOL strategy."[10]

We can see that KMOL is more than a fad, yet it still has a long way to go to make its way into the core of the business process. Although the CEO may claim that knowledge and learning are critical to the future success of the enterprise, KMOL is one of those complex behavior-driven programs that most executives don't feel comfortable managing.

If we go back to Chapters 4 and 5 on leadership, it was very clear that tomorrow's leaders are going to have to learn how to deal with these messy, unpredictable, and uncontrollable human development and knowledge organization issues. They cannot be pushed off on human resources. They are everyone's business. People like to talk with others who share common interests and problems. People want to learn and grow. Training can help, but communities of practice and BDAL are more effective media. In the final analysis, knowledge organization and learning are core competencies that must be mastered for success in e-world

REFERENCES

1. Regis McKenna, *Relationship Marketing* (Reading, Mass.: Addison-Wesley, 1991).
2. Jac Fitz-enz, *The 8 Practices of Exceptional Companies* (New York: AMA-COM, 1997).
3. Alvin Toffler, *The Third Wave* (New York: William Morrow, 1980), p. 27.
4. *Organization Design for KM* (Los Angeles: Center for Effective Organizations, USC, 1999).
5. Peter Senge, *The Fifth Discipline* (New York: Doubleday/Currency, 1990).
6. Alan Webber, "Will Companies Ever Learn?" *Fast Company,* October 2000, pp. 276–282.
7. Ibid., p. 276.
8. Yury Boshyk, ed., *Business Driven Action Learning* (New York: St. Martin's Press, 2000).
9. *Best Practices in Knowledge Management and Organizational Learning Handbook* (Lexington, Mass.: Linkage Inc., 2000).
10. Ibid., p. xvii.

Chapter 14

E-Human Capital Summary and Scorecard

THE KEY HUMAN CAPITAL ISSUE in e-world is not the shortage of qualified people. It is how an enterprise deals with its people. There is a plethora of research supporting the claim that companies that understand people have little trouble finding and keeping them. Consider this: The top executives typically come from sales and marketing, finance, or production. None of them comes from a field that focuses on human capital. As a result, only a few CXOs (CEO-COO-CFOs) have in-depth knowledge of the needs and desires of their staffs. They read the articles about talent being critical, and most of them believe it. Then, they turn to human resources and tell them to do something about it while the CXOs return to the issues they understand. Unfortunately, many human resources managers understand program management better than business management.

People today are human beings just as were their grandparents. They want many of the same things. However, the world obviously is different, and this affects how they go about getting the things they want. Fundamentally, people are social beings who would like to survive and advance their needs through their work. Because of the pressures of constant change and inconsistency on the part of many executives, people are taking more control of their lives than did their forebears.

We've touched on the leadership failures in previous chapters. Now let's look at solutions. The single most important factor by a couple of light-years is communication. Wrapped around that is corporate culture. The two are so tightly integrated as to be inseparable. If we want to solve the talent shortage, we cannot do it through more money and benefits. We have to do it by becoming an employer of choice. This implies creating a culture that attracts and holds people. At its core is a two-way communications system. It is not a passive system that claims our door is always open. It is an active program of listening and talking openly about the important issues of the enterprise.

The arrival of the Web has stripped every executive naked. People have access to so much information that leaders cannot hide behind platitudes and half-truths. They have to come out and talk to the people as directly as possible. The first step to effective communication is to get someone's attention. Although attention is the item in shortest supply in e-world, management has an edge because its actions have so much effect on people's economic well-being. After gaining the associate's attention, management has to create interest in its message. This is simple. Talk about the topic in terms of what it means to the audience. For example, a financial report is exceptionally boring and often incomprehensible to well over half the people in the company. It needs to be translated into WIIFM (what's in it for me?). This can be accomplished by telling the people what the key features are in whatever we are communicating. Then show them what the benefits are for them.

The Web is an excellent communications tool. We can send text, pictures, and sound. Maybe one day we can send some form of smell and taste. But the Web is not the only tool and it cannot be used in situations where personal contact is necessary. A daily flood of e-mail text messages from HQ is quickly relegated to the *open later* list. Each medium has its strong points. Decide which medium is best for each communication you make. Effective communications have to be planned and implemented just like a production run or an administrative process. Associates are more than economic units. They are thinking, feeling beings who are a lot more perceptive than management sometimes realizes.

Two factors that block management initiatives more than any

other are fear and ignorance. A smart executive can remove both blocks.

- **Fear.** It is natural to be anxious about the unknown. E-world is a massive unknown, and it is engulfing us. Many people fear that they are dealing with an electronic Tyrannosaurus Rex that is about to consume them. Management has to get out of its offices and walk among the people. We have to learn what it is that bothers them. Then we have to come up with solutions and deliver them. I'm talking about support. The traditional support systems of the United States are in disarray, so people look to their employer to play a support role. This is where some of the new benefit programs like day care and fitness centers come in. *Fortune's* "100 Best Companies to Work For" can help show the way. When you wrap it up, you see that the essentials of financial security, time, personal support, and health are taken care of. No wonder people want to work there.

- **Ignorance.** The other basic block that effective leaders remove is lack of knowledge. Ignorance can relate to skills, general information, new technology, or organizational changes. All of these can be addressed through communication, training and education, and mentoring. Over the past decade many companies have been spending large sums on training, typically 2 percent or more of payroll. That, combined with an open communications program and consistent behavior on the part of all levels of management, has turned many companies around.

In the final analysis, successful management of human capital rides on clear vision and values, open communication, a collaborative culture, and opportunity for personal growth and advancement.

MEASUREMENT IN E-WORLD

The issue of managing human capital from a return-on-investment standpoint was treated in great depth in my last book.[1] Here, we look specifically at managing and measuring human capital in e-world. Our attention is focused more on the so-called soft side of e-world—that is, from a management practices viewpoint. This complements the strong emphasis placed on financial return in that previous work. In Chapter 15, on how to align the enterprise in e-world, we will recombine the quantitative and qualitative sides in some new measures.

Figure 14-1 is a list of pertinent questions regarding human capital management in an e-world environment. It deals with issues of communicating e-strategies with associates, stimulating creativity among associates, teamwork, effects on employees of introducing e-business, and similar issues.

The ten items can be considered key drivers, imperatives, or checkpoints. The scales give us the degree to which we are focusing management time to these. I use the term *drivers* because these items drive associates at all levels to greater commitment and productivity. Failure to deal with any of them can impair competitive advantage.

REFERENCES

1. Jac Fitz-enz, *The ROI of Human Capital* (New York: AMACOM, 2000).

Figure 14-1. Human capital scorecard.

1. *Vision*   1   2   3   4   5
                                                Low   High

   Management's vision of e-business is widely communicated and thoroughly understood by our associates. There are regular communiqués, meetings, and discussions of e-business changes. We periodically check the associates' level of comprehension through formal and informal channels.

2. *Structure*   1   2   3   4   5
                                                Low   High

   We are restructuring the company to support e-business. The structure takes into consideration the needs of associates to interact freely across business unit boundaries fostering collaboration, teamwork, and creativity.

3. *Culture*   1   2   3   4   5
                                                Low   High

   The corporate culture has shifted from i-world to e-world. Associates understand the similarities and differences between the two as they relate to practices and relationships internally and relationships with external factors such as customers, suppliers, competitors, and the communities in which we operate.

4. *Attraction*   1   2   3   4   5
                                                Low   High

   Our e-business initiatives help in attracting top talent. E-business activity is woven into our staffing strategies and programs. E-business products and successes are prominently displayed in recruitment advertising and highlighted in interviews with all candidates.

5. *Careers*   1   2   3   4   5
                                                Low   High

   We have established career paths focused on e-business. Associates are informed as to the skills, knowledge, and attitudes required to build a career in an e-business setting. Management and professional progression pathways have been clearly defined and published.

6. *Learning*   1   2   3   4   5
                                                Low   High

   Associates understand that continual learning is a requirement of e-world. Their growth is supported with a wide variety of formal training programs, project assignments, and stretch goals.

7. *Innovation*   1   2   3   4   5
                                     Low   High

Associates are encouraged and incented to be creative. They are aware that e-business requires constant innovation to find new values for customers and gain competitive advantage in the e-marketplace.

8. *Management*   1   2   3   4   5
                                     Low   High

The importance of supervisor-associate relations is understood by our supervisors and by management. Significant and continuous investment is maintained in supervisor training and mentoring.

9. *Communication*   1   2   3   4   5
                                     Low   High

Recognizing the importance of communication in times of change, there is a major associate communications program. Continual surveying of associates' questions guides the design of communication.

10. *Future Look*   1   2   3   4   5
                                     Low   High

As we restructure the company, we are concurrently reviewing competencies required in the near future. Changes in technology and markets guide us in identifying needs and preparing associates to meet them.

Part V

ALIGNING YOUR ENTERPRISE

FOR E-WORLD

Chapter 15

How to Align Your Enterprise for E-World

THE NEW NEW-LOOK

What business are we in? What makes this company unique? What are our core competencies? What are our key assets? How does the latest technology affect our market?

E-world demands that we reconsider who we are, where we are going, how fast we want to get there, who our major competitors are, where new competition might come from, and how we need to releverage our capabilities to compete. Although the fundamentals of business are the same—get and keep a customer—the best way to do that has changed. Whom we have to look out for certainly has changed; ask Barnes & Noble, Compaq, Sears, and other franchise brands that were knocked sideways by Amazon.com, Dell, and Wal-Mart, each of which brought a new perspective, a new New-Look to their market.

Everyone does not have to become a dot-com company to survive, but each of us has to look at the potential of the Web to serve us or kill us. General Management Technologies (GMT) conducted a study of 166 companies in the summer of 2000 regarding the application of e-business initiatives and

> *Everyone does not have to become a dot-com company to survive, but each of us has to look at the potential of the Web to serve us or kill us.*

tools.[1] They focused on success rates and trends and factors that contribute to success. Their conclusions were twofold:

1. Executives are just beginning to learn about e-business. They are struggling to understand the rules of the New Economy. They are asking themselves how their organizations can apply e-business tools with some confidence that they will be successful.
2. There were success stories that were laying down the first principles of e-business success. Both the winners and those still seeking positive results agreed on the success factors (which are discussed later).

MANY PATHWAYS TO E-BUSINESS

GMT found that executives are testing a wide range of approaches in search of what will take advantage of the opportunities that the e-world market offers. It is a trial-and-error process, and the following early trends are emerging:

*   E-business is new to most executives; 91 percent reported that their programs were less than two years old.
*   The future lies within e-business. Only 59 percent agreed that e-business is "important" or "very important" to their organizations today, yet 93 percent said that e-business will be critical to their growth in the future.
*   E-business has no single, common source within the organizations. Only 27 percent of the respondents had a manager dedicated solely to e-business efforts. The CEOs, vice presidents, and project managers all have assumed leadership of programs, with marketing, planning, and IT being the locus of most efforts.
*   E-business has no singular form. Only 25 percent of the responding companies have separated their e-business efforts into distinct units. In most cases, e-business is a cross-functional responsibility, an ad hoc effort, or a group integrated into an existing marketing or IT function.
*   E-business has many objectives. Most executives invest in e-business to enhance customer service (80 percent) and to streamline communication (74 percent) rather than to improve procurement (28 percent) or increase direct sales (30 percent).

We can see from these results that e-business clearly is a new idea. Will it be another management fad? That is not likely since this is not another management theory. It is an idea that takes a form and is being burned into the infrastructure of the company. One can't easily and cheaply invest in e-business and abandon it without significant repercussions.

BARRIERS TO STRATEGIC SUCCESS

Experience has demonstrated four barriers to strategic success: development, acceptance, communication, and implementation. Let's look at them.

The first is a development barrier. We know we need a strategy to guide the enterprise, but we don't know how to design one. Part of the reason for this is that between 1989 and 1995, we decimated the ranks of seasoned managers by downsizing. Today, the people who would have been ready for the executive floor are gone. Younger, smart but less experienced people have been thrown into strategic thinking positions, and they aren't ready for them. At this point we all might have to hire a consultant and pray.

The second barrier to strategic success is acceptance. In this case, the CEO is ahead of the executive group in formulating a strategy but is unable to get buy-in. Many companies that I have been involved with suffer from some variation of the buy-in barrier. Without a CEO who can get commitment from the top team, the other senior managers spend a good deal of their time maneuvering rather than collaborating. Everyone salutes, but few march, and fewer charge.

The next barrier is communication. Even when the top team buys in, they may not know how to get a clear message across to subordinates. In today's environment, where the intelligence of everyone is key to success, it is imperative that the senior executives find a way to get the word out to everyone and gain commitment to the plan. The entire organization needs to know exactly what the enterprise goals really are and how they are expected to contribute to them.

Finally, we have the implementation barrier. Even when things are clear, the troops don't always know what to do. This is especially true today as more organizations move from command and control to participative systems. People are not used to thinking for themselves in those cases. They are standing around waiting for marching orders. There is a big gap between the CEO's vision and the operations of the business units.

EARLY SUCCESS SIGNS

In its study, GMT asked responding executives about their general approach to e-business and the factors behind their e-business performance. Surprisingly, both the highest and lowest performers named the same factors as keys to success:

- Well-defined strategy is the single strongest determinant. Nearly 60 percent of executives who had achieved e-business success attributed it to an initial clear strategy. A weak e-business strategy was cited by more than half of those reporting a lack of e-business success.
- A widely shared vision is the attribute most critical to e-business success. Other cultural factors, such as employee empowerment, advancement opportunities, and an entrepreneurial environment, marked at least 75 percent of the successful cases. Companies with lower levels of success reported these cultural attributes much less frequently.
- Planning and preparation are critical. Successful executives built their e-business program on competitive and internal assessments, brainstorming sessions, e-model design, and detailed implementation planning.
- Adequate funding and executive involvement are essential. Not surprisingly, the larger the budget was, the more top executives personally supported the program, and the higher the incidence of success.

ARE YOU READY TO USE THE WEB?

Cisco Systems is arguably the most e-enabled company in the world. Since its business is to build products on which the Internet runs, it has given a great deal of thought to organizational issues.

Cisco's Web site displays two questionnaires that give an organization a glimpse of how ready it is to use the Web as a major structural tool. The first, the Net Readiness Scorecard, contains fifty-seven questions. A manager can fill in the questionnaire online and within a few minutes get back her organization's scores, which show its state of readiness. The second instrument is the Internet Quotient Test. Aimed at senior management, it shows an organization's current potential for using the Web. A score is obtained by submitting online answers to twenty yes-no questions covering the following topics:

1. Management Vision
2. Customer Connectedness
3. Adaptive Technology Infrastructure
4. Ecosystem Potential
5. Executing in Real Time
6. Ecosystem Partnership
7. Internet Standards
8. Developer Community
9. Market Innovation
10. Venture Capital Endorsed
11. Business/IT Partnership
12. E-Learning
13. E-Commerce
14. Employee Empowerment
15. Internet Returns
16. Market Vision
17. Community Building
18. Global Presence
19. Market Position
20. Strategic Investment

I have filled out both of these questionnaires on my company, and the results can be sobering. They showed me how well or poorly management was connecting with associates and customers. The data revealed what are usually issues of secondary importance in management's mind, such as community relations. They showed where we were in terms of understanding our market—something we all take for granted that we know, and then have often fallen behind. Probably as important as anything was what we weren't doing around supporting associate communities of interest and associate learning. I saw where we stood and I saw how we compared to the norms. Now, I know how far we have to go in each area to be competitive. The results gave me a map that I can follow to build an e-business. Anyone who wants to know what is involved in establishing an e-enterprise should go to Cisco's Web site and submit his opinions. The data are kept confidential and so far no salesperson has called on me. You can find the questionnaires online at www.cisco. com.

ALIGNING FOR E-WORLD

There are four steps to building and operating any competitive enterprise. They are (1) having clear vision and values, (2) developing a strategic plan, (3) building a structure that complements the plan, and (4) executing the plan. This is not new. What is new is the world in which we are operating: e-world.

As pointed out in Chapter 2, i-world and e-world are merging, and already there is a good deal of overlap. This was evident after the April 2000 meltdown of the dot-com mania, when the market came to its senses and recognized that a Web site is not a business. Despite that, we have to keep in mind that what worked yesterday probably won't work well tomorrow, and that goes for either extreme. If we don't adapt to the new market forces and opportunities, we may not be driven out of business in the near term, but we certainly won't be competitive for long. At best, we will spend the rest of our existence as one of the zombie companies—the living dead.

The Web-Acknowledged Strategy

Yesterday, today, tomorrow—there is no one best way to do something. This goes back to the benchmarking caution. Management by imitation seldom succeeds. Each of us must learn as much as we can from every source and then adopt our own strategic methods. Once we have commitment to our vision and values, we can move to the essentials of planning and execution. One without the other leaves the job half done. Rethinking our strategic model and plan with the potential of Web technology is absolutely necessary. Next, resource commitment must be suitable for the new strategy and the objectives that issue from it. Shortchanging the input shortchanges the output. Finally, like everything else, important programs need the personal

> *Yesterday, today, tomorrow—there is no one best way to do something. Management by imitation seldom succeeds.*

support of important people, the CXOs. Figure 15-1 lays out an alignment structure for e-world.

In this structure, the Web is the background within which the strategic model is developed. That's the major distinction from the disconnected past. The rest of the model is not radically different from what we already know, except for one absolutely critical imperative. It rests on the assumption of a truly direct, visible alignment from the Strategic Goals through Operating Objectives to Resources. We have been talking alignment for years, yet in practice, alignment is seldom an unbroken chain from top to bottom. That is why we chase fads, waste resources, fail to achieve strategic goals, and frustrate our associates and ourselves. Those wonderful human traits—

Figure 15-1. An alignment structure for e-world.

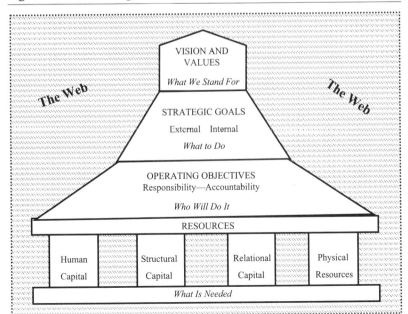

fear, ignorance, greed, spite, and self-centered ambition—break the chain. And it isn't the associates who are to blame. As Pogo so wisely put it, "We has found the enemy and they is us," namely, management at all levels.

Before we jump into the Web strategy model, I want to point out the subtle differences between this model and the traditional i-world model.

- Strategic Goals (or strategy) has been subdivided into External and Internal. External refers to the typical market and financial goals. Internal refers to the restructuring needed to operate in e-world. This internal focus will be there for the foreseeable future because e-world is changing faster than we can adapt to it. We saw in the GMT survey described earlier in this chapter how companies are already lagging behind. If we have the courage to take the Cisco online tests (also discussed in this chapter), we will undoubtedly find specific evidence of our gaps.

- In the Operating Objectives section, Responsibility and Accountability have been highlighted. My experience in big companies is that accountability is often dodged. Failure is always someone else's fault, and it is always easy to push off because of the lack of initial commitment to a visible line of sight from top to bottom. There is always room to slide through the gaps. This denial of accountability is reasonable if we stop to think of how organizations really work.

  In most organizations, competition rather than collaboration is the modus operandi. If you disagree with that assertion, show me an organization where engineering and sales, R&D and marketing, and IT and general managers consistently work together. Because competition is the nature of commercial enterprises, people find it in their interests not to fully commit. When someone stumbles, she is seldom given another chance because someone else is ready to take her place rather than help rescue her. Many companies are "we versus they" institutions. We can never erase that, but we can mitigate it with a different value system, culture, and structure. Only the CEO can make this happen.

THE WEB STRATEGY MODEL

Vision and Values

As always, everything starts with communication leading to alignment. The vision and values must reflect the realities of e-world. The connective power of the Web affects both vision and values. Everything must be glued together, from the strategic set provided by the CEO to the foundation resource support pillars of intellectual and physical capital. I chose the word "glued" rather than "nailed" or "cemented" to emphasize that we can no longer cast organizations in rigid forms. In fact, the glue should be rubber cement so parts can be easily loosened, moved, and reglued as conditions change.

Strategic Goals

Under the vision and values come the strategic goals. These top-level targets are usually focused on financial gains, market penetration, internal structure improvements, and talent growth. The goals can be pursued through decisions about how to improve operations, engage in mergers, or make acquisitions of technology and talent to capture markets. What is new in strategic planning is the arrival of the Internet. At the risk of being redundant, the informational and connective nature of the Web has to be factored into every strategic business plan. Equally important is consistency. Stanford professors Charles O'Reilly and Jeff Pfeffer brought to bear over two decades of experience in management education and consulting in their book *Hidden Value*.[2] One of their conclusions is that there must be absolute alignment of values and practices and consistency of managerial behavior. In their study of eight companies (Southwest Airlines, Cisco Systems, The Men's Warehouse, SAS Institute, PSS World Medical, AES, Nummi, and Cypress Semiconductor), O'Reilly and Pfeffer looked at six management practices aimed at ensuring that values would be reinforced. Those six are:

1. Values, culture, and strategy alignment
2. Hiring for fit
3. Investing in people
4. Widespread information sharing

5. Team-based systems
6. Rewards and recognition

They found that when any of the companies failed to practice these, they floundered. When they stuck with them, the enterprise prospered.

Operating Objectives

The enterprise's goals come alive in the operating objectives of the various business units. Allegedly, these are aligned, but quite often they are not. History shows that midway toward our goals, we often divert our efforts to chase the latest management nostrum. This action might help us achieve near-term operating objectives, but it is seldom obvious what power it has to serve our goals. The reason we do this is twofold. First, we are paid for short-term performance. The only long-term incentive we have is stock options. Most people opt for money today versus promises about tomorrow. The second reason is that we are still wedded to the industrial age, where process and activity rather than transformation and results were the objective. We don't take time to analyze. Often our arguments are based more on self-preservation and personal advancement than on the goals of the company. If we are going to compete, we have to keep the goals in front of us while objectively deciding what is the most direct pathway, what tools are needed, and who is responsible and accountable. This last point is critical for future competitiveness.

Resources

Success depends on the management of the organization's intellectual capital and physical resources. This is where execution of the business plan takes visible form. This is putting the fuel in the engine of management. Without it, the vision, values, goals, and objectives are inert documents. It is also where i-world is shifting toward e-world. The hardheads have to go beyond the clichés about people's importance and fervently embrace the new truth that the greatest leverage of the e-economy is human intelligence. This is not an aberration of Silicon Valley. The e-economy is not found exclusively in computer hardware and software companies. Practically every business now depends on human intelligence for its competitive advantage. Even mom-and-pop stores can use the resources of the Web for better merchandising ideas. In lieu of keeping longer hours and working harder to compete with the chain stores, they can apply their intelligence to learning how to surf the Web. Every i-world enterprise from iron foundries to paper suppliers is turning to technology and human creativity, looking for better ways to compete.

Machines can't tell us better ways. Physical assets are listless. They don't move; people move. One of the oldest tools in the world is the lever, but the lever is just an inert, heavy iron bar that lifts nothing by itself. It takes a human being to create leverage, to exploit the potential power and value of that tool. Tools without intelligence are useless. It is the user who makes the difference. This is not a novel idea. The point is that now intelligence plays a more powerful role because when it is combined with technology and information, the leverage is greater than when intelligence is applied to simple hand tools or assembly lines. Taylorism is dead, and reengineering is its pallbearer.

THE E-WORLD NETWORK MODEL

Figure 15-2 offers an operational model that complements the strategic model described above. The model is founded on accountability. This is the essential innovation. The enterprise structure, instead of being the usual series of connected boxes laid out in a linear and hierarchical style, features an internal network embedded in the Web. In the traditional hierarchical model, we can escape accountability because of the cultural and communications protocols designed into the model. It is very difficult to collaborate in the industrial model, which was designed to support Taylor's one-best-way to do something.

Now that e-world is driving us from linear formats to networks, it makes sense to have an operating model that reflects reality rather than antiquity. Value chains are giving way to value networks. The principal difference in nets over hierarchies is connectivity. In a net-

Figure 15-2. The e-world network model.

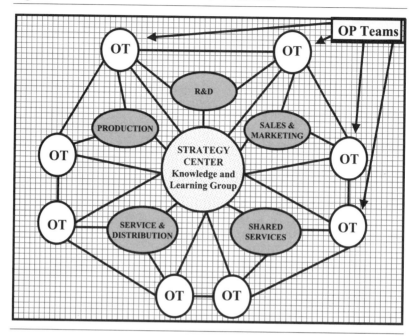

work, everyone has a direct connection to everyone else on the net. There are no delaying protocols that prescribe acceptable communications paths. In the net, all communication is acceptable. And in a network, power resides on the periphery, not at the center. Energy must be committed to supporting the value-adding activity on the edges rather than the resource consumption going on at the center.

Value chains are giving way to value networks. The principal difference in nets over hierarchies is connectivity.

Why have we always talked about general and administrative functions being expense centers? Because that is what we set them up to be. It was rather stupid to create a unit whose responsibility is to consume resources without being accountable for contributing measurable value-adding results. If accounting, IT, and human resources cannot be managed to add value, we shouldn't have them. (Incidentally, they can be set up to contribute measurable value-adding results, but nine out of ten companies have not figured out how to do it yet.)

Figure 15-2 shows the e-world network model in place. Following are its parts.

Strategy Center

The Strategy Center of the net is where the CEO, CFO, and COO reside. The COO is accountable for enabling the strategic vision of the CEO. The COO directly manages a Knowledge and Learning (K&L) Group within the Strategy Center, which is composed of a small group of strategists and highly skilled professionals plus thought leaders and enabling consultants as needed. Their job is to support two sets of groups: (1) the Function Groups, which report to the COO; and (2) the Opportunity Teams (Op Teams), which are ad hoc strike forces set up to take advantage of opportunities to make the enterprise more competitive.

Function Groups

Surrounding the Strategy Center are the Function Groups. These are the traditional operating units: R&D, Sales and Marketing, Production, Service and Distribution, and Shared Services. The heads of the functions are accountable to the Strategy Center for achieving the operating objectives. The CXOs set and monitor alignment of the enterprise goals with the operating objectives. The Shared Services Group, which is a different kind of staff support group, houses the General and Administrative services that are not outsourced. As many support services as possible should be outsourced. This includes *almost all* functions usually budgeted for under G&A, including the transactional services within IT, accounting, and human resources.

Many management theorists argue for outsourcing everything that is not core. However, most of them have never had K&L responsibility or been accountable for organizing anything as complex as a two-car parade. Still, I agree with the proposal and I have started and run a business for a couple of decades. The issue is how to decide which functions should stay internal in what form and which should be contracted out. The Strategy Center contracts for and manages the outsourcers. The counterargument—that we can't manage service contracts as well as we manage internal staff operations—is simply a save-my-job campaign. Up to the late 1980s, we did such a great job managing staff that we found ourselves so overloaded we had to banish a couple of million loyal employees to make ourselves competitive again. Then, while we were still downsizing, the economy took off and we didn't have the foresight to hire or train enough people to fill our needs. Rather than take on a new model of staff management, we stayed behind the innovation curve mired in industrial age thinking. Are we good staff managers, or what?

Opportunity Teams

Teams are a phenomenon of the last two decades of the 20th century. They came about in response to the need to make change happen more quickly than it could within the protocols and barriers of the traditional hierarchical structure. They brought with themselves new management and reward problems, some of which have been resolved and many of which have not. In the e-alignment model, these are ad hoc groups of any size that are supported by the CXOs and/or the Function Group heads and are partnered with the Knowledge and Learning (K&L) Group. This partnering is a key element for the following reasons:

1. It serves as a support mechanism for the Op Teams, providing the best professional or technical advice available.
2. It ensures that whatever learning comes out of the exercise is captured for the benefit of the larger enterprise.
3. Furthermore, as new Op Teams are formed, the knowledge gained in the past is pushed out to the team to avoid redundancy.

This model is truly participative in that *anyone* can form an Op Team by delivering a value proposition regarding an opportunity to make the enterprise more competitive. Funding can come from the Function Group head or the CXOs. The team is given resources in the form of a budget and support personnel from the K&L Group as needed. The Op Team is held accountable for a return on investment and has incentives based on ROI performance.

Op Teams are a key concept. Up to now, teams usually have been formed by upper-level managers to cut expenses, solve problems, or develop new products. This worked well in many cases.

However, teams are not inherent parts of the traditional i-world structure. They are merely tools. In this e-world model, Op Teams are a natural entity. They are continually being formed, performing, morphing to something new, or being terminated after having achieved their objective. They are a reflection of the fluidity of e-world. Some might work together for only a few weeks; others could go on for a year or more. They are run on business-driven action learning principles. The expectation is that CXOs and Function Group managers see to it that at all times dozens of Op Teams are exploring, fixing, testing, adding, or cutting something. The essential requirements are that:

- Their objective has to support directly one of the enterprise's goals.
- They are accountable for measurable value-adding results.
- They make a closing report of their learning that is entered into the knowledge exchange maintained in the Strategy Center.

The K&L people look for opportunities to push the learning out to areas where it can be exploited either by teams or ongoing operating units. This helps to make K&L active rather than reactive work. The U.S. armed forces have significantly improved their operations by a variety of such after-the-exercise reports. These are write-ups of what went right and wrong, and what was learned as a result. This intelligence is shared through a knowledge exchange system.

ENABLERS: TALENT AND TECHNOLOGY

People First

Since e-business depends more on the mix of talent and information than the industrial era did, it is logical to build a strategy based on investment in intellectual capital backed by physical resources rather than the other way around. This is still a tough sell in many companies. Management knows how to invest in machinery and how to procure materiel. Hardware and software are necessary, but from there on the incremental advantage is going to go to the company with the best talent. Mixing relevant information into an empowered, stimulating culture yields the best chance for success.

A study sponsored by Andersen Consulting and carried out in 2000 by Saratoga Institute and Canada's McMaster University made it unequivocally clear that value alignment and management of intellectual capital (human, structural, relational) leads to exceptional performance.[3] The study was unique in that it started with management perceptions integrated with current financial data. Participants included seventy-six senior executives from thirty-six companies in the financial services industry. The objectives of the research were:

1. To determine the relationships between human activity and financial outcomes by linking economic measures with perceptual measures of human capital management
2. To benchmark the relative standing of participating organizations so their human capital could be reallocated more effectively
3. To set a baseline for trending and norming human and financial capital links

The findings threw light on the relationship of management capability and employee factors with financial business performance. The basic connections are shown in Figure 15-3. Note especially the intellectual capital set (human capital, relational capital, structural capital), the employee set (employee satisfaction, employee commitment, employee motivation), and the knowledge set, particularly knowledge sharing. In order to make this complex diagram more understandable, I have emphasized the pathways that are most strongly correlated with business performance. Correlational values range from 0.43 to over 0.72. Here are the key findings:

- The development of senior management's leadership capabilities is the key starting ingredient for the retention of key employees. Effective leadership sparks knowledge sharing, helping senior management align values throughout the organization.
- The effective management of all forms of intellectual capital (especially human and relational) yields higher financial results per employee. The education level of employees and their overall satisfaction positively influence the development of the enterprise's human capital bank.

Figure 15-3. The connections and pathways among people, knowledge, and performance.

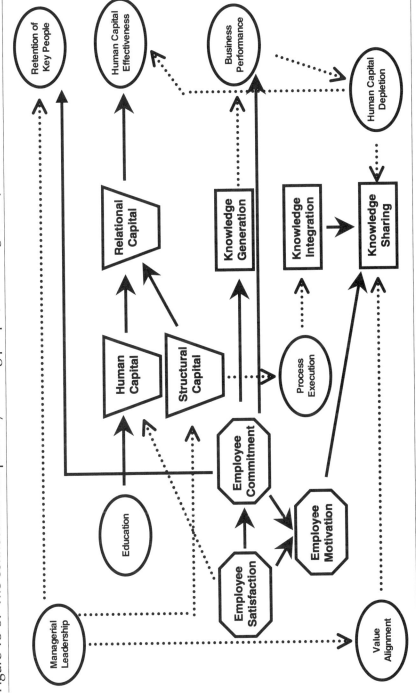

- Employee sentiment—as defined by satisfaction, motivation, and commitment—can be traced to intellectual capital management, to knowledge management, and ultimately to business performance.
- Knowledge management initiatives can decrease turnover rates and support business performance if they are coupled with HR policies.
- Business performance is positively influenced by employee commitment and their ability to generate new knowledge. This subsequently acts as a deterrent to turnover, which in turn positively affects performance.

The central point is that by using perceptions directly linked with economic factors, a connection becomes clear. Perceptual data alone are weak. The value of these findings is that management can be specific in its commitment to various actions, confident that it will obtain an acceptable ROI and be servicing the goals of the enterprise.

Technology Support

There are two technical and one sociological challenge for the information system designers. One technical challenge is that information must be available *now*. The other is that the information is constantly changing. The sociological challenge is to persuade people to use the data and the capability of the software to make themselves more productive and effective.

> *Most software programs are over-featured. People typically want to do three or four things with their computer; capability beyond that is wasted.*

First, the technical issues. The information system must enable every employee to easily access whatever he or she needs quickly from a 24/7 platform from any point in the world. While the operative term is speed, ease of access problems have inhibited many systems. After repeated failures to navigate the system, people give up in frustration and go back to their old, less efficient but more effective methods. Simplicity is preferred over complexity. Most software programs are overfeatured. People typically want to do three or four things with their computer; capability beyond that is wasted. If I want to drive from home to the grocery store, I don't need a Ferrari or a tank.

Second, the half-life of useful information is short. How short is an irrelevant question; it is short with a capital *S*. Yesterday's information may be obsolete already. For example, consider the constant flow of titillating articles about technological advancements. By the time such prognostications are published, a significant portion of them are already out of date. Projections are that within ten years, half the new information we get will be obsolete within twenty-four hours. Therefore, state-of-the-art information must be *constantly* discovered, configured, and put literally at the fingertips of the employee. This is another argument for simplicity. Complex systems simply cannot be maintained.

Then there is the sociological challenge. The human issue is even more complex than the technical. Saratoga Institute has conducted a number of studies for software vendors on how their customers are using the capabilities built into the programs. *In every case*, the finding has been that the customer is using only a small part of the potential. This problem has three parts. One is clearly that people are so stressed that they don't feel they have the time to learn all the system has to offer. Another part of the problem is that most programs are overfeatured, as mentioned above. Typically, people want to improve one capability or solve one problem, but engineers want to solve many problems or offer many capabilities within one elegant solution. These are incompatible goals that generate paradoxical outcomes. The more technological capability that is built into a product, the more it ends up inhibiting human usage through overload. The third part of the problem is that the industrial model taught people to focus on their individual task rather than on looking for ways to innovate and contribute to the enterprise goals. You can walk through any company in North America and ask people at random what the top three enterprise goals are, and you will be lucky to find one in ten who can tell you something specific. Until companies throw out the industrial model in favor of the e-model, this problem will continue to be baked into the brains of employees.

CONCLUSION

Leadership and management have become simultaneously more important and more difficult since the arrival of the global marketplace some thirty years ago. In the emerging new economy, the pace, complexity, and size of the market are overwhelming us. Obviously, a model developed midway through the industrial age is not going to be serviceable in e-world. We all have a lot to learn and it starts with the CEO, whom many employees claim is confused and failing to provide a clear vision.

There are clear maps that can be followed to e-align the enterprise. Along with formulating and communicating a clear vision, the senior executives have to design a new structure and define a strategy that is embedded in the connectivity of the Web. This is the seminal difference between i-world and e-world: connectivity. It must be the essential characteristic of our structure. Slow, inhibited connections are noncompetitive. We can't be afraid to try new forms because if we don't, we will inevitably fall behind those who are innovating in organizational design as well as products and customer service.

Taking in information from throughout the organization is the

> **It is an undeniable fact that our associates know more about the operating issues of the day than the top executives who are sheltered from them.**

best approach for developing our strategy. It is an undeniable fact that our associates know more about the operating issues of the day than the top executives who are sheltered from them. We cannot build our strategy through management by imitation. We need to start by rethinking the profile of our enterprise in light of e-world. Then, we can gather data from the marketplace on effective practices. Fitting our uniqueness to the elements underpinning effective practices can help in strategy formulation.

One more time, let me point out how critical it is to ensure the direct, visible links among enterprise goals, operating objectives, and resource management. Not having these links is the major cause of organizational inefficiency. It is also a key contributor to the depletion of talent. Frustrated, confused people cannot commit to unknown goals and perplexing objectives. Transformation rather than process improvement is the imperative of the new millennium. Incremental gains are useful, but they do not keep pace with the rate of change in e-world. We need teams of people who are working on transformational issues and feeding the learning and knowledge into the system for others to leverage. Finally, accountability has to be reintroduced into the system. The purpose is not to be able to hang people who fail. It is to force clarity and commitment as well as have a valid method for assessing and rewarding performance.

Financial performance and enterprise viability are dependent on management of our intellectual capital. Constant accumulating and sharing of information is the bedrock of the e-aligned enterprise. Our associates are the talent of the enterprise. They have to be both learners and teachers. To accomplish this, we have to make learning and knowledge a central part of our daily work. If we want someone to do something, what do we have to do to make it happen? We have to communicate the reason for doing it. We have to provide the learning and the tools to do it. We have to explain it in terms of WIIFM. Then we have to build a system of rewards and punishments that incent it. Finally, we have to commit unequivocally to it and model it within the executive group.

Our associates are the pivotal point of the enterprise. For the most part they want to learn, grow, and contribute. The only things that can hold them back are the system into which we thrust them and the attitudes of the people who manage them. Outdated systems based on outdated attitudes and fearful managers are a disastrous combination. However, this does not need to be the case. There is a very small difference between the top performers and the rest of the pack. This is it:

Top performers realize that what they did yesterday that made them so successful has absolutely nothing to do with what they need to do today to make the enterprise successful tomorrow. As managers, we have to learn and grow first before we can expect associates to do the same.

REFERENCES

1. *E-Business Benchmarking Study* (Pittsburgh, Penn.: General Management Technologies, July 2000).
2. Charles O'Reilly and Jeff Pfeffer, *Hidden Value* (Cambridge, Mass.: Harvard Business School Press, 2000), pp. 237–239.
3. Nick Bontis, *Human Capital Valuation Study* (Santa Clara, Calif.: Saratoga Institute/Andersen Consulting, 2000).

E-Alignment Scorecard

THE SCORECARD OF AN E-WORLD organization contains all the measures listed on the previous scorecards. For the sake of differentiation and clarity, I will refer to them as micro measures. In addition, there are macro measures that are based on the same values as the micros, while extending them. Finally, there are several human-financial macro measures that we have found useful for assessing the relative movement of human capital versus financial performance trends. There is a natural alignment throughout the system from the micro to the macro, from the tactical to the strategic, from the human to the financial.

Figures 16-1and 16-2 lay out a sample of the types of qualitative and quantitative macro metrics that are essential to measuring progress in the e-economy. In addition, there is a format for tracking the metrics over time. In every case, the macro metrics are the end product of creating a composite measure or an index of micro measures around a seminal issue. Collectively, the micros define the macro. At this level, that is the most efficient way to operate.

Consider this example. A reporting period rolls around and we want to know how we are doing on a set of business objectives. We start by scanning along the macro level, the single number that shows the trend. If this is a critical issue or one in which the trend

Figure 16-1. Qualitative metrics to measure progress in the e-economy.

	Last Period	This Period	Change Percent	Goal Percent	Industry Mean	Comments
Customer Satisfaction						
Associates						
Culture						
Innovation						
Knowledge & Learning						
Collaboration/Alliances						
Management						
Technology						
Brand Strength						
Quality						
Community/Environmental Relations						

Figure 16-2. Quantitative metrics to measure human and financial variables in the e-economy.

	Last Period	This Period	Change Percent	Goal Percent	Industry Mean	Comments
Human Capital ROI						
Human Capital Value Added						
Human Capital Cost						
Human Economic Value Added						
Human Market Value Added						

has changed or is not immediately evident, we can drill down into the micro measures from previous chapters or other sources that underpin the macro. Say we want to know why the macro measure of Customer Satisfaction is declining. Which related micro measures from the Leadership, Strategy, or Human Capital Scorecard might point the way? In the customer service department, we find that the mean time to respond and repair has risen. We see the number of complaints rising regarding the Service Center. Why is this happening? It is similar to looking at the trend in cash on a balance sheet. If we see cash declining, we want to know why, so we look at receivables, and we might look at receivable aging. We study revenue growth and any other metric that might yield clues to the decline in cash. Most metrics can be evaluated by looking at related forces that influenced the observed result.

Figure 16-1 offers a number of qualitative issues.

- **Customer Satisfaction.** This is the number one measure in business. Without customers, we have no business. This measure looks into the past to tell us how well we have done with our customers up to now. The score is also a good predictor of what we can expect from the customers in the near future. Happy customers tend to stay with us.
- **Associates.** The ability and motivation of associates is the active ingredient of any business. It can be measured as a combination of job satisfaction, morale, commitment, voluntary turnover, satisfaction with career opportunities, supervisory support, and many other things. If we construct effective employee attitude surveys, we obtain most of the data. Then, by adding an exit interview program—preferably conducted by an outside party—we gain a different perspective. The combination of employee surveys and exit interviews should yield data that can be aggregated into an Associate Index. In addition, we should be watching contingent labor. What is the ratio of contingent labor to regular employees? Where are the contingents concentrated? Some companies have found that contingents are holding down many of their key technology jobs. What happens when they leave? Answer: They take the learning and the ability to compete out the door.

- **Culture.** All activity takes place within a field of cultural values. Most of the other macro measures are the result of the play of cultural values. We have seen it in the great companies of the past century. When their cultural values were sound, the financial results were exceptional. When they lost touch with what they were about, economic performance suffered. We can develop associate perspectives of culture with the same employee attitude surveys mentioned in the previous topic. Ask questions about the corporate culture's values and see how many people can answer them correctly. A wrong answer is an indictment of management. We may not have done a good job of communicating the values.

- **Innovation.** The key imperative of e-world is innovation. The company that continually responds to market trends with new or improved products or services ahead of its competition usually will win the battle. Innovation is the responsibility of everyone and must become a cultural hallmark. It is often measured in terms of sales of new products. What other measures tell us how well we are innovating? Are we operating from a new business concept, à la Amazon.com or Dell, or just making incremental process improvements? How sensitive are we? Look back at the Cisco test for topics. How open are our systems? Ask the associates: Are we setting or following standards? By definition, innovation metrics cannot be restrictive. We innovate our measurement system just like our product line.

- **Knowledge & Learning.** With people being the primary profit lever of e-world, we need to know how well we are supporting them with information and opportunities to improve their skills. K&L are essentials for optimizing the leverage potential of our human capital. When we design our information strategy, it should be derived from knowledge and learning requirements, and we should always *think network*. We can ask associates if they have easy access to the information they need for two challenges: (1) responding to the customer today, and (2) looking ahead to how they can innovate. On the learning side, we can query associates regarding the training and education they need to serve the customer and advance their own skill bases and careers. What is the level of satisfaction? We know from exit interview data that career opportunity is a major retention factor.

- **Collaboration/Alliances.** Partnering and allying are proven ways to leverage resources and bring ideas to market quickly. Set a strategy of creating partnerships around key opportunities. Monitor the partnerships or alliances in terms of value added. Knowing how many formal alliances we have is interesting, but the central question is, "So what?" The most common mistake made in metrics is to simply count the number of things occurring and assume that is some surrogate for effectiveness or value added. What are the correlations between financial performance and the number of partnerships, MBAs, reengineering projects, quality meetings, or improvement teams we have? In most cases there is none, and the senior executives consistently fail to ask this question.

- **Management.** How can we measure the strength of our management? Let me give you a clue. It has nothing to do with the graduate school managers attended or the degree they earned. It has a lot to do with the results they obtained. And the most often ignored question is what by-products did they create in pursuit of those results? So we measure management as a function of a number of primary and secondary outcomes. The scorecards in Chapters 6, 10, and 14 provide sample metrics.

- **Technology.** What does top management need to know about its technology investment, including what all those acronyms mean? How close we are to owning state-of-the-art technology is not a good indicator. Take a page from Japanese management, which views technology merely as an enabling tool. Investment trends, carrying costs, and ROI would be three good metrics. Carrying costs include all expenses associated with the technology, including labor costs. Pay, benefits, contingent and contractor expenditures, and their cost of capital are a good start for determining labor costs.

- **Brand Strength.** How do we assess brand strength? The most obvious way is by sales; declining sales are a sign of a weakening brand. Another way is to conduct surveys. (I am always wary of surveys conducted by the advertising agency that has our contract. Would we expect them to tell us that the millions we just spent on advertising and marketing had no effect?) A third method, which is simpler and cheaper, is to monitor the mention of our brand against competitors in the media. Who is getting the most positive "ink"? The best way is to construct an index consisting of multiple measures taken from the point of view of customers, suppliers, and competitors.

- **Quality.** Quality has long been defined as meeting customer expectations. In manufacturing, there are clear, objective measures of error or defect rates. In service, quality is what the customer says it is at the time the service is being provided. In the second half of the 1990s, customer expectations of service rose in some cases almost to unreasonableness. Typical service quality measures are responsiveness, reliability, integrity, empathy, and anticipation.

- **Community/Environmental Relations.** Depending on our business, we need to select a small number of micro measures that paint the macro picture of our community relations. In addition, we need to keep our environmental record in front of us. The combination of community involvement and environmental accountability make up a nice macro measure.

Figure 16-2 offers a set of quantitative macro metrics linking human and financial variables. These provide a broad view of the relationship and the trend of the enterprise.

- **Human Capital ROI.** This measures the return on capital invested in pay and benefits. The formula is:

$$\text{Human Capital ROI} = \frac{\text{Revenue} - \text{Nonhuman Expenses}}{\text{Pay and Benefits}}$$

Pay includes all money spent on regular and contingent labor.

- **Human Capital Value Added.** This uses a similar formula to Human Capital ROI but divides by the number of full-time equivalent employees (FTEs). The formula is:

$$\frac{\text{Human Capital}}{\text{Value Added}} = \frac{\text{Revenue} - \text{Nonhuman Expenses}}{\text{Full-Time Equivalents}}$$

This yields a profit per FTE. These two measures are views of the profitability attributable to human effort.

- **Human Capital Cost.** This is simply the average pay per regular employee. The formula is:

Human Capital Cost
$$= \frac{\text{Pay} + \text{Benefits} (+ \text{ Contingent Labor Cost})}{\text{Full-Time Equivalents}}$$

It can be augmented by adding in contingent labor in parentheses. In that case, we would take total regular employee labor expenses, including benefits costs, and divide by FTEs, including contingents.

- **Human Economic Value Added.** This is net operating profit after tax, minus the cost of capital divided by FTEs, including contingent labor. The formula is:

Human Economic Value Added
$$= \frac{\text{Net Operating Profit After Tax} - \text{Cost of Capital}}{\text{FTEs}}$$

- **Human Market Value Added.** This divides market capitalization by FTEs, including contingents. The formula is:

$$\text{Human Market Value Added} = \frac{\text{Market Capitalization}}{\text{FTEs}}$$

In all cases we are looking at the effects of human capital on financial performance.

Over the Horizon

WOULDN'T IT BE GREAT IF we knew what was coming—how e-world will evolve? Besides heading for Las Vegas or going online to trade stocks, we could deal more effectively with our associates and position our company ahead of the competition. Unfortunately, whoever has knowledge of the future is not sharing it with us, so we just have to stand on our tiptoes and look as far over the horizon as we can.

WHAT A VIEW

The new millennium presents a mind-numbing array of possibilities. Think how it would have been if we had been standing on the threshold of January 1, 1900, trying to see what was ahead for the 20th century. Would we have envisioned a man on the moon, the Internet, organ transplants, or robotics? Looking on toward 2100, we can already see world population and environmental degradation problems that could destroy life on the planet unless they are solved. We can see new dynamics that support GDP growth at double or even triple 20th-century rates. Will hypergrowth expand the gap between the skilled and unskilled? Will people work two hours a day—as predicted in 1890, with robots picking up the load—or twelve hours as we run to keep up? Will government continue to move toward Big Brother or a more benign model? Will education come in Cliff's Notes tablets or injectable doses of specific topics (give me 100,000 units of anthropology please)? Will all disease be eradicated and many people live to over 100?

It is clear that silicon-based processing will give way to molecular storage units and light as a data transmission medium. The chokepoint of bandwidth disappears in an optical network. George Gilder offers an eye-popping look in that direction: "The Internet is best imagined as a virtual point of light into which will be distilled all commerce and culture of the race."[1]

At work, optics technology will make instantaneous communication a common process. We'll sit in an ergonomically designed chair—with built-in massage, of course—speaking rather than typing. A blink of an eye opens and closes all circuits for each type of communication. Converters take inputs and change them into voice or text as we choose (in any language). Databases and people-friendly systems retrieve any information we need. Artificial intelligence interprets the data, relating the information to the questions we have. Communications devices, computers-telephones-pagers-PDAs that can be carried in our pocket, are integrated with add-on features. All day, they are absorbing information from our experiences whether we make a conscious entry or not.

At home, we insert that communications device into a slot on the wall. It updates our life-database, learning from today's experiences so it knows how to configure our abode for our state of mind and body. On comes Beethoven's "Pastoral Symphony," soothing us in house-around sound. Space at tonight's game, concert, or square dance is reserved automatically because the device can sense our needs and desires. When we enter our dressing room, the appropriate refreshment is poured into the glass as we disrobe and step into our rejuvenation chamber for a quick ion fix that rehabs our skin and drives away the wrinkles that today's problems created. Dinner is prepared automatically to suit our tastes, mood, and metabolic needs. After we are relaxed, whatever type of experience we need—intellectual or physical—is cued up in the Happy Chamber. What a day.

BE PREPARED

Since we can't foresee the future except in the broadest terms, we have to prepare ourselves for what we can see. How do we prepare for the next decade? Review the fundamentals.

- **People will drive it.** CEOs report in survey after survey that finding talent is the major barrier to future success. Sources of contingent labor have to be cultivated. Internships for students, relations with contingent labor sources, offshore contracts, outsourcing, and contracting with retirees will help solve the talent shortage.

- **Information will be the chief nonhuman resource.** Develop an information strategy based on knowledge and learning requirements, and *think network*. Thoroughly investigate the many software vendors. Look at functionality, integration, experience, service and support capability, and financial viability. Develop strategic partnerships with the ones that meet your criteria. Partners are more responsive than vendors because they have more to lose from the termination of a relationship.

- **We must integrate knowledge and learning.** It's more efficient, cost-effective, and useful. It eliminates redundancy and encourages collaboration. Develop a knowledge culture and strategy that looks to the future as well as the present. Employ a futurist periodically to help evaluate your strategy. Train people to manage and apply the knowledge that you are collecting and organizing. Use self-paced and distance-learning technology. Focus learning on essentials.

- **We must remake line management.** Drive relentlessly toward a collaborative culture and use opportunity teams to accelerate innovation. Make managers as accountable for learning and knowledge management as they are for budgets and production.

Although there are myriad details to be managed, they will follow naturally as by-products of these central issues.

THE KEY TO LIFE IN E-WORLD

The most difficult challenge of e-world will be to find balance. It is necessary for all living things to maintain balance. We witness it in the simple biological principle of homeosta-sis. Plants practice heliotropism because they need the sun for photosynthesis. Photosynthesis pro-vides them with the energy input to manufacture

> *The most difficult challenge of e-world will be to find balance.*

nutrients and eliminate waste by-products. So long as they keep this in balance, they can survive to the end of their natural life span. Animals, without consciously being aware of what they are doing, search for the foods in the environment that they need to maintain a healthy balance, be it a salt lick or a bit of roughage.

It is the same for humankind. We seek the inputs we need to maintain physical and mental health. It is the latter that separates us from the photosynthetic searchers. But don't confuse balance or equilibrium with a static state. On the contrary, *balance is the highest state of readiness for a person*. You know that when we are physically or mentally out of balance, we are not efficient. In extreme cases, we can become totally dysfunctional and even catatonic. When we are at optimum physical and mental balance, we talk about being "in the zone." To fulfill the biblical mandate that by the sweat of our brows shall we earn our bread, we must find gainful employment. This is as true for the thief as it is for the corporate striver. In e-world, the imbalance and alienation from nature that technology produces must be countered. If we cannot find a way to live in harmony with tech-nology, we will eventually be morphed into a robotic form, doing without thinking.

As we are propelled into e-world, we must decide, day by day, which decisions support balance and which do not. History has docu-mented for us the shallow, soul-deadening result of a mindless pur-suit of wealth. To seek to become the richest person in the world is the most self-destructive goal imaginable. Wealth has only one value, and that is to provide the necessities of life so that we might pursue the full development of our potential as thinking and caring human beings.

The greatest challenge for the executive is to grow an organization that is balanced in all respects. It must meet the imperative of making an acceptable return on all participants' investments. Stockholders, lenders, suppliers, employees, and customers must all benefit from the executive's decision. When short-term gain is consistently chosen over the creation of an institution of lasting value, customers and employees are eventually shortchanged. Inevitably, the market value of the enterprise begins to decline, driving stockholders out and sooner or later taking the executive with them. We saw it most recently in the crash of the dot-com, fund-and-flip value system. The fundamentals of economics, just like the fundamentals of health, must be maintained in order for an enterprise's life to continue.

Every value system has natural outputs. We must choose our value system wisely. It is a death or life matter.

REFERENCES

1. Eric Pfeiffer, "Gilder on Optics," *Forbes ASAP,* August 21, 2000.

Three Levels of ROI Measurement

INVESTORS ARE PAST THE EUPHORIC stage of ever expanding market valuations. They have had their fill of hot technology hype—at least for the moment. Bored with sound bites about number of *hits* or *eyeballs,* they now want to see profits. There is no question that gaining market share is absolutely critical to the financial success of a company. However, unless we can afford to operate for several years at a loss, it is imperative that we act as though we are running a business within e-world. Basic business activities such as competitive analysis, brand building, and financial measurements need to be brought back into focus. While the latest Great Idea is exciting technicians and providing fodder for marketers, executives have to keep their feet on the ground. It is time to get back to basics: setting goals, designing objective-based data-collection systems, collecting performance data on a regular basis, and measuring progress along the profit path.

The focus here is to review and update performance measurement in business, especially as it will be done in e-world conditions. Managers have been measuring manufacturing and administrative processes for longer than anyone can remember. However, as intangibles take on more importance in the new economy, most organizations need some help assessing their value in economic terms. In this

Appendix we lay down the fundamentals of performance measurement. Part V looked at examples of metrics for e-world specifically. We need to be grounded in measurement methods for intangibles, which will enable us to develop metrics beyond the examples in Part V.

Financial measurement is never about absolutes. There is no interest in metrics that are as refined as necessary in academic research. We don't care if something is provable at the .05 level of statistical significance. We simply want to know about relationships. How do we stack up to the competition, and which way are the numbers moving? It is all about relationships and degrees of change.

STARTING AN ROI MEASUREMENT PROGRAM

Return-on-investment measurement occurs at three levels: corporate/enterprise, business unit, and resource management. ROI measurement starts at the corporate level. We'll see below how the whole process works across the three levels, but before we do that, we need a quick review of performance measurement. As you know, the basic elements of measurement are cost, time, quantity, quality, and reaction of people. The first four are self-explanatory. The fifth, reaction of people, covers how customers and associates feel about the processes in which they are involved and the results of those processes. The outcomes of the processes are generically labeled service, quality, and productivity.

Figure A-1 is a display of the performance measurement matrix. I have been using this matrix as the foundation for performance measurement for over twenty years. I have found that it can be applied to any human activity, business or personal. I'm certain you can see how it applies to business situations. At a personal level, if you are the analytical type, your experiences can be viewed the same way. The only difference is the setting and the desired objectives. If you really want to push it, consider for a moment how the matrix can be applied to something as personal as making love. What did it cost you to get to this point? How long is it taking to achieve . . . shall we call it *results*? How much or how often is this happening? How well does it meet the standards you set for lovemaking? And the age-old

Figure A-1. The performance measurement matrix.

Process / Change Indicator			
COST			
TIME			
QUANTITY			
QUALITY			
REACTION			

question, "Was it good for you?" Fess up, you've always made those judgments before, haven't you? I would never kid you when it comes to measurement.

For a more mundane example of the matrix, see the sample in Figure A-2. I've selected the three basic functions of resource management: acquiring, maintaining, and developing or enhancing a resource or asset. In the Acquire column, we can record in the Cost row the cost of buying, renting, leasing, borrowing, or hiring a physical or intellectual asset. The resource can be real estate, equipment, cash, an employee, or a patent/copyright/trademark. For the Time row in the Acquire column, we can track how long it took to conduct the process of purchasing and receiving delivery, to rent space, to work with the lender to obtain a loan, to hire an employee, or to complete research and register a patent/copyright/trademark. The Quantity row is obvious. How much or how many of these things are we talking about? Quality is a matter of meeting a standard or specification. How close did we come to achieving that? Finally, the Reaction row is how satisfied with the process or result the internal customer who needed the resource is. I should mention that these are only examples, and I do not expect you to keep track of all these possibilities. You do only what makes sense in terms of understanding and improving resource management.

The same method applies across the other processes. For the Cost row of the Maintain column, what is it costing us to maintain the resource, whether it be real estate space, equipment, people, or the patent/copyright/trademark? For Quantity, how much space or equipment, how many people or patents/copyrights/trademarks are we handling with a given input of staff? Quality is how well we are doing it as measured in terms of clean and safe space, up-time of equipment, problems with employees (e.g., absenteeism or turnover), or error-free filing of patent/copyright/trademark updates. Reaction is again a matter of how someone feels about the maintenance process or results. Then, in the case of the Develop or Enhance column, what does it cost to upgrade any of the above or to train associates?

From that list, you can select the activities and monitor performance strictly on a resource management or efficiency basis. Next, we'll see next how to track and measure the application of those

Figure A-2. Sample measurement matrix for resource management.

Change Indicator \ Process	RESOURCE MANAGEMENT		
	ACQUIRE	MAINTAIN	DEVELOP or ENHANCE
COST			
TIME			
QUANTITY			
QUALITY			
REACTION			

resources to the operations of the company and ultimately the effects the subsequent operations have on corporate management goals.

MULTILEVEL MEASUREMENT

As mentioned above, there are three levels at which change can be measured and related to other levels. If our goal is truly to understand the dynamics of performance and what drives it, this method will accomplish that. The key is always to start at the corporate or enterprise level, not with process improvement. Executives whose improvement programs focus first on processes often find they have spent a lot of resources improving something that has minimal or no noticeable effect on corporate financial or market goals. It is this habit that frustrates managers and associates and is behind the 65 percent failure rate of improvement programs.

Before performance measurement can have meaning, it must have targets. The principal targets are the goals of the enterprise. These goals most often reflect financial or market targets. In e-world, customer and human capital goals are in ascendance, joining the traditional financial and market goals. Executives are coming to realize that human beings, not cash, are the principal lever of profits. Cash is inert. We can have the key to Fort Knox, but if someone doesn't pick up the key and unlock the door, all that wealth is still beyond our reach and useless. Even if we open the door, the gold bars are not going to jump up and do something. Managers and associates have to be energized to invest their resources in the pursuit of a business goal. They do this by applying corporate resources to innovate and to build customer relationships externally. How well they do this is found ultimately in the degree to which they have impacted corporate goals. This brings us to the second level of measurement: the business unit.

At this level we are looking for changes in business unit service, quality, and productivity results. All business objectives can be classified as service, quality, or productivity. These are the measurable results of activities that take place in R&D, production, sales, service, and the so-called support functions like finance, IT, and human resources. All changes can be measured through a combination of cost, time, quantity, errors or defects (quality), and human reactions. Whether we are talking about production costs, sales volume, service quality, or support function leverage, this is where the data show how we have performed in relation to operating objectives.

The third and most basic level of measurement is resource management. It is here that all intellectual and physical capital resides. In the most basic sense, these are the tools that managers and associates employ in the course of their daily activities. Measurement tells us how efficiently and effectively they applied these resources or tools.

Resource management can be viewed and measured at two levels. The first is internal resource management efficiency. We had an example of this above in the introduction to measurement, where the matrix in Figure A-2 is a template for assessing internal resource management efficiency. For each resource selected, a business unit can look at what it cost to acquire the resources. For example, what is the unit cost of some physical item such as a part, a machine, or a new hire, or an intellectual item such as a training program or an internal software application program, whether purchased or written in-house? (We could argue about whether a new hire is a physical or intellectual asset, and the answer is probably both, depending on how we expect to employ his/her muscles or brain.) Then, how long did it take to acquire that resource or asset? How many did we need? What is their level of quality (against a specification or standard)? How satisfied are we as managers of the process with our work and the result of the acquisition exercise? The same applies to the maintenance and development processes.

The second measure of resource management is effectiveness. This is where resource management and operating performance interface. After they were acquired, how well were the resources employed and leveraged to achieve business unit results? *How well* is measured by the same five indicators seen in Figure A-1.

Most people grasp how to measure physical items and their effects on operations. The barrier for some is applying this to intellectual capital. They don't know how to find the economic value of intellectual property, infrastructure, and corporate culture, as well as that of associates' behavior and customer relationships. I grant that it is not as self-evident as physical resources. Nevertheless, it can be accomplished at a level sufficient to determine how well we are making progress toward business goals. After all, isn't this all we really need to know? Let the academicians work on theories and models; businesspeople just need to continually improve economic performance. Figure A-3 lays out the elements and connections among resource management, operations management (operating objectives), and corporate management (corporate goals).

Since the greatest leverage comes from people, learning how to measure the effectiveness of our human capital resources is paramount. This topic was dealt with in great detail in my last book, *The ROI of Human Capital*.[1] That work showed the connections between human capital management and line functions in terms of serving operating objectives and corporate goals.

APPLICATIONS

Let's look at a scenario of a corporate goal and how resource management supports the operational processes that underpin it. Assume our goal is to increase market share by a given percentage. Many corporate improvement programs start with cost reduction, which is usually the most visible and easiest way to show gains. There are countless cases of improvement through cost reduction. During the 1990s, American businesses reduced their size and improved their efficiency. Total quality management (TQM), downsizing, and reengineering have all contributed to cost reduction and improvement in competitive positions. Clearly, if we can cut costs, we can reduce prices and perhaps gain market share. Unfortunately, the competition can probably do that also, and after a short time we find that our competitive edge in unit cost has eroded.

Conversely, a greater opportunity can be found on the revenue-generating side of the income statement. When we discover we can't cut much more out of the business without impairing our ability to serve customers, what do we do? There is only one pathway left. We have to concentrate on innovations that will attract customers—otherwise known as *grow the top line*—and retain them, thereby reducing sales and marketing expense. With the arrival of the Internet came the realization that the medium had transferred power from the provider to the customer. This brought customer service onto

Figure A-3. The elements and connections among resource management, operating objectives, and corporate management.

Resource Management	Operations Management	Corporate Management
Intellectual & Physical Capital	Service—Quality Productivity	Financial & Market Goals
Intellectual Property	R&D	Leadership
Infrastructure	Production	Strategy & Planning
Human Capital	Sales	Governance
Relationship Capital	Marketing	Coordination
Plant and Equipment	Service	Performance Management
Cash & Credit	Administration	& Measurement
Material and Inventory		

the radar screen in bright flashing lights. The central question surfaced immediately: How do we serve customers better? In most cases, the first step was to turn to technology, hence the rise in customer relations management (CRM) systems. This put a tool into the hands of the associates that made it easier for them to anticipate and respond to customer needs. Then, the more insightful executives caught on to the fact that CRM systems are only part of the remedy. We can spend hundreds of thousands of dollars on the best tools and not get a nickel's worth of value in return. We all know how to do that. Tools are passive. Our associates are the action levers. Given better tools plus training and perhaps incentives, our associates should produce substantial gains. Gains from this approach outstrip cost reduction gains and do not quickly reach the point of diminishing returns. By George, I think we've got it!

People (customers and associates) are the real drivers of successful businesses.

In the final analysis, business is a people game. The path to long-term success is through the effective combination of human capital, infrastructure, and equipment in service to customers.

Figure A-4 is an example of the pathway from resource management—infrastructure (incentives and processes), human capital (associates), and physical capital (CRM software)—to better customer service, resulting in a measurable improvement in market share goals.

You can say, "There is nothing new here. We do this every day." And I would say in reply that you must be different from the thousands of companies I've encountered over the last three decades that manage their assets in a very broad and loose manner. They talk of alignment but under questioning cannot find most of the connections. In practice, executives often find it difficult to locate the specific drivers of improvements. Typically, because they are beset by a multitude of demands and because the measurement of intangibles is not easy, they give up and just charge myopically onward as best they can. Most often, they set corporate goals and attack in a very broad and familiar manner devoid of verifiable point-to-point links. They adopt and endorse some improvement process and hope for a bottom-line payoff. Even when they get it, they can't say with any degree of confidence what caused it. In the end, there is no way to learn which

Figure A-4. The pathway from resource management to market share.

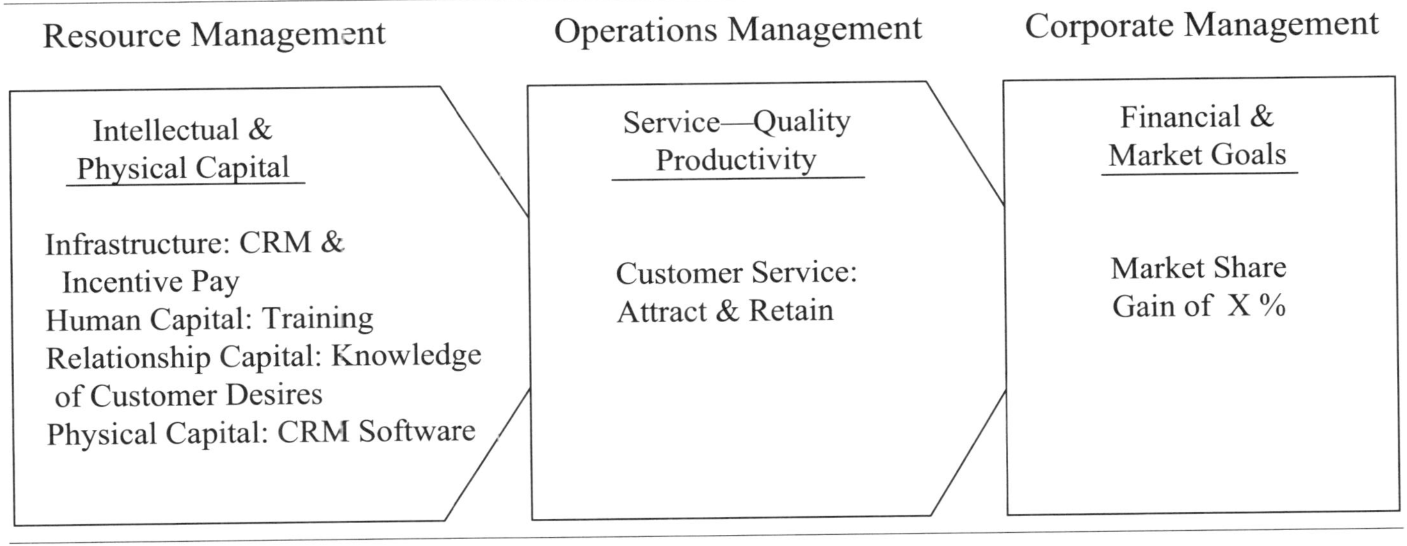

Resource Management	Operations Management	Corporate Management

Intellectual & Physical Capital

Infrastructure: CRM & Incentive Pay
Human Capital: Training
Relationship Capital: Knowledge of Customer Desires
Physical Capital: CRM Software

Service—Quality Productivity

Customer Service: Attract & Retain

Financial & Market Goals

Market Share Gain of X %

action generated the most value. So the next time around they have to start from scratch again.

The first problem with this hit-or-miss approach is that there are too many misses. How many times have you heard the lament, "We never have time to do it right, but we always have time to do it over when it doesn't work"? This is a very inefficient and demoralizing way to run a business. It is a direct contributor to high operating costs and highly stressed associates.

The second problem is that we seldom learn as efficiently as we could from both our successes and our failures because going in we didn't have a clear idea which resource might be the most powerful driver. Each manager—customer service, marketing, human resources, and IT—believes that her investment is the key. More time is spent arguing about who is going to be the savior than on carrying out an effective and objective analysis of the problem or opportunity. In the end, win or lose, no one really knows why and how the goal was achieved or the mark missed. I suppose it is not important if we have a monopoly, but if we are running a competitive business, e-world demands that we learn from our actions so that we can keep up.

So how do we know what was the principal driving force? To understand the result, we have to understand the problem. In this case, what is the problem? Is it simply a need or desire to have greater market share, or is it a last-gasp, do-or-die play? What if we don't significantly increase market share? Can we grow revenue simply by matching the growth rate of the market? Or do we have to make some type of quantum leap? Figure A-5 is an analytic method that helps us understand:

- The nature and severity of the issue
- The probable cause of the problem
- Potentially the best solution
- After the fact, the principal driver of the result

In this simple example, we are building visible links from the corporate-level problem (market share) down through operations (customer service deficiencies) to resource management (people and equipment) and back up to the corporate goal of market share gain. With these direct links it is possible to assess results in more explicit

Figure A-5. An example of path value analysis.

1. Goal: Increase market share.
2. Requirement: Attract and retain more customers.
3. Alternatives: *Path A.* Cut product cost and reduce prices.
   Path B. Understand and serve customer needs better.
4. Decision: Follow *Path B.*
5. Analysis: a. Conducted market study of customers' current and future needs.
   b. Surveyed customers to learn current satisfaction levels.
   c. Learned that customers are unhappy with time to respond to calls for service.

   Investigation determined that slow response time is a function of three deficiencies: inexperienced customer service personnel; inefficient dispatching system; inefficient organization of field service territories, resulting in long travel times to some customers.
6. Actions: 1. Train customer service personnel.
   2. Invest in more powerful dispatching system.
   3. Reconfigure service territories
7. Measurement: Survey customer satisfaction. Compute difference between initial and subsequent scores. Estimate the value in terms of customer retention between initial and subsequent satisfaction levels.

terms, learn, and continue to raise the standards of customer attraction and retention.

We may learn as a result of the actions taken that each contributed to customer satisfaction or that one was the dominant contributor. We discover this by surveying the customers at the earliest reasonable point after taking the action. Surveying too early does not give the remedy time to take effect; all medicines need time to effect a cure. We may find that we did effect an improvement, but it was insufficient to meet the enterprise goal of market share increase. So, is there an underlying problem that was not uncovered by the customer satisfaction program? Do we have product problems around competitive price and performance that the satisfaction program did not discover? Were we simultaneously working on improving our sales and marketing programs? Were we continuing or initiating product innovations?

In practice, we usually attack on several fronts, but that is not always the case. If we are going to be competitive, we have to work concurrently from every angle possible. When we achieve our goal, we can go back and learn what action or combination of actions drove us to success. Statistical proof of the efficacy of one remedy over another is not our objective. Nevertheless, without analysis, we learn nothing and are condemned to repeat the effort in the future. Effective analysis helps us learn quickly and be more efficient on the next round.

REFERENCES

1. Jac Fitz-enz, *The ROI of Human Capital* (New York: AMACOM, 2000).

Bibliography

Allee, Verna. *The Knowledge Evolution*. Newton, Mass.: Butterworth-Heineman, 1997.

Barham, Kevin, and Claudia Heimer. *ABB: The Dancing Giant*. London: Financial Times and Pittman, 1998.

Baron, Talila. "IT Talent Shortage Renews Interest in Mentoring." *Information Week*, April 24, 2000.

Bayers, Chip. "The Inner Bezos." *Wired*, March 1999.

Bennis, Warren, and Patricia Ward Biederman. *Organizing Genius*. Reading, Mass.: Addison-Wesley, 1997.

Bontis, Nick. "There's a Price on Your Head: Managing Intellectual Capital Strategically." *Business Quarterly*, Summer 1996.

Boshyk, Yury. "Beyond Knowledge Management: How Companies Mobilize Experience." *The Financial Times*, February 8, 1999.

Boudette, Neil. "How a Software Titan Missed the Internet Revolution." *Wall Street Journal*, January 18, 2000.

Byham, William C. "Executive Help Wanted, Inquire Within: The Leadership Dearth Is the Real Dilemma." *Employment Relations Today*, Autumn 1999.

Charan, Ram. "Opinion—Why So Many CIOs Fail." *Information Week*, November 1, 1999.

Citron, James, and Thomas Neff. "Digital Leadership." *Strategy and Business*, First Quarter 2000.

Crainer, Stuart. "Grow Your Own Global Leader." *hrworld,* March/April 2000.

Crawford, Richard. *In the Era of Human Capital.* New York: Harper-Collins, 1991.

Dauphinais, G. William, and Colin Price, eds. *Straight from the CEO: The World's Top Business Leaders Reveal Ideas That Every Manager Can Use.* New York: Simon & Schuster, 1998.

Davenport, Thomas H. *Information Ecology.* New York: Oxford University Press, 1997.

Dell, Michael. *Direct from Dell: Strategies That Revolutionized an Industry.* New York: HarperCollins, 1999.

Dertouzos, Michael L. *What Will Be: How the New World of Information Will Change Our Lives.* New York: Harper Edge, 1997.

Dotlich, David, and James Noel. *Action Learning: How the World's Top Companies Are Re-creating Their Leaders and Themselves.* San Francisco: Jossey-Bass, 1998.

Downes, Larry, and C. Mui. *Unleashing the Killer App: Digital Strategies for Market Dominance.* Boston: Harvard Business School Press, 1998.

Edvinsson, Leif, and Michael Malone. *Intellectual Capital.* New York: Harper-Collins, 1997.

Gates, Bill, with N. Myhrvold and P. Rinearson. *The Road Ahead.* New York: Viking, 1995.

Goleman, Daniel. *Emotional Intelligence: Why It Can Matter More Than IQ.* New York: Bantam, 1995.

Handy, Charles. *The Age of Unreason.* Boston: Harvard Business School Press, 1989.

Heifetz, Ronald, and Donald Laurie. "The Work of Leadership." *Harvard Business Review,* January/February 1997.

Hesselbein, Frances, Marshall Goldsmith, and Richard Beckhard. *The Organization of the Future.* San Francisco: Jossey-Bass, 1997.

Hiebeler, Robert J. "Benchmarking Knowledge Management." *Strategy and Leadership,* March/April 1996.

Horibe, Frances. *Managing Knowledge Workers—New Skills and Attitudes to Unlock the Intellectual Capital In Your Organization.* Etobicoke, Ontario: John Wiley & Sons, Canada Ltd., 1999.

Junnarkar, Bipin. "Creating Fertile Ground for Knowledge at Monsanto." *Perspectives on Innovation,* Issue 1: *Managing Organizational Knowledge.* www.businessinnovation.ey.com

Kao, John. *Jamming: The Art and Discipline of Business Creativity*. New York: HarperBusiness, 1997.

Kaplan, Robert, and David Norton. *The Balanced Scorecard*. Boston: Harvard Business School Press, 1996.

Komenar, Margo. *Electronic Marketing*. New York: John Wiley & Sons, 1997.

Kouzes, James, and Barry Posner. *Credibility*. San Francisco: Jossey-Bass, 1993.

Kurtzman, Joel. "An Interview with Rosabeth Moss Kanter." *Strategy and Business*, Third Quarter 1999.

Lipnack, Jessica, and Jeffrey Stamps. *Virtual Teams: Reaching Across Space, Time, and Organizations with Technology*. New York: John Wiley & Sons, 1997.

"Make Yourself a Leader." *Fast Company*, June 1999.

Marquardt, Michael J. *Building the Learning Organization*. New York: McGraw-Hill and American Society for Training and Development, 1996.

Martin, Chuck. *Net Future: 7 Cybertrends That Will Drive Your Business, Create New Wealth, and Define Your Future*. New York: McGraw-Hill, 1999.

McDougall, Paul, and Marianne Kolbasuk McGee. "How to Survive as a CIO." *Information Week*, November 1, 1999.

Mottil, Judith N. "Unusual Perks Give Workers More Free Time." *Information Week*, April 3, 2000.

Mulgan, Geoff. *Connexity: How to Live in a Connected World*. Boston: Harvard Business School Press, 1998.

Murphy, Chris, with Jennifer Mateyaschuk. "Still Not Enough IT Workers—The Survey Says: Lots of IT Jobs, Not Enough Workers." *Information Week*, April 17, 2000.

Neilson, Gary L., Bruce A. Pasternak, and Albert J. Viscio. "Up the (E) Organization." *Strategy and Business*, First Quarter 2000.

Nevins, Mark David, and Stephan A. Stumpf. "21st-Century Leadership: Redefining Management Education." *Strategy and Business*, Third Quarter 1999.

Nonaka, Ikujiro, and Hirotaka Takeuchi. *The Knowledge Creating Company*. New York: Oxford University Press, 1995.

O'Toole, James. *Leadership A to Z: A Guide for the Appropriately Ambitious*. San Francisco: Jossey-Bass, 1999.

Petrash, Gordon. "Dow's Journey to a Knowledge Value Management Culture." *European Management Journal,* August 1996.

Prokesch, Steven E. "Unleashing the Power of Learning." *Harvard Business Review,* September/October 1997.

Revins, Reginald. *The ABC of Action Learning.* London: Lemos and Crane, 1998.

Ruggles, Rudy, and Dan Holtshouse. *The Knowledge Advantage.* Dover, N.H.: Capstone, 1999.

Sapal, Pepi, ed. "Shooting to the Top." *hrworld,* March/April 2000.

Savage, Charles M. *5th Generation Management.* Newton, Mass.: Butterworth-Heinemann, 1996.

Schwartz, Evan. *Digital Darwinism: 7 Breakthrough Business Strategies for Surviving in the Cutthroat Web Economy.* New York: Broadway Books, 1999.

Seybold, Patricia. *Customers.com: How to Create a Profitable Business Strategy for the Internet and Beyond.* New York: Times Business, 1998.

Sittenfeld, Curtis. "Report from the Future—Leadership Is Hell." *Fast Company,* August 1998.

Stewart, Thomas A. *Intellectual Capital.* New York: Doubleday Currency, 1997.

Sveiby, Karl Erik. *The New Organizational Wealth.* San Francisco: Berrett-Koehler, 1997.

Tapscott, Don. *Growing Up Digital.* New York: McGraw-Hill, 1998.

Tissen, Rene, Daniel Andriessen, and Frank Lekanne Deprez. *Knowledge Dividend.* London: Financial Times/Prentice Hall, 2000.

Tobin, Daniel. "Buckman Labs Focuses on Engaging the Customer." *Knowledge Inc.,* June 1997.

Toffler, Alvin. *The Third Wave.* New York: William Morrow, 1980.

"The 21st Century Economy." *Business Week,* August 31, 1998.

Ulrich, Dave, Jack Zenger, and Norm Smallwood. *Results Based Leadership.* Boston: Harvard Business School Press, 1999.

Vision 2010: Designing Tomorrow's Organization. New York: The Economist Intelligence Unit in cooperation with Anderson Consulting, 1997.

Wheatley, Margaret J. *Discovering Order in a Chaotic World.* San Francisco: Berrett-Koehler, 2nd edition, 1999.

Zemke, Ron, and Tom Connellan. *e-service.* New York: AMACOM, 2001.

DR. JAC FITZ-ENZ IS ACKNOWLEDGED WORLDWIDE as the father of human performance benchmarking and assessment. He carried out the breakthrough research on the measurement of human capital in the 1970s. Under his direction, Saratoga Institute publishes benchmark data on employee productivity, best human capital management, and retention practices. Saratoga clients include ninety of the Fortune 100 companies and many major multinationals.

Dr. Fitz-enz has written more than 130 articles and reports, as well as six previous books:

How to Measure Human Resource Management (1984) set the international standard for quantitative evaluation of human resources operations. Currently going into its third edition, it is still the seminal text on this topic.

Human Value Management won the 1991 Book of the Year Award of the Society for Human Resource Management (SHRM). In it, Dr. Fitz-enz foretold the reengineering movement, showing how to radically redesign HR as a value-adding function.

Benchmarking Staff Performance (1993) took performance improvement technology to a new level, demonstrating how staff departments use benchmarking to drive competitive advantage in their organizations.

The 8 Practices of Exceptional Companies (1997) describes the results of five years of research on 1,000 companies that yielded the factors common to the top human capital managing companies around the world.

A New Vision for Human Resources (1998), coauthored with Jack

Phillips, describes in detail how to manage and measure the value added of a human resources department.

The ROI of Human Capital, winner of the 2000 SHRM Book of the Year Award, presents the next generation of human capital performance measurement by connecting HR services to operational objectives and corporate performance.

Dr. Fitz-enz has trained more than 50,000 managers in forty countries. He and the Saratoga network remain "The Source" for human capital performance measurement for the American Management Association, the Society for Human Resource Management, the American Productivity and Quality Center, the International Quality and Productivity Centre, the U.S. and Canadian Conference Boards, the major multinational consulting firms, and most trade associations.

Saratoga Institute has offices throughout Asia Pacific, North and South America, Africa, and in the United Kingdom. These offices have data collection capabilities in more than twenty countries.

Prior to founding Saratoga Institute in 1977, Dr. Fitz-enz had twenty years of business experience in several line functions and held human resources vice presidential positions at Wells Fargo Bank, Imperial Bank, and Motorola Computer Systems.

The Saratoga Institute, Inc., is located at 3600 Pruneridge Avenue, Santa Clara, California 95051. Telephone: 408-556-1150. Fax: 408-556-1155. E-mail: jacfitz-enz@saratoga-institute.com.